Personality Types: A Modern Synthesis

Personality Types

A Modern Synthesis

Alan Miller
University of New Brunswick

University of Calgary Press

© 1991 Alan Miller. All rights reserved

ISBN 0-919813-77-1

University of Calgary Press
2500 University Drive N.W.
Calgary, Alberta, Canada T2N 1N4

Canadian Cataloguing in Publication Data

Miller, Alan, 1938–
　　　　Personality types

Includes bibliographical references.
ISBN 0-919813-77-1

1. Typology (Psychology)　2. Personality.　I. Title.
BF698.3.M54 1990　　　　　　　155.2′64　　　　　　　C90-091638-9

Cover design by Rhae Ann Bromley

Printed in Canada

♾ This book is printed on acid-free paper.

To my parents
Robert Miller and Jenny Muckles

Contents

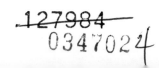

Foreword

IN RECENT TIMES, the heroic task of understanding personality largely has become a series of careful fine-grained empirical studies. The professional journals are filled with earnest scientific endeavours that, in respecting the demanding rules of modern research technique, are inexorably pushed into attention to details. That is one reason no one seriously interested in the overall nature of human personality, from the well-read layperson to the undergraduate who has a first course in personality to the senior scholar, can afford to ignore Alan Miller's new treatise.

The purpose of his book is nothing less than to offer an entirely new view of personality. To be sure, as Miller's sub-title indicates, this new view is not composed of strange, green concepts; rather it is a fresh integration of ideas that have surfaced and re-surfaced for centuries. In brief, the synthesis is derived from the classic domains of cognition, motivation, and emotion, each of which receives chapter-length treatment that will be of interest to scholars in those fields who care about how their topic relates to personality. Cognition is the basis of an analytic–holistic dimension, motivation the basis of an objective–subjective dimension, and emotion the basis of a stable–unstable dimension. The first two dimensions yield four types: reductionist, schematist, gnostic, and romantic, each with stable and unstable versions (the third dimension). Thus, Miller's synthesis would re-organize our conception of personality using familiar building blocks that, surprisingly, have never been assembled in quite this way.

Perhaps the most striking feature of the synthesis is its wide-ranging basis in scholarship. Miller not only fully grasps the key issues and findings in contemporary personality theory and research, as the reader has a right to expect, but evinces a strong grounding in the literatures of cognitive science, emotion, and motivation. Miller's voyage toward the ultimate conceptualization of personality is commendable for its inclusiveness and wholeness.

The Miller perspective has admirable breadth in another way. More than any other book I've see, it offers fair and equal treatment to ideas from both sides of the Atlantic. Finally, the book manifests unusual depth; Miller happily acknowledges classic sources from Theophrastus to Allport.

Some personality manifestos have been just that: broadsides marred by self-serving dogmatism and unconscionable blindness for alternative views. One thing that kept me humming through this book was Miller's very generous treatment of competing and complementary theories. The dominant tone is not "this is the way it is," but "given that X's studies found this and Y's theory says that, it seems reasonable to me that the truth of the matter is...."

Not every reader will agree with Miller's new synthesis. Some are committed to another view; others may disagree with what seems reasonable to him. However, this is precisely why everyone who cares about personality should read the book: its wide-ranging, solid scholarship requires that the tenets of Miller's synthesis are examined, discussed, and debated. Because of the virtual necessity of specialization in a time of data overload, I expect there are few readers, even among our most senior colleagues, who will not learn something important from the breadth and depth of these chapters. It becomes incumbent on those who hold established views of personality to show how this synthesis is *not* superior (if they can!).

Unlike most contemporary typologies, Miller's synthesis has been developed rationally rather than empirically. In chapter five, after outlining the present state of the field and developing the three key dimensions of his theory, Miller discusses its similarities and differences with other type theories, from Jung to the interpersonal circle. Next, Miller illustrates his types with fascinating case histories in ways that will please those who have asked, with Ravenna Helson, "Where is the person in personality?"

Finally, Miller tackles the problem of his theory's usefulness. He offers particularly telling examples of how it might be used in clinical, vocational, and environmental contexts. As a sometime environmental psychologist, I am especially impressed by the convincing aptness with which Miller's typology applies to the characterization of professionals who are charged with managing and improving the natural environment.

The Miller typology is compelling as a bold hypothesis on the nature of personality. In an age of research specialization and occasional slavery to numbers, it is a brave and well-informed foray into the land of giants such as Freud, Murray, and Allport, where creative, far-seeing scholars dare to describe the landscape of personality in its entirety. Students of personality will soon wish to progress from debates over the merits of Miller's typology to empirical tests of its postulations.

Robert Gifford
University of Victoria

Preface

THIS BOOK HAS its origins in my demoralizing experiences as a graduate student in ecology during the early 1960s. As a somewhat naive young man, untutored in interpersonal politics, I was baffled by the mutual incomprehension that existed between my supervisor and myself. Attempts to communicate served only to make matters worse as it became apparent that we agreed on little of significance. The prospects for reaching some working compromise were dashed by the hostility which pervaded our every interaction. I realize now, of course, that we subscribed to fundamentally different values about the nature and conduct of research. It was only later that I came to understand how common such conflicts are in academic and professional life. Rychlak (1968), for instance, in describing the autobiographical origins of his own book on personality theory, explains: "It all began with the fact that I came up against people—highly competent people—with orientations so foreign to my own regarding the nature and goals of psychology that we could not really communicate without losing our tempers" (p. ix). At the time, however, the experience left me puzzled and confused, so much so that, even though I did manage to graduate (due largely to the intervention of a more sympathetic faculty member), I drifted into an introspective limbo from which I emerged several years later determined to grasp the nettle and embark on graduate work in psychology.

I soon learned that work in psychology was quite different from what I had been used to in biology. While there is some consensus about the taxonomic and conceptual systems that impose order on biological phenomena, psychology appeared to be utterly chaotic on first impression. My early years in the discipline, therefore, were spent in a fruitless search for some ordering principle that might reconcile the competing schools of personality theory or, at the very least, provide a structure within which empirical studies might be integrated. Gradually, I came to realize that no such ordering system existed and, worse, none of the prevalent personality theories spoke meaningfully to the issues that concerned me, namely the personality and behaviour of professionals. It became evident that I would have to develop my own "ordering principle"—hence the personality typology described here.

The model emerged slowly as I identified, and worked with, some promising personality dimensions. To begin with, my interest in individual differences in professional thinking and problem solving led me to the enormous amount of literature on cognitive styles and the *analytic–holistic* distinction which I came to adopt as the cognitive dimension of my typology. In Chapter 2, I indicate how this older research on cognitive styles can be integrated with more recent findings in cognitive psychology to formulate a generic cognitive style dimension. Since I had learned to my cost that there is more to the practice of academic (professional) life than some detached rationality, I realized that I would have to find an appropriate way of depicting the emotional and value components of personality. After much trial and error, I found myself drawn increasingly to some of the oldest ideas in personality theory, notably that of temperament (emotionality) and the Tough-Tender distinction, which latter I chose to interpret as a difference in values. Thus, in Chapter 3, I discuss the many and varied conceptions of emotionality, indicating how a recent version of the concept, *affect intensity,* can be used to portray individual differences in the experience and expression of emotions. In turn, Chapter 4 describes the way in which I have reformulated the Tough-Tender dichotomy into a more empirically grounded *objective–subjective* dimension, one that helps in understanding why professionals of different stripes have so much difficulty establishing common ground. Finally, in Chapter 5, I integrate the preceding three dimensions into what I trust is a plausible personality typology. The decision to develop a typology rather than some other personality model was due, in part, to my personal preference for simplicity and the desire to make the model of practical value in applied areas such as educational and clinical psychology. More technical reasons for choosing a typology are discussed in Chapter 1.

Although the present model was developed with a particular purpose in mind, it has proved to be more widely applicable than I had anticipated. In other words, it is a more generic model than its origins in describing individual differences in professional behaviour might imply. In support of this contention, I include examples in Chapter 5 of the way in which it can be used to understand, for instance, the nature and relationships between the various DSM–III personality disorders, as well as the origins of environmental disputes. In addition, I believe that the model applies equally to both men *and* women, and is not a theory devised by a man to describe men. To underscore its applicability to women I have chosen deliberately to illustrate the main prototypes postulated by the model with case studies of women.

While the typology is, at its most abstract level, relatively simple, the arguments in support of it are not. Since I draw on a wide range of concepts and empirical evidence, the reader will need an extensive background in psychology if he or she is to profit from the discussion. It follows that this is not an appropriate book for introductory courses in personality. On the other hand, it is eminently suitable for courses at the advanced undergraduate and graduate levels, as well as a source of hypotheses for a wide range of scholars interested in an integrated approach to personality studies. I suspect, however, that the book will find its most attentive audience amongst practitioners in occupational and educational psychology, especially those involved in the education and counselling of professionals. This suggests that the book may also be of interest to scholars and practitioners in the fields of administration and psychiatry, both of which entail the categorization and management of various types of individual.

Acknowledgements

I WOULD LIKE to thank Marilyn Jacques and Janet Olmstead for their tireless efforts in typing the many drafts of this book; Murray Linton for his help with the book's figures and, most of all, Janet Stoppard for her encouragement and support.

This book has been published with the help of a grant from the Social Science Federation of Canada, using funds provided by the Social Sciences and Humanities Research Council of Canada.

Chapter 1

A Trait-Type Theory of Personality

ALTHOUGH PERSONALITY typologies have a venerable history, they have fallen into disrepute in recent times. In academic psychology, the intellectual credibility of personality dispositions has been thrown into doubt and the typologies derived from them dismissed as an even more dubious form of theorizing. As a consequence, attempts to discuss personality typologies are commonly met with amused contempt, as if one were dealing with some mediaeval horoscope.

This low point in the history of personality typologies reflects a more general malaise in personality theory, a direct result, it seems, of the ascendancy of positivist–behaviourist views during the first half of this century. For much of the period, speculation about psychological structures and processes, the very substance of personality theory itself, was deemed unwise, a form of intellectual folly (Feshbach, 1984; Maddi, 1984). However, psychology, like other disciplines, is conducted within, and influenced by, the prevailing intellectual *Zeitgeist*, one that has been shifting away from the more extreme forms of positivism for some time (Capra, 1982). Indeed, there are signs that psychology is beginning to respond to the changing climate, as previously unfashionable views reassert themselves, much to the chagrin of Skinner (1987) who asks: "Whatever happened to psychology as the science of behavior?" At the same time, personality theory is experiencing something of a renaissance as long-standing disputes are reassessed and new non-positivist directions explored (Houts *et al.*, 1986; West, 1986). Not that such a trend is greeted with universal delight, of course, the sharp interchange between Carlson (1984) and Kenrick (1986) being a case in point.

One result of this ferment is that it is now academically respectable, at least in some circles, to talk about the stability and consistency of behaviour in terms of personality dispositions. The question that follows from this is whether one should take the matter one step further and attempt to resurrect personality types, or should the type be recognized as a relic of a pre-scientific era best left to historians of psychology? Also, if one is interested in reappraising personality typologies, is there anything new to say after all these centuries of speculation, or would one invariably rehash conventional wisdom?

In what follows, I assume, along with Bem (1983), Eysenck and Eysenck (1985), Millon (1981), and Wiggins (1980), that personality types do have practical and theoretical utility. Such utility would be enhanced were it possible to integrate some of the more traditional ideas about types with recent findings in experimental and personality psychology, something I attempt here. To begin with, therefore, I shall review some of the problems that have arisen in the conceptualization of traits and types before proceeding to outline briefly the personality typology which is discussed at length in subsequent chapters.

PERSONALITY DISPOSITIONS

Since personality structures and processes cannot be observed directly but must be inferred from behaviour, the vagaries of inference play a central role in disputes over the credibility of personality dispositions. At one point during the 1970s, research on social judgment appeared to have established the fact that human beings are flawed judges, so prone to error and bias that our subjective judgments of personality are unusable as a source of personality data (Funder, 1983). Thus, the more behaviourally inclined researchers were apt to reject subjective data in favour of direct measurement of relevant behaviours.

In keeping with the changing times, however, the research on which this rather extreme position had been based has itself been subjected to extensive criticism. In particular, the emphasis on "artificial" laboratory situations, in which subjects were required to judge strangers, is thought to have underestimated the level of accuracy of which people are capable in more natural circumstances (Kenrick & Dantchik, 1983). A more reasonable position to take on the question of inference, therefore, is that, while inferences are prone to error, they "can be rich sources of data with a substantial component of validity and usefulness" when skillfully made by knowledgeable observers (Funder, 1983, p. 353).

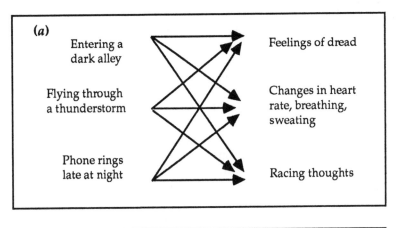

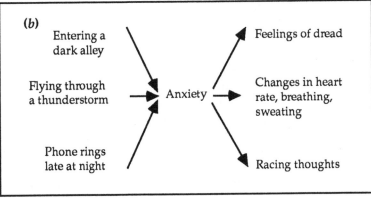

Figure 1. Empirical and theoretical generalizations. (Modified from Ross, 1987).

Level of Inference

I believe that differences of opinion over the validity of subjective inferences are unlikely to go away, for the very reason that they may be influenced less by the available evidence than by the individual's ideological preferences. Coan (1979), for instance, has identified coherent clusters of epistemological beliefs, amongst psychologists of differing persuasions, that reflect radically different assumptions about what is right and proper in the conduct of psychological research. What he calls the *restrictive* orientation includes the belief that inferences should be kept close to the observable data, limiting generalizations to the kind depicted in Fig. 1a. In contrast, those who adopt a *fluid* orientation are more willing to accept the more speculative inferences involved in the use of hypothetical constructs to simplify interpretations of empirical generalizations (Fig. 1b).

It follows that the common distinction between what Hirschberg (1978) calls summary and dispositional traits, which differ in the *level* of inference involved in their formulation, may be an attempt to develop conceptions of traits that satisfy different ideological predilections. Summary traits, also referred to as surface traits (Phares, 1988) or act trends (D. Buss & Craik, 1984), are observations that certain behaviours tend to be correlated, with no implication that the trait either explains or "causes" such behaviours. On the other hand, dispositional traits, which are sometimes referred to as source traits, are regarded as underlying structures having an explanatory and causal role in behaviour. When used in this way, a trait implies some inner mechanism that influences the behaviour of the person.

For example, when you say that a pill is water-soluble, you mean more than just the tendency to dissolve in water. You also mean that the pill has the sort of *internal* chemical structure that causes it to dissolve when water is present. The same applies with causal use of traits—you are implying that there is some internal psychological structure that causes the person to behave in a certain way *when situational conditions are appropriate* (Hirschberg, 1978). Dispositional traits, therefore, refer to the causal make-up of people and, as such, may involve speculation about physiological and other processes.

For instance, Eysenck's conception of Extraversion is a multilayered concept that links overt behaviours with brain structures and processes. Clearly this kind of construct involves considerable speculation, too much perhaps, for those whose tolerance is already stretched by the limited inferences involved in summary traits. This is unfortunate, since dispositional traits play a major role in the formulation of personality types.

If one adds to this the fact that a personality "type" is usually conceived of as a superordinate construct, a higher-level abstraction that subsumes lower-order traits, then one can see why typologies generate so much controversy. They are far too speculative for those who are ideologically committed to a more restrained form of inference. To be fair to this latter group of psychologists, however, there has been great difficulty in obtaining empirical verification of the extant typologies, so the matter is not purely ideological. We shall return to these issues shortly.

Since the typology developed here is a higher-order abstraction composed of dispositional traits, all I can do to justify my approach is to say that I take great pains to temper my inferences with empirical data. Whether this will satisfy those who adopt Coan's (1979) *restrictive* orientation is another matter.

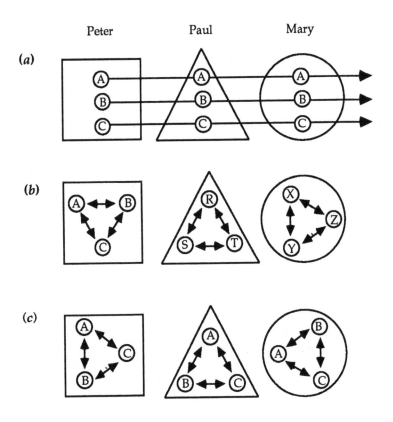

Figure 2. Conceptions of traits. Small circles represent personality traits; different traits in individuals are indicated by labels. Arrows show interactions between traits. (Modified from Smith, 1974.)

Breadth of Inference

The purpose of a personality typology is to provide a systematic way of dealing with individual differences, one that allows you to compare and contrast individuals by allocating them to distinctive categories. For this purpose, it is necessary to identify, or to formulate, personality dispositions that are meaningful when applied to the population being studied. In other words, you need to infer what Allport (1961) refers to as *common* traits, dispositions that are relevant in describing everyone. The usual strategy, in this *nomothetic* approach, is to assume that individuals vary only in degree on the traits in question (Fig. 2a). Little or no attempt is made to explore the interaction, patterning, or qualities within the individual (Hermans, 1988).

Unfortunately for those interested in typologies, the nomothetic approach has been subjected to sustained criticism from two directions. Behaviourists and situationists have argued that nomothetic traits are both unstable and relatively unimportant as predictors of behaviour (A. H. Buss, 1989). As I have mentioned earlier, such views played a major role in limiting the credibility of personality theory in the recent past. How these criticisms have been rebutted is a matter that deserves a separate discussion and, therefore, will be dealt with shortly.

Criticisms of nomothetic traits coming from the opposite tack, from "personologists" such as Carlson (1985), maintain that nomothetic traits fail to catch the uniqueness of the individual. Eysenck's trait of Extraversion, for instance, is composed of nine different kinds of behaviour, including sociability and sensation-seeking (Eysenck & Eysenck, 1985). However, the relative significance of each of these components is likely to vary from one individual to another, an aspect of individual uniqueness that is difficult to accommodate in nomothetic conceptions of traits.

Since nomothetic generalizations are derived from group data and seek to represent some hypothetical "average" behaviour, they are not applicable to each and every individual (Allport, 1961; Lamiell, 1987). For this purpose, one needs to formulate *idiographic* traits. These traits, which are sometimes referred to as *personal* traits, are thought to be unique to each individual and are largely irrelevant when applied to others. A typical idiographic strategy is to identify the pattern of personal traits that characterize the individual through the study of biographical and life-history data (Fig. 2b). Recently, Lamiell (1987) has developed a quantitative approach to idiographic research in which subjects not only estimate the extent to which they exhibit certain behaviours but also determine the significance to be assigned to them, thereby avoiding the imposition of an average weighting derived by the investigator from some nomothetic rule. Clearly, however, these approaches do not lend themselves to the development of typologies, for one cannot easily relate findings from one person to another. For instance, Repertory Grid methods are excellent tools for idiographic research, for they enable you to study the pattern of personal constructs used by an individual in construing significant others (Fransella, 1981). However, each grid is unique, based on an idiosyncratic constellation of personal constructs. Consequently, the only way in which grids can be compared across subjects is by requiring them to use common, as well as personal, constructs in their judgments. That is, one has to introduce some nomothetic features into the assessment.

Difficulty in generalizing findings is only one of many problems incurred by the idiographic approach (Runyan, 1983). For instance, an issue related to the question of generalization, and one that is particularly relevant to the importance of typologies, is the assumption of individual uniqueness, which implies that each *new* individual must be studied afresh. For many practical purposes, such as allocating students to educational programmes, the resources simply are not available to undertake extensive individual assessment.

The dilemma for typologists is how one can combine the practical efficiency of the *nomothetic* approach with at least some of the *idiographic* concern for uniqueness and pattern in the individual life (Hermans, 1988). One possible compromise has been suggested by Bem (1983) in his interpretation of the so-called *morphogenic* approach. Bem suggests that the effectiveness with which lay people judge others comes about through their efforts to identify patterns of nomothetic characteristics in those around them (Fig. 2c). Typologies based on this strategy, therefore, would be interested in the interaction of nomothetic traits within each type of person. Hypotheses about these interactions could serve as guidelines for more detailed idiographic studies of individuals (Hermans, 1988; McReynolds, 1989). The attractive feature of such a conception is that it combines the strength of both approaches, using nomothetic generalizations to map out the terrain and idiographic particulars to fill in the detail. It is on these grounds that I justify the use of nomothetic traits in the typology developed here.

Stability of Inference

If an individual's behaviour changes from one situation to the next, with no apparent consistency, then there is little justification for inferring stable personality dispositions. This is precisely the claim of *situationists*-psychologists who emphasize the role of situational forces rather than personality dispositions in determining behaviour. Apparently, the difference of opinion between "personologists" and "situationists" is, like many disputes in psychology, ancient. Bem (1983) points out, for instance, that one of the earliest proponents of the self-evident truth that people *are* consistent in their behaviour was Theophrastus (372–287 B.C.), while an advocate of the self-evident truth that people are *not* consistent was Michel de Montaigne (1533–1592). The most recent outbreak of this dispute is attributed to Mischel (1968), who claimed that if you look at research that compares the behaviour of groups of people in two similar situations, the correlation between these two sets of behaviours is generally less than 0.3, an indication of relatively low levels of consistency. Obviously, this is damaging to those who are interested in the credibility of traits and types. The response of the latter to this dilemma takes several forms:

1. *Aggregation*. Personologists suggest that the research referred to by situationists in claiming low levels of consistency is flawed, because it looks only at single acts or items of behaviour:

> [I]n almost all cases the correlations were based on single items of behavior. Such correlations actually have little relevance for the existence of traits, as no trait theorist believes that a trait can be inferred from a single instance of behavior. A trait is a generalized tendency for a person to behave in a certain manner over a sufficient sample of events and does not imply that he or she will exhibit trait-relevant behavior in all situations or even on all occasions in the same situation. (Epstein, 1979, p. 1102)

In other words, you have to observe many different kinds of behaviour across many situations before you can infer the presence of a trait. Even then, you end up making inferences about a general tendency, not an automatic behaviour that shows itself invariably in all situations.

The personological argument can be illustrated by reference to a classical study on honesty carried out many years ago on 8,000 school children. A team of researchers assessed the children on about twenty measures of honesty, including: cheating in the classroom; cheating during a game; stealing money; lying; falsifying records; and so on. When scores on these behaviours were intercorrelated in pairs, only low correlations of around 0.23 were found. Being a classical study, this finding is often cited in support of the situationist position. According to Epstein (Epstein, 1979; Epstein & O'Brien, 1985), however, what is commonly overlooked is that, when the same data are *aggregated* (the scores of several tests of honesty combined into an aggregate score) then the correlations obtained rise dramatically to 0.7 or above. One conclusion that can be drawn from this is that you can find either consistency or inconsistency in behaviour depending on the way in which you collect and analyse your data, which leads us to the next point.

2. *Genotypic-phenotypic*. When you are trying to demonstrate that a person shows a particular trait, it is natural to look for *consistent behaviour*, or what researchers might call multiple acts. For instance, you may decide that a child is honest after observing honest behaviour in many diverse situations. In doing so, you have established *phenotypic* consistency-behaviour that *on the face of it* appears to be consistent. However, what about a child who is quiet and obedient at home but unruly and difficult at school? Phenotypically, there is no apparent consistency here, nor is there evidence of a trait. Is it possible, though, that there is some "underlying" consistency that ties these apparently

contradictory behaviours together at a *genotypic* level? One could speculate that the child has decided that the best way to obtain attention is to behave as a model child at home, while school requires more assertive behaviour. It would seem plausible, in such a case, to propose some kind of motivational trait, such as *need for* attention. Thus, the personologists argue that situationists are overly concerned with phenotypic consistency and summary/surface traits, thereby overlooking the kinds of genotypic consistency that exist.

However plausible the argument for genotypic consistency might sound, it is important to remember that it is open to abuse. Since genotypic traits are based on speculations about the way in which disparate behaviours are related, it is easy enough to allow one's imagination to run riot. Some critics see this as a major problem in psychodynamic theories of personality in which, for instance, a son or daughter who shows great solicitude for their elderly parents, constantly proclaims his or her love for them, and spends a great deal of time attending to their needs, could be interpreted as showing the defence of *reaction formation*, i.e., trying to cover up an intense hatred of his or her parents by behaving in exactly the opposite way. Clearly, speculation about underlying genotypic traits needs to be carefully controlled.

3. *Some people more than others.* When the correlation of 0.3 is quoted in support of low cross-situational consistency in behaviour, the coefficient is based on the scores of a *group* of subjects. Such a procedure may obscure the true levels of consistency that actually exist because research has demonstrated that some people are more consistent in their behaviour than others (Kenrick & Dantchik, 1983). Correlations from an unselected group are, therefore, average figures which tell you little about the range of consistency in that group.

Gangestad and Snyder (1985) have found, for instance, that people vary greatly in their level of *self-monitoring*, which is the tendency to monitor one's own behaviour and to behave in a way that suits the demands of the situation, thereby presenting oneself in the best light. Those who score high in self-monitoring are very sensitive to situational demands, taking pains to adjust their behaviour accordingly. As a result, their behaviour is more variable, more attuned to the nuances of each situation in which they find themselves. It follows that it would be more difficult to identify trait-like consistency in such individuals, as compared to those who score low in self-monitoring. The latter appear to lack either the ability or motivation to bother about adjusting their behaviour to each and every situation they come across and so are more likely to show cross-situational consistency.

Thus, the notion of a stable personality trait may be applied appropriately to some people more than others. Typologies are likely to concentrate on such consistent individuals, particularly when a *prototypical* approach is advocated, as it is here.

4. *Apportioning variance.* In arguments about the stability and import-ance of personality traits, situationists claim that the variance attributable to personality variables is usually smaller than that attributable to situational and interactional components. Put another way, this argument implies that personality variables, such as traits, are not as useful as situational variables in helping explain why people differ in their behaviour. A typical personological response to this is:

> [T]he proportion of variance attributable to any one factor, such as individuals, is always influenced by the range of variability represented by the other factors. Thus, if situations are selected over a wide range of variability and individuals over a narrow range, the proportion of variance for individuals will be smaller than that for situations. It is evident that depending on how one selects individuals and situations, and how the two are selected in relationship to each other, individuals, situations, or their interaction can be made relatively large or small. (Epstein, 1979, p. 1102)

In other words, both situationists and personologists can find evidence in support of their positions because research studies are designed differently and, inadvertently, produce contradictory findings.

These, and other arguments along the same lines, have enabled personologists to reassert their belief in the utility of a trait approach to the study of behaviour (A. H. Buss, 1989; Carson, 1989; Kenrick & Funder, 1988). Given the ancient nature of the dispute, however, it is unlikely that the disputants have been persuaded of the folly of their ways. One has the sense that the current round of argument has faded away because everyone is bored with it or, as Maddi (1984) implies, because it no longer serves any purpose within psychological politics. Extremes of personology and situationism have given way at least to the appearance of a more moderate interactionist view which asserts that behaviour is best understood as a function of the interaction between both personality *and* situational characteristics.

Within such a framework, however, one is still faced with the task of characterizing the person (Bem, 1983). Perhaps the most useful attitude to adopt on the question of traits, therefore, is that of Hampson *et al.* (1986) and Zuroff (1986), who suggest that we turn our attention to determining how broadly and narrowly defined traits might be used appropriately. Given my interest in typologies, I am attracted to A. H. Buss's (1989) conclusions on the matter that, if one's goal is a comprehen-sive picture of personality, broader traits are preferable simply because there are fewer of them. The search for such broad traits and how they might be incorporated into a typology is something to which we shall return later in the chapter.

PERSONALITY TYPES

In a general sense, a *type* is a group or category of things distinguished by the common characteristics of its members. A *personality type*, therefore, is a category of people who exhibit a particular combination of psychological characteristics, the assumption being that this combination is unique and distinguishes the type from others.

Since ancient times, there has been a great deal of speculation about types of people. One of the earliest, and most influential, personality typologies comes to us from ancient Greece where a number of scholars, such as Aristotle, Galen, and Hippocrates, contributed to the development of a typological theory of temperament based on the doctrine of "humors." The four humors (blood, black bile, yellow bile, phlegm) were seen as bodily substances that combined in various ways to produce four types of temperament. This is not quite as ridiculous as it might appear for, in modern times, we can talk legitimately about the influence not of humors, but of hormones on temperament. Thus, in ancient times, a preponderance of blood was said to lead to a *sanguine* or enthusiastic temperament; the sadness of the *melancholic* was attributed to an excess of black bile; an over-abundance of yellow bile produced the irritability of the *choleric*; and finally, the slowness and apathy of the *phlegmatic* was due to the influence of phlegm. Since the humors were thought to leave their mark on the body, particularly the face, each type could be recognized by its characteristic physiognomy (Fig. 3). Thus:

> the slenderness and delicate texture of the *melancholic* type is given by nature, but the downcast eyes and vertical furrows in the brow reflect acquired habits of withdrawal and unpleasant thought. Similarly, the *choleric* face betrays natural vigor and strength of temperament plus acquired habits of open-eyed responsiveness to the environment and a heavy seaming due to intense emotional feeling. The *phlegmatic* face is lethargic in build, inattentive in habit; and lines on the face are due to fat rather than feeling. The *sanguine* face is normal enough in bony structure, but is not marked by lines indicating deep or lasting emotional experience. (Allport, 1961, p. 40)

The important feature of this typology is the fact that it is *categorical*; it depicts discrete personality types that do not overlap with one another or share common psychological characteristics. In other words, the four temperaments are qualitatively different from one another, as well as being mutually exclusive, so that a person can be identified with only one type (Peterson, 1988). This categorical tradition is still to be found in

1. Melancholic   2. Choleric

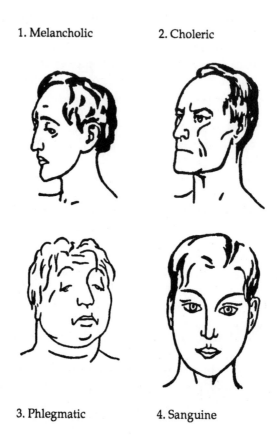

3. Phlegmatic   4. Sanguine

Figure 3. Physiognomic representations of the four temperaments. (From Allport, 1961.)

modern psychiatry where personality disorders are classified into qualitatively different types (Widiger & Kelso, 1983), although the situation does appear to be changing (Millon, 1986a,c).

As the discipline of psychology became more established in the late nineteenth century, however, it became apparent to researchers that psychological characteristics tend to be both continuously and normally distributed. Relatively few people obtain extremely low or high scores, while the majority cluster in the central part of the dimension. It is unusual to see discontinuities in the distribution. For those interested in typologies, the obvious implication was that, in attempting to develop models of personality, they would need to take this new understanding into account, basing their typologies on personality dimensions, rather than using the older categorical approach. An early attempt to do so can be found in Wundt's "dimensionalization" of the ancient Greek theory of temperaments (Fig. 4a; Eysenck & Eysenck, 1985). This has been elaborated further by Eysenck based on his conception of introversion–extraversion and neuroticism–stability (Fig. 4b), a typology that has achieved considerable popularity, especially in Britain, because of its practical usefulness.

Both categorical and dimensional approaches to personality typologies have run into difficulties, however, because of the assumptions on which they are based. Both of them assume that in devising a personality typology, one should try to identify a discrete category of people which can be differentiated from others by a precise list of personality characteristics. In this sense, the type or category would be homogeneous (composed of people who share all the defining attributes) and distinct (clearly different from other types) (Livesley, 1985). This *classical* conception of a category is borrowed from the field of logic and has been the prevailing view in psychological research. When applied to personality theory, however, it creates a number of significant problems (Widiger & Frances, 1985).

Problems with Classical Types

In practice, the identification of classical categories is difficult to achieve, because in most cases people grade into one another to such an extent that it is not clear where to draw the line between one "type" and another. Thus, finding a homogeneous group of people who share all the characteristics they are supposed to exhibit is often impossible, for individuals may show some, but not all, of the defining features of a "type." Problems of this kind have been complicated further by the modern tendency to look for dimensional types, a strategy that makes the question of continuity/discontinuity an issue of crucial importance. Thus, if it is not possible to demonstrate some form of discontinuity between people, "the notion of a type becomes a verbal convenience rather than a meaningful mode of categorization" (Mendelsohn *et al.*, 1982, p. 1159). This is a matter we need to look at more closely.

There are at least three ways to define classical types using psychological dimensions (A. R. Buss & Poley, 1976). If one uses only a single dimension, it is possible to describe the extremes as "types" (Fig. 5a). However, this is possible only if some arbitrary cut-off points are used, so that people who score beyond these points are included in the types. As you can imagine, this is unsatisfactory because there is frequently little rational basis for deciding where the cut-off points should be. Essentially, you could put them anywhere and, therefore, include

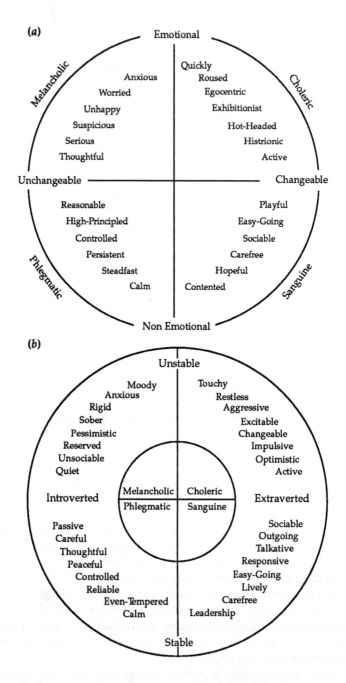

Figure 4. Dimensional representations of the ancient Greek temperaments. (From Eysenck & Eysenck, 1985.)

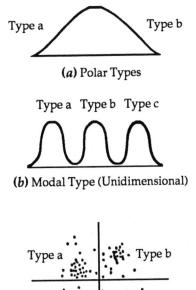

(*a*) Polar Types

(*b*) Modal Type (Unidimensional)

(*c*) Species Type (Modal Multidimensional)

Figure 5. Dimensional types. (From Buss & Poley, 1976.)

virtually anyone in the "types" you are trying to establish. If the distribution of scores on the personality dimension in question was multimodal (Fig. 5b), i.e., showing some natural grouping of people, then the problem might be eased somewhat. Unfortunately, however, multimodal distributions are uncommon. Finally, the use of two or more dimensions to define a type (Fig. 5c) suffers from the same problem found in using a single dimension. Unless there are clearly defined areas of density, you are still faced with having to make an arbitrary decision about who is to be included in your "type."

This preoccupation with establishing discontinuity, and the methodological arguments it generates (e.g., Block & Ozer, 1982; Hicks, 1984; M. Miller & Thayer, 1989; Weiss *et al.*, 1982), is, I believe, wasted effort. For, in defining typologies in terms of classical categories, and seeking empirical evidence to support such typologies, psychologists may have been setting themselves an impossible task. The reason for this is that recent research on *natural categories* (i.e. categories we use to classify things in everyday life) suggests that they are organized around *prototypes*. One conclusion from this research is that, while classical categories are eminently suitable for certain kinds of research in logic and science, natural categories most adequately represent the world around us, and the people in it. Thus, rather than dismissing personality types as a lost cause, a more reasonable conclusion might be that, while it is difficult to demonstrate the existence of *classical* personality types, other forms of typology may be quite legitimate. We should, perhaps, be thinking of personality typologies in terms of *prototypes* (Broughton, 1990).

Prototypes and Natural Categories

A *prototype* is the best example of a category. For example, when you use the category "bird," the most typical example of a bird, in your mind, is likely to be something like a robin, sparrow, or blackbird, and not something like an ostrich or penguin. Thus, some members of a category are more typical than others, which allows us to conclude that a robin is a *prototype* of the category "bird." Eleanor Rosch has demonstrated that natural categories are organized around a central cluster of prototypical examples with less typical examples (such as penguins) located at the margins of the category (Rosch,1978).

An important feature of prototypes is that, while they are the best examples of a category, they do not exhibit *all* the characteristics of *all* the members of a category. They show only typical characteristics. Or to put it in another way, the prototypical bird (robin) flies, chirps, has feathers, wings and clawed feet, but ostriches have only some of these features, while penguins have none. Yet, you would still classify ostriches and penguins as birds because they share some important features with robins, such as reproducing by laying eggs, as well as having beaks and other anatomical similarities. These peculiarities of prototypes means that *natural* categories are quite unlike *classical* categories. Natural categories are not identified by some definitive list of necessary and sufficient psychological characteristics but, rather, the requirement for membership is only that a prospective member (penguin) should exhibit some of the typical features of the prototype (robin). Thus, the decision about whether or not to include something in a natural category depends on its similarity to the prototype for that category. In some cases, an object or event may be included in a category even though it shares only one or two characteristics with the prototype (as in the case of penguins). These marginal members of a natural category can, therefore, overlap with other categories without calling into question the value of, for example, the category "bird." Thus, the preoccupation with distinct boundaries, homogeneous membership, and lists of defining features, which is so important in the case of classical categories, becomes less important when dealing with natural categories. Separation into types, therefore, is achieved by considering each category in terms of its clear cases, rather than in terms of its boundaries (Livesley, 1985, 1986).

Implications of Prototypes for Personality Typologies

There is now a great deal of research in support of the idea that we all use personality prototypes in judging others (e.g., Cantor & Mischel, 1977, 1979). Each prototype is based on a store of knowledge about the traits, behaviours and situations associated with a particular type of person. Just as in dealing with other natural categories, we use these prototypes as standards or templates against which to judge some new acquaintances. The fact that the use of personality prototypes is commonplace in everyday life does not, of course, mean that such a strategy should be taken in developing personality theory. The reason I suggest so here is that I believe that there is no alternative. There appears to be no prospect of developing personality typologies based on classical categories and I am convinced by Rosch (1983) that the kind of complex, fuzzy data associated with our impressions of others can *only* be dealt with by using prototypes. An additional advantage in using prototypes is that they allow one to reconcile categorical and dimensional views of personality. Since prototypal assumptions do not require the demonstration of discontinuities for the definition of types, categories can be defined in dimensional terms by using, for example, the trait clusters or profiles exhibited by prototypical exemplars (Kiesler, 1986; Romney & Bynner, 1989; Widiger *et al.*, 1987).

Not everyone, of course, will find such an argument acceptable, notably the tough-minded psychologist who might have the following objections. First, personality prototypes are just another way of referring to social stereotypes which, as everyone knows, tend to be crude oversimplifications that easily lend themselves to biased and prejudiced ways of thinking. This is certainly not the route that scientific psychology should follow. Second, we should persevere with classical categories because their clarity and precision provide the only satisfactory basis for scientific classification. After all, they have been used with enormous success in scientific taxonomies so there is no reason, in principle, why similar success should not be achieved in dealing with people.

The counter-argument runs something like this. It is not inevitable that personality prototypes should degenerate into crude social stereotypes. Indeed, it is the responsibility of personality psychologists to devise prototypes that avoid this problem. In addition, as we shall discover in Chapter 2, some classification tasks are best approached using the analytic precision of classical categories whereas other tasks are not. For instance, when classification can be based on clear, readily definable attributes of the kind involved in classifying chemical elements, then classical categories are appropriate. On the other hand, where it is difficult to select and define some mutually agreeable set of attributes, then another classification strategy, such as the use of prototypes, is necessary. Such is the case in dealing with the classification of personality types. As Wiggins (1982) notes, Neisser (1979) exemplifies this view in his discussion of the problems involved in deciding what we mean by an "intelligent person":

> In my opinion, then, *intelligent person* is a prototype-organized Roschian concept. Our confidence that a person deserves to be called "intelligent" depends on that person's overall similarity to an imagined prototype, just as our confidence that some object is to be called "chair" depends on its similarity to prototypical chairs. There are no definitive criteria of intelligence, just as there are none for chairness; it is a fuzzy-edged concept to which many features are relevant. Two people may both be quite intelligent and yet have very few traits in common—they resemble the prototype along different dimensions. (in Neisser, 1979, p. 223)

What Neisser is saying is that, while we all have a conception of what an intelligent person might be, we differ amongst ourselves in the exact meaning of the phrase and so, find it difficult to pin down what we mean with any precision. It follows that we would also have problems in both defining and measuring the concept.

Where does this leave us? If you are inclined toward the tough-minded view, you may consider what follows in this book as a dubious form of psychology, one that is arguing for fuzzy ideas and rather unscientific forms of classification. If, on the other hand, you are persuaded by the argument, then you may be more willing to accept the usefulness of personality prototypes. In either case, what we need to turn to now is the business of identifying and describing personality prototypes, and the question becomes how one might undertake such a daunting task. My approach to model-building is not confined to, or by, the results of empirical studies but involves a more eclectic strategy, aptly described by Maddi (1976) as:

> [P]ersonality theories are not based solely ... on empirical knowledge. To my mind, this state of affairs is neither surprising nor disadvantageous. When

set alongside the richness and complexity of people and their lives, the empirical knowledge available to the personologist is scanty and sometimes so partisan as to be severely limited in generality. Under these conditions, how can it possibly be surprising that personality theories would not be based completely on empirical knowledge? Far from being disadvantageous, the inclusion in personality theories of statements not firmly based in empiricism is a potentially fruitful procedure.... It is true that the theorist risks being wrong, but he will find out soon enough when the empirical development of the field catches up ... meanwhile, the theorist can feel justified that the statements he makes ... will spur his colleagues to make observations and plan experiments that they might not have envisioned otherwise. (Maddi, 1976, p. 10)

Thus, along with Maddi, I see theory development as a speculative exercise, one that uses a mixture of intuitive, rational, and empirical knowledge. My intuitive sense of what is important in personality theory comes from a reading of both venerable and modern sources. The rational element is described below as a search for a conceptual framework with which to guide the selection of traits, and more modern empirical findings serve to clarify and elaborate personality conceptions, such as "emotionality," that have been used for millenia. I recognize that this approach may not satisfy the tough-minded positivist who would prefer a more data-driven theory. However, as Hogan (1983) and others recognize, theory is as much a product of the person as it is of the available evidence. Although I recognize the merits of positivism, I think it is a mistake to regard it as the only acceptable epistemic basis for theory construction.

Thus, the model of personality developed here had its origins in my informal observations of individual differences amongst academics and professionals, and the intuitive sense that distinct prototypes were clearly evident. My study of the psychological, and other, literature, therefore, has been to determine whether others have reached similar conclusions and to find ways in which such prototypes might be parsimoniously described and validated. It is to one element of this search that we now turn.

IN SEARCH OF GENOTYPIC TRAITS

As mentioned earlier, *genotypic* traits (also known as source and dispositional traits) are hypothetical constructions that refer to fundamental characteristics of the person and reflect what Allport (1961) calls the core-dynamics of personality. In contrast, *phenotypic* (surface, summary) traits are more superficial, since they entail simple summaries of the person's behaviour devoid of any causal or explanatory meaning.

A great deal of effort has been expended over many decades in pursuit of acceptable conceptions of genotypic traits. The resulting diversity of opinion seems to be a natural consequence of the widely differing approaches to the task which range, according to A. H. Buss and Finn (1987), from atheoretical factor analytic studies (e.g., Cattell; Guilford) to conceptual invention (e.g., Jung) and various mixtures of the two (e.g., Eysenck; Wiggins). Many observers of the scene find the end-products of all this effort profoundly disappointing. Millon (1981), for instance, observes that little consensus has been achieved about the number or kind of dimensions needed to represent personality adequately, a consequence of the excessive subjectivity of researchers whom, he suggests, simply invent traits to suit their predilections. The net result is that "catalogs of convenience have replaced meaningful taxonomies of personality traits amongst most of the current generation of social/personality researchers" (McCrae & Costa, 1987, p. 81). Such a melancholy situation need not persist, however. While it is true that all traits are "inventions," in the sense that they are hypothetical constructs, this does not mean that one has to accept taxonomic chaos. If it were possible for trait theorists at least to agree on the implicative meaning (Wiggins, 1973) of their inventions, then steps could be taken to determine whether such traits have some "existence" in the "real" world. Traits do not have to remain as figments of a feverish imagination.

One of the more promising methods for achieving consensus on the implicative meaning of traits is factor analysis. Champions of the approach argue that it is an excellent tool with which to determine the underlying structure of data sets (McCrae & Costa, 1984). Blashfield (1984), for instance, recognizes its merits in constructing personality dimensions. Critics of factor analysis have two qualms, however. First, there is the endless squabbling amongst factor analysts over nuances of technique and interpretation (Mershon & Gorsuch, 1988). The thirty year "debate" between Cattell, Eysenck and Guilford (Eysenck & Eysenck, 1985) is a case in point, with each theorist steadfastly defending his own framework, claiming errors and conceptual problems in the others' work. Something of the flavour of the debate is caught by Digman and Inouye (1986) who state that "no one has been able to replicate Cattell's dozen or more factors ... there is the further suspicion that [they] were founded on clerical errors that plagued factor analysis in the precomputer era" (p. 121). The same authors claim, of course, that their factor solution is preferable. In contrast, Cattell (1970) maintains that his source traits have been replicated and confirmed on numerous occasions. Needless to say, this internecine warfare does not imbue one with confidence in the field.

Second, there is the problem alluded to above, the question of the meaningfulness of factorially derived traits. Factors are statistical entities, convenient fictions that may or may not be psychologically meaningful.

Both Revelle (1983) and Brandt (1982) claim that many psychologists are apt to forget this, instead, tending to reify the products of factor analysis. Revelle, in particular, is doubtful about the usefulness of factor analysis in creating meaningful concepts. He argues, for instance, that the hierarchical structures generated by factor analysis do not imply that such structures "exist" in nature; replicability of factors simply may imply an identity of method and assumption; factor analysis may produce hypotheses about "underlying structure" but cannot determine if this interpretation is correct; similarly, one cannot conclude that factors "cause" patterns of data; and finally, all you can do with factorial models is accept or reject them, you cannot determine whether they are correct in some sense. Eysenck and Eysenck (1985) are more sanguine about establishing the meaningfulness of factorial traits, however, something they regard as a matter for research beyond the confines of factor analysis. One approach, for instance, is to compare factorial traits with those based on clinical judgment. When one does this, the results are equivocal. Clinicians are inclined to conclude that the two sets of factors do not correspond very well (Phares, 1988). However, Cattell (1970) believes that the discrepancy between these two domains is more apparent than real, a result of the resistance amongst clinicians to what they see as the rather arcane products of factor analysis. The fact of the matter, says Cattell, is that his factors bear striking resemblance to the traits used in clinical work, despite their rather unfamiliar labels.

What can be concluded from all this? One accepts, of course, that factors and traits are convenient fictions and that factor analysts will tend to argue over the details of factorial solutions. If, however, some degree of consensus emerges, from a variety of unrelated studies, then at least the implicative meaning of a particular set of traits has been established. The question of the "realness" of such traits is, as the Eysencks point out, a matter for further deliberation. Fortunately for my purposes here, and despite the apparent confusion in the search for genotypic traits, a substantial degree of unanimity is emerging around what have become known as the "Big 5" factors.

The Big 5 (or 6?) Factors

The factorial systems of Cattell, Eysenck, and Guilford, together with the tests derived from them (16 PF, EPI and the Guilford–Zimmerman Temperament Survey, respectively) have, along with the MMPI and the California Personality Inventory, dominated the field of personality assessment and research (McCrae & Costa, 1985). This is unfortunate since the various disputes referred to above have deflected attention from

TABLE 1. THE ROBUST PERSONALITY TRAITS[†]

United States	United Kingdom
Surgency	*Energy*
talkative–silent	talkative–silent
sociable–reclusive	sociable–unsociable
adventurous–cautious	adventurous–cautious
Agreeableness	*Affection*
good natured–irritable	trusting–suspicious
mild–headstrong	affectionate–hostile
cooperative–negativistic	cooperative–uncooperative
Conscientiousness	*Conscience*
responsible–undependable	responsible–irresponsible
persevering–quitting	persistent–quitting
tidy–careless	order–disorder
Emotional Stability	*Neuroticism*
calm–anxious	calm–anxious
composed–excitable	composed–excitable
poised–nervous	poised–nervous
Intellect	*Intelligence*
intellectual–nonreflective	general intelligence ("g")
imaginative–simple	cognitive ability
artistically sensitive–insensitive	analytical capacity
	Will
	independent–dependent
	dominating–submissive
	strong willed–weak

[†] Modified from Digman and Inouye (1986) and Brand (1984).

some interesting new developments in factor analytic approaches to personality structure.

Conley (1985a), Costa and McCrae (1988), Digman and Inouye (1986), and McCrae and Costa (1985, 1987) summarize extensive recent work in the United States confirming the earlier findings of, among others, Norman (1963), that the personality domain can be represented adequately by five robust factors (Table 1). In an independent review from a primarily British perspective, Brand (1984) comes to similar conclusions (Table 1). The difference between the two models is due to the preference of some researchers for splitting the energy/surgency/extraversion factor into sociability and willfulness components (McCrae & Costa, 1987). In addition, cross-cultural studies of personality trait usage in the Dutch, German and Japanese languages offers additional support for the generality of the Robust Traits (John *et al.*, 1988).

The question is, of course, whether the five (or six) factors in these schemes are as important as their advocates claim. Some critics argue that, while the Robust Traits may correspond to the popular, lay, view of personality, experts should be able to make finer distinctions than the average person. Thus, research and clinical practice might be better served by models composed of thirteen to eighteen factors (Mershon & Gorsuch, 1988). However, my sense of this argument is that it is taking place between what Holton (1978) calls "lumpers" and "splitters" and, as such, may reflect cognitive style rather than some empirical reality. A second criticism of this work is that it deals merely with language labels rather than "genuine" psychological characteristics. This is a version of the meaningfulness problem discussed earlier. That is, the strategy used by Norman, as well as Cattell, was to seek out the factorial structure underlying trait terms commonly found in the English language (John *et al.*, 1988). As McCrae and Costa (1985) point out, however:

> The argument that personality is exhaustively captured by the evolution of natural language is appealing, but by no means compelling. One might argue that the research of psychologists in the past century has uncovered important aspects of personality that were not encoded in the language. No one would imagine that an analysis of common English terms for parts of the body would provide an adequate basis for the science of anatomy; why should personality be different? (McCrae & Costa, 1985, p. 74)

The same authors point out that, until 1985, the five-factor solution remained empirically isolated and its promise as an adequate personality taxonomy awaited attempts to link these linguistically based factors to other approaches to a comprehensive personality system. The most recent research reported by Digman (Digman, 1989; Digman & Inouye, 1986) and McCrae and Costa (1987, 1989a,b) has established such links, thereby enabling one to be more confident that the five factors are as robust as they are claimed to be. What I have done in my own theorizing is to adopt these five (or six) factors as hypotheses about genotypic traits and use some of them in developing a three-dimensional typology.

TOWARD A NEW PERSONALITY TYPOLOGY

One problem with trait lists, such as those in Table 1, is that there is no indication of meaningful relationships amongst the traits listed. One of the strengths of a typology, however, is that it *does* attempt to portray the relationships between selected traits. In developing a typology, therefore, one is faced with the problem of how many, and which, traits should be incorporated into the model. As might be expected, theorists deal with the dilemma in various ways. Wiggins (1980), for instance, has constructed an "Interpersonal Circumplex" around two orthogonal traits of *power* and *love*, his choice being influenced by Sullivan's interpersonal theory of personality. (See Chapter 4 for a more detailed discussion.) Additional traits, related obliquely to one another and to the two generic dimensions, complete the model. In a similar vein, Eysenck's (Eysenck & Eysenck, 1985) three-dimensional model is derived in part from historical precedent, confirmed and elaborated by factor analytical and experimental studies of normal and clinical populations. Millon (1986a-c), too, has generated a three-dimensional representation of personality after combining his study of historical precedent with extensive clinical experience. A significant lesson to be drawn from all this is that the authors of these influential typologies have opted for relatively simple models based on a small number of generic traits selected on the basis of historical precedent, personal predilection, and recent empirical findings. Clearly, from my earlier comments, I am in sympathy with this approach and intend to follow it here. However, one significant refinement needs to be made. The models of Wiggins, Eysenck, and Millon do not cover the whole personality domain, one notable omission being the absence, in all of them, of a cognitive dimension. In constructing a typology, therefore, one is faced with the problem of finding some way in which to cover all of the most important aspects of personality without making the model either too complex or too simple. In seeking an organizational principle that would accommodate these demands, I am attracted, along with A. H. Buss and Finn (1987), to the old tripartite system that has informed psychology over the centuries, one that recognizes three psychological domains: cognition, affection, and conation. The use of this system and the selection of one genotypic dimension to represent each domain, would result in a relatively simple but comprehensive three-dimensional typology. The question is whether this would be a sensible approach.

The Tripartite System

Interest in the tripartite system has waxed and waned over the years. During the nineteenth century, for example, it was the dominant classificatory system providing the foundation for faculty psychology (Hilgard, 1980). Ultimately, this association led to its downfall, however, when it became apparent that one could not talk about psychological processes as totally independent faculties, each replete with its own laws and development. This disfavour has persisted into the twentieth century, a fact that cannot be accounted for solely by the behavioural dominance of psychology for, despite the reintroduction of dispositional concepts ushered in by the cognitive revolution, the affective and conative (motivational) domains have received short shrift (Pervin, 1983; Sorrentino & Higgins, 1986). However, the intellectual climate in psychology is changing and one sees, for example, recent attempts to incorporate aspects of all three domains in current research on personality disorders (Benjamin, 1986) and adaptive behaviour (Dweck & Leggett, 1988). In doing so, these authors implicitly endorse the old tripartite system, stripped of its "faculty" connotations. Of course, this is not to everyone's satisfaction. There are those who argue that the recognition of cognition/affection/ conation as separate processes seriously misrepresents the unity of psychological functioning and, worse, once you have broken the individual into pieces you are faced with the unenviable task of putting Humpty-Dumpty back together again (Bruner, 1986; Lazarus *et al.*, 1984; Revelle, 1983; Santostefano, 1986). Rather than reverting to an outmoded way of thinking, they say, it would be better to find other ways of dealing with the multiple processes within each of us. While this is an admirable sentiment, until other ways are found one has recourse only to more traditional approaches which involve the analytic separation of processes followed by attempts to describe their many interactions. My personality typology, therefore, is composed of cognitive, affective, and conative dimensions.

The Selection of Genotypic Traits

In developing the model, I assume that the Robust Traits provide a convenient starting point from which to construct appropriate dimensions. Accordingly, I have modified some of these trait conceptions and discarded others in light of my understanding of the broader personality literature. The details of these changes, and the reasons for them, are described in Chapters 2 to 4. Only a brief summary is offered here.

The identification of an intellectual factor as an important genotypic trait (Table 1) underscores the need to include a cognitive dimension in the typology. Unfortunately the precise composition of this factor remains controversial. From Brand's (1984) British perspective, it is depicted as general intelligence, "*g*," and assessed in terms of mental ability. In contrast, the U.S. work on the *intellect* factor is based, not on ability measures, but on reports of the qualities thought to be associated with intelligence, which include artistic and intellectual interests, cultural sophistication, inquiring intellect, and openness to experience. As a result, American factor analysts have had great difficulty in achieving consensus on the nature of this fifth factor, although there is agreement that it is not a matter of ability. We are presented with something of a dilemma, therefore, whether to represent the cognitive dimension as general intelligence or in terms of the non-intellective correlates of intelligence. I have chosen to do neither, preferring, instead, to think of the dimension in terms of *cognitive styles*. There are two reasons for this. First, ability and intellective conceptions of "intelligence" refer to *what* people are capable of or what they prefer to "cognize." In other words, they are *content* aspects of personality. Unfortunately, the content domain is so large that it is difficult to decide how best to represent it. For instance, there are many kinds of "intelligence" and much dispute over the most suitable ways in which to assess each kind (Eysenck & Eysenck, 1985). In contrast, the stylistic aspects of behaviour (i.e. *how* people behave) can be represented parsimoniously by relatively few variables (Royce & Powell, 1983). Second, the available evidence appears to indicate that cognitive styles exhibit strong cross-situational consistency and are (according to Bem, 1983) among the most promising genotypic traits one might include in a personality typology.

The most suitable cognitive style dimension, for my purposes, almost selects itself, for as Brand (1984) notes: "A serious possibility is that there are omnipresent differences between people in whether they attend narrowly to (self-) selected aspects of reality or whether they are more broadly attentive" (p. 195). The distinction alluded to here, between cognitive narrowness and broadness, is ancient and is one that has not only recurred over the centuries but also continues to play a major role in the way that cognitive differences are depicted (Coan, 1979). Of the many labels that could be used for this style dimension, I prefer *analytic–holistic*, a distinction that is discussed at greater length in Chapter 2.

Two of the Robust Traits have an emotional flavour, namely: surgency/energy and emotional stability/neuroticism. Indeed, they are identical to Eysenck's Extraversion and Neuroticism, respectively, which are considered to be dimensions of temperament or emotional style. The possibility of representing the affective dimension of the model in terms of emotional styles is appealing for, like cognitive styles, they offer a parsimonious way of depicting a specific personality domain. Given that two generic traits have been identified, however, the question is which should be selected for inclusion in the model. My decision has been to use both. Since the reasoning behind this is too convoluted to summarize here, suffice it to say that the affective dimension, labelled *emotional stability–instability*, combines elements of both Extraversion and Neuroticism into an *affective intensity* dimension. The matter is explained further in Chapter 3.

The term *conation* appears to have dropped out of common usage along with the demise of faculty psychology and has been replaced by the more

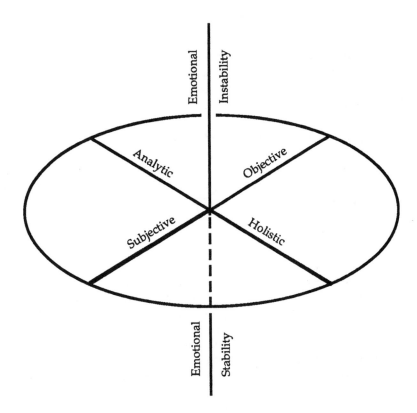

Figure 6. A three-dimensional typology. (From A. Miller, 1988.)

familiar term *motivation*. However, *conation* and *conative* carry implications of an effortful, striving, self-willing form of behaviour rather than the expression of some biological urge or a mechanical response to situational pressures. In other words, conation has to do with *volition*, a psychological concept that has languished in the backwaters of psychological theory for decades and is only now beginning to resurface (Westcott, 1985). The selection of a conative dimension for my model is aided by Brand's (1984) observation of what he calls a certain negative tension between his will and affection factors which suggests the possibility of a higher-order *will–affection* dimension that is clearly conative in nature. The contrast he has in mind is between striving for autonomy/power/masculinity (will) and dependence/cooperation/femininity (affection). Recent reinterpretations of the conscientiousness factor (Table 1), by such American factor analysts as Digman (1989), emphasize its "will" component and therefore support the possibility of a higher-order conscientiousness (will)–agreeableness factor. However, the inclination of Wiggins (1980) and other circumplex theorists is to retain an orthogonal relationship between the two factors. One of the interesting features of a *will–affection* dimension, however, is that it bears a striking resemblance to William James's tough–tender mindedness (James, 1907), a dichotomy that is said to date back to the Socratic–Sophist dialogues of ancient times and continues to the present day in various guises (Kimble, 1984). Given that I am predisposed to ancient precedent, I include a more modern version of the dimension, relabelled *objective–subjective*, in my model and elaborate it further in Chapter 4.

A Three-Dimensional Personality Typology

The model that results from all this (Fig. 6) depicts personality in its simplest and most abstract form. As we examine it in more detail, however, it will become clear that each genotypic dimension is actually rather complex, as are the types derived from them. The model allows one to identify eight types, selected examples of which will be discussed in Chapter 6.

There is nothing quite like this typology among the dozens extant, although it overlaps with many. For instance, in emphasizing objectivity–subjectivity, it shares a concern for the difference between external and internal orientations with such theorists as Heymans, McDougall, and Jung (Millon, 1981). The use of an emotionality dimension is also common enough among some of the older typologists such as Heymans (Van Der Werff, 1985) as well as in the more modern work of Eysenck (Eysenck & Eysenck, 1985) and McCrae and Costa (1984). Virtually no typologist, however, has included a purely cognitive dimension in their model. Jung's two functions of thinking–feeling and sensing–intuiting come close to my analytic–holistic style, but appear to be a mixture of cognitive and conative processes. Perhaps the closest to my model are the relatively unknown typologies of Conley (1985b), Cotgrove (1982) and Gittinger (in Bem, 1983), all of whom include separate cognitive and conative dimensions resembling those in Fig. 6.

In what follows, I discuss each dimension under the heading of personality *structure*, before looking at how they interact in the section on personality *dynamics*. This provides the necessary foundation for an elaboration of the structure and dynamics of personality *prototypes* in their normal and abnormal forms.

Chapter 2

The Cognitive Dimension

A T FIRST GLANCE, the decision to represent the cognitive dimension of my personality model as a *cognitive style* may seem unwise for, after a flurry of activity in the 1950s and 1960s, interest in cognitive styles appears to have faded away (Sternberg, 1987). This decline was, in part, a matter of unfortunate timing. Attempts to develop conceptions of cognitive styles as broad, stable dispositions were gathering momentum at precisely the same time as the person-situation debate in psychology was fermenting yet again. The subsequent dominance of situationist-behavioural views (Chapter 1) created a climate that was uncongenial to the notion of stylistic traits. In addition, interested parties were having difficulty in sorting out the many overlapping conceptions of cognitive style that appeared on the scene and even greater difficulty providing credible evidence in support of their favoured "style" (Messick, 1984). However, the *coup de grâce* appears to have resulted from the loss of the field's leading figures, either through death or the decision to seek fresh pastures (Kogan, 1983). Consequently, the vast literature on cognitive styles gives the impression of being both dated and stale, hardly a promising source of ideas for personality theory. Fortunately, some recent developments make the situation less discouraging. There is, of course, the return to favour of personality traits, which affords some added credibility to speculation about styles. However, more important is the growing interest of cognitive psychologists in "higher-order strategies" and the recognition that the older work on cognitive styles may provide some useful insights into these executive processes. One finds, therefore, a number of attempts to incorporate notions of cognitive style into mainstream cognitive theory (Baron, 1985; Baron *et al.*, 1986; Messick, 1987; A. Miller, 1987; Sternberg, 1987), the net result of all this being that an

29

apparently moribund concept is showing signs of life, albeit in a somewhat different form.

The purpose of this chapter, therefore, is to show how the older conceptions of cognitive style can be combined with more recent findings in cognitive psychology to construct a generic *analytic–holistic* dimension. To this end, I have developed an information-processing model in which cognitive styles represent individual differences in specific cognitive processes. In some instances, the link between style (*e.g.*, field independence) and process (*e.g.*, selective attention) is easily made, since both areas of research are well-developed. This is not always the case, however, for there are places in the model where individual differences have received little or no attention. For instance, no traditional cognitive style has been associated with analytical reasoning and, in such cases, I have had to "invent" appropriate styles. Despite these difficulties, I believe that the model is a plausible and coherent way of depicting individual differences in cognition. For the moment, however, the point to bear in mind is that the model is organized around the assumption that its eight pairs of styles and processes are subordinate components of a broad, superordinate *analytic–holistic* dimension. In what follows, I discuss each pair of styles and processes in turn, beginning with those involved in perception, then moving to memory, and, finally, to thought/ reasoning.

What is a Cognitive Style?

Before getting too involved in a discussion of the analytic–holistic dimension, it might be useful to pause for a moment to clarify the distinction between cognitive styles and cognitive abilities. In doing so, we may not be able to lay this thorny issue to rest, but we can, at least, settle on a working definition of cognitive style. I draw heavily on Messick (1984) in what follows.

1. *Content v. manner.* The concept "ability" refers to the *content* of cognition and is used in answering the question: what kind of information is being processed by what operation, in what form and how well? In contrast, the term "style" refers to the *manner* or *mode* of cognition, reflecting the *way* in which information is processed. For instance, two individuals may show equal ability in solving analogy problems but may differ dramatically in how they go about doing so. One may be logical and systematic, the other impulsive and intuitive. Hence, they show the same ability but different styles.

2. *Competence v. propensity.* In measuring ability, one seeks to assess maximal performance, emphasizing the accuracy and correctness of responses. You are interested in how well someone is *able* to perform. On

the other hand, styles are *propensities*, typical performances that are likely to be shown in a given situation. The implication is that, while people may have the ability to perform in a certain way, they may not always do so. Messick offers the example of the individual who has the ability to use either broad or narrow categories in making perceptual judgments, yet tends consistently to favour one kind of category. Messick refers to these stylistic tendencies as *generalized habits* that cut across ability domains, rather than using the term *preference* which he believes implies an easy flexibility in the use of styles. In at least some individuals, styles are embedded in personality in such a way that they may not be able to change their prevailing styles even though they may wish to do so.

3. *Unipolar v. bipolar*. Abilities are unipolar, ranging from low to high levels of a particular quality, with increasing levels implying more of the same. One's standing on an ability dimension, therefore, reflects one's proficiency with regard to that ability. Style dimensions, on the other hand, are bipolar, contrasting qualitatively different kinds of cognition. The implication is that the more you show of one kind, the less you are likely to show of the other form of cognition. Bipolarity, therefore, refers to a contrast between polar opposites, two mutually exclusive forms of perceiving and thinking. It follows that, while the high end of an ability dimension is normally considered to be more valuable (more of an ability is better than less), attempts have been made to emphasize that both stylistic poles are of equal value, each having adaptive qualities in different situations. In practice, though, this value-free notion of styles has been difficult to sustain, especially in the case of field dependence–independence, where the independence pole was originally imbued with a monopoly on virtue.

4. *Specific v. general*. Abilities are specific to a given cognitive domain, as in "verbal ability," "spatial ability" and so on, acting as *enabling* variables by facilitating performance in an area of content. Styles, on the other hand, are conceived of as broader concepts cutting across cognitive and other personality domains. As mentioned earlier, they are now being referred to as higher-order (*i.e.*, more general), executive principles that "recruit," or control, lower-order (*i.e.*, more specific) abilities and strategies. In other words, a person who is said to show an analytic cognitive style is likely to select, from his or her cognitive repertoire, primarily analytic abilities and strategies when faced with some problem situation. Royce and Powell (1983) have developed these ideas at greater length. Taking these considerations into account, a useful working definition of cognitive style may be advanced. The term *cognitive style* refers to consistent individual differences in the manner or mode of cognition that are intimately interwoven with other personality structures and which function as general organizing and controlling mechanisms.

THE ANALYTIC–HOLISTIC DIMENSION

Although the various cognitive styles that have been identified over the years appear to be quite disparate, some form of analytic–holistic dichotomy commonly underlies the way in which they are conceptualized (Fowler, 1977; Kagan & Kogan, 1970; Missler, 1986; Morais, 1982; Moscovitch, 1979). Whether this reflects some "real" distinction between opposing styles, or whether it is simply a conceptual habit deeply engrained in human thought, is a matter for debate. Certainly, the tendency to account for human behaviour in terms of simple polarities such as "destructive–constructive," "diversifying–unifying" and "disordering–ordering" is an ancient tradition (Coan, 1974). Similarly, two qualitatively different types of thought are commonly recognized:

> Among the terms used to describe one type are analytic, deductive, rigorous, constrained, convergent, formal and critical. Representative of the terms used to describe the other type are synthetic, inductive, expansive, unconstrained, divergent, informal, diffuse and creative. (Nickerson *et al.*, 1985, p. 50)

However, the tendency to seek simple dichotomies often is dismissed as reprehensible, a form of intellectual primitivism that seriously hinders intellectual progress. On the other hand, while polarities like analytic–holistic are simplifications, they do not have to be used in a simple-minded way. What I shall argue in this chapter, therefore, is that the analytic–holistic distinction is a generic principle that can be used to organize many of the "traditional" cognitive styles. To develop this argument, we need to clarify the meaning of "analytic" and "holistic" processes before moving on to an examination of the way in which they exhibit themselves at different points in cognitive processing.

Analytic, Holistic (and Synthetic) Processes

The dichotomy I refer to as analytic–holistic has also been labelled by others as analytic–synthetic, articulated–global, and differentiated–integrated. In all cases, the distinction being made is between a tendency to focus on parts (analytic) as opposed to wholes (holistic). It is a relatively easy matter, therefore, to define *analytic* processing as the breakdown of a configuration of some sort into its constituent parts, with each part being studied as a discrete entity in isolation from all other parts and their surrounding context. This concern for detail plays an important role in everyday cognition as well as in more specialized tasks such as finding errors or faults in complex systems (Henneman & Rouse, 1984). Taken to an extreme, however, one finds individuals virtually paralyzed by a preoccupation with minutiae, so narrowly focused that they lose touch with the broader reality. We shall return to these issues later. Meanwhile, I assume that the terms *analytic, articulated,* and *differentiated* are synonymous.

The contrasting mode of thought, however, is more difficult to define for I suspect that two quite different processes are being confused. Although the terms *holistic, global, synthetic,* and *integrated* are used loosely and interchangeably, it seems more reasonable to distinguish holistic/global, from synthetic/integrated, thought. For instance, Widiger *et al.* (1980) conclude that global processing implies the absence of *both* analysis and synthesis. Similarly, many theories of perception posit the occurrence of a primitive holistic/global stage that precedes analysis (Robertson, 1986). Holistic/global processing can be defined, therefore, as the immediate, primitive apprehension of wholes without prior breakdown into parts. What seems to be involved is the extraction of the "configural features" of a stimulus array, rather than the extraction of partial, local features that occurs in analytic processing (Morais, 1982). The ability, and inclination, to see patterns and configurations is, of course, a necessary complement to analytic thinking, as well as being at the root of many forms of creativity (Bastick, 1982). Like analysis, however, it too can be taken to extremes. When holistic thinking takes the form of avoidance of detail, as in the vague, impressionistic thinking of the hysterical personality (Shapiro, 1965), then the individual also loses touch with what one might call empirical reality. In what follows I shall take *holistic* and *global* to be synonymous, both meaning relatively *undifferentiated* thinking.

Synthetic/integrated thinking, however, is far from being undifferentiated. When these terms are used in theories of cognitive development, for example, they denote an advanced form of thinking incorporating both global *and* analytic processes (Harvey *et al.*, 1961; Loevinger, 1976). Thus, in synthetic thinking, previously differentiated parts are combined with intuitively sensed wholes to form complex patterns, thereby fashioning order out of chaos. Synthetic/integrative thinking, then, is the epitome of creative thought, the synthesis of analysis and intuition in the production of novel insights (Coan, 1974; Samples, 1976). At a more prosaic level, everyone exhibits synthetic thinking to some extent, otherwise we would be unable to adapt to even the simplest of life's tasks. Perhaps the more creative among us know when to switch styles in response to task demands and are more effective in each specialized mode.

What I am suggesting, therefore, is that analytic and holistic thinking are the more basic processes, while synthetic/integrated thinking involves their integration into a higher-order capability. It follows that there should be at least three generic cognitive styles, comprising specialists in analytic or holistic processing as well as generalists who can alternate between, and thereby integrate, the two. The latter are variously referred to as versatile (Pask, 1976), hybrid (Hudson, 1968), creative (Coan, 1974) and mobile (Witkin & Goodenough, 1981). The existence of the stylistically versatile creates problems in attempts to demonstrate the stability of styles, as we shall see shortly but, for the individuals themselves, versatility is viewed as an unmitigated blessing, a state of grace toward which education should strive (Entwistle, 1981).

Although the assumption of a triad of cognitive styles composed of a basic polarity and a higher-order synthesis may seem plausible, not everyone would agree that this is empirically correct. Brumby (1982), for instance, suggests that at least four different conceptions of the relationship between analytic and holistic styles can be found in the literature: a bipolar dimension along which individuals occupy a fixed position; a bipolar dimension along which people vary according to task-demands; a true dichotomy in which you are either analytic or holistic; and, two independent, orthogonal dimensions. Brumby's research on problem-solving styles among biology students leads her to favour the latter viewpoint, an orthogonal relationship between two independent analytic and holistic dimensions. She bases this conclusion on the presence of a number of subjects in her sample who showed high levels of both analytic *and* holistic thinking—something, she points out, one would not expect to find if the two styles are mutually antagonistic forms of thought. However, I have just suggested above that such findings are not inconsistent with a bipolar view and that subjects who show high levels of both are merely versatile. The question is, how does one choose between these apparently contradictory views? One approach might be to examine the way in which analogous conceptual problems in other areas of psychology have been resolved. For instance, the debate over the relationship between masculinity, femininity, and androgyny bears striking resemblance to the problem being discussed. Much of the early work on androgyny assumed masculinity and femininity to be orthogonal dimensions, with arguments ranging around whether androgyny should be seen as a balance between masculinity and femininity or as a combination of high levels of both (Babladelis, 1984). Of interest to us is subsequent research which appears to have demonstrated that, while some aspects of masculinity and femininity are orthogonal, other aspects are genuinely bipolar. In other words, components of the masculinity–femininity distinction, such as aggression and dependence, are implicitly opposed, generating tensions within the individual that are difficult to resolve (Babladelis, 1984).

I assume that a similar situation pertains with regard to the analytic–holistic distinction. Unfortunately, it is not known which aspects are orthogonal and which bipolar, nor is the proportion between them known. Given this state of ignorance, I can only offer a personal surmise. I agree with Prentky (1979) when he concludes his review of analytic and holistic processing with the comment: "It does not seem plausible, from the standpoint of personal anecdote or research, that the same individual would naturally migrate between relatively *extreme* methods of processing information" (p. 34). In other words, there does seem to be a genuine opposition between these two forms of thinking as exemplified, perhaps, in the contrast between the compulsive and the hysteric. Furthermore, given the embeddedness of styles in personal dynamics, it is difficult to see how an individual could alternate between *extremes* of functioning. Is it reasonable to expect, for instance, that an extremely obsessive-compulsive individual would easily and repeatedly switch to a more clinically hysterical form of behaviour? Not likely, I think. A reasonable conclusion would seem to be that analytic and holistic styles are mutually opposed (*i.e.*, bipolar) forms of cognition and, while some degree of integration is possible, an inherent tension militates against a flexible alternation between extremes.

Cognitive Processes and Cognitive Styles

Underlying the assumption of a generic analytic–holistic dimension is the implication that individual differences of an analytic–holistic kind are likely to occur in all phases of cognition. To explore this further we need an organizing framework within which the matter can be systematically discussed. What I propose to do is to represent cognition in the traditional way as an interaction between perception, memory, and thought (Fig. 7), each of which can be conveniently subdivided into component processes (Fig. 8). The rationale for this classification will become clear as the story unfolds.

I should point out that several attempts at this kind of analysis have been made in the recent past, with varying degrees of success (Fowler, 1977; Kagan & Kogan, 1970; Royce & Powell, 1983). They, as well as I, faced two problems in doing so. First, as mentioned earlier, there is very little information on individual differences in the cognitive psychology literature. One is forced, therefore, to use any scraps of information that happen to be available, the result being an uneven discussion in which some topics are covered more convincingly than others. Second, as Messick points out:

> [T]he relationships between cognitive styles and information-processing phases are by no means perfect or even orderly because some cognitive styles influence information-processing sequences in more than one way and at more than one point. [For] example ... extensiveness of scanning affects

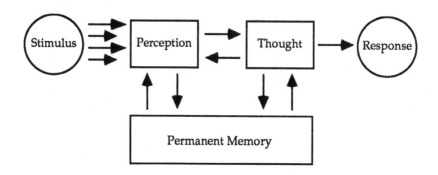

Figure 7. An information-processing model of cognition. (From A. Miller, 1987.)

> information search of both external stimulus fields and internal memory fields, thereby influencing both perception and memory retrieval. (Messick, 1987, p. 53)

What this means is that the relationships indicated in Fig. 8 between cognitive processes (left of figure) and cognitive styles (right of figure) are a simplification of what is in reality a less static, more dynamic situation.

What follows, then, is a combination of empirical review and speculative essay in which I link "traditional" conceptions of cognitive style with more recent theoretical work in cognitive psychology. More specifically, I outline the ways in which subordinate styles can be viewed as individual differences in the various subcomponents of an information-processing model.

PERCEPTUAL STYLES

Perception is the process whereby stimuli registered by our senses are interpreted in light of previous knowledge and prepared for use in more complex mental activity. It is common to distinguish between *preattentive* and *attentive* components. In the former, stimuli are held in raw form for a short period of time while being subjected to preliminary analysis in what is known as *pattern recognition*. This is thought to be an automatic process largely under the control of stimulus properties but also responsive to a variety of personal biases operating at an unconscious

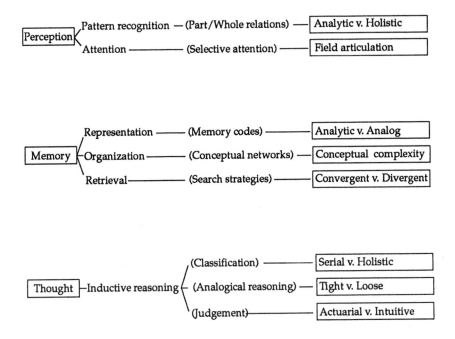

Figure 8. A model of cognitive styles and cognitive processes. (From A. Miller, 1987.)

level (Bargh, 1984). The net result is a continuing flow of relatively crude percepts only some of which are attended to. *Attention*, then, is a highly selective process of limited "channel capacity," involving the deliberate choice to focus on some percepts rather than others (Mandler, 1985).

As in all areas of psychology, there are many controversies over the precise nature of these perceptual processes, two of which are of interest to us in our pursuit of individual differences. First, opinions differ over both the timing and extent of attentional control of the "perceptual flow." While the more esoteric details of these arguments need not concern us, what is important is the implication that people may differ in the relative balance they maintain between preattentive and attentive processes. For instance, those who impose early attentional control on their perception of events may achieve high levels of perceptual selectivity, while those who do not exert control may be prone to distraction by "irrelevant" information. Second, perception theorists differ over which is the more primitive, the processing of parts or the processing of wholes (Delis & Ober, 1986). The controversy simply may reflect the fact that individuals differ in the emphasis they place on each strategy, a possibility that underscores the significance of analytic–holistic differences in perceptual style, to which we now turn.

Pattern Recognition

Pattern recognition is an elementary phase of perception in which the things that you sense are recognized and identified. There appear to be two theories about the ways in which this comparison of incoming stimuli with stored knowledge can be undertaken. *Feature analysis* is the process whereby stimuli are recognized in terms of their distinctive elementary features and the relationship between them. In this case, pattern recognition follows an analytical process in which you look at different aspects of the object, comparing these one at a time with a list of features in your memory of similar objects. *Prototype matching*, on the other hand, involves the comparison of whole stimuli with stored templates or mental copies of the object—a more holistic strategy it would seem. Although both theories are usually presented in cognitive texts as alternative explanations of pattern recognition (Howard, 1983; Matlin, 1983), it seems reasonable to speculate that everyone uses both processes to some degree but that people differ in their preference for, or skill in the use of, either one.

Unfortunately, there is relatively little information bearing on the hypothesis that stylistic differences may be involved. Psychometric theories of intelligence identify individual differences in perceptual "abilities," but their methods of assessment tell you nothing about the individual differences in perceptual strategies underlying such abilities (*e.g.*, Guilford, 1967). Similarly, research on perceptual styles is virtually non-existent in cognitive psychology. However, Fletcher (1981) and Gathercole and Broadbent (1984) have identified what appear to be analytic (discrimination of features) and holistic (non-selective processing of wholes) strategies in stimulus identification tasks. In both studies, however, the two strategies are discussed as alternative responses to task demands rather than a persistent quality of the individual subject. That is, they are seen as strategies rather than styles. A more stylistic interpretation of perceptual differences can be found, however, in the extensive research programme of Lynn Cooper (Cooper, 1982; Cooper & Mumaw, 1985). In a typical experiment, Cooper required subjects to decide as quickly as possible whether or not the items in a series of irregularly shaped patterns matched a standard pattern. Over the course of many repetitions, Cooper was able to identify consistent individual differences among the experimental subjects, who seemed to exhibit one of two styles. *Analytic* subjects were defined as those who showed an effect of the difficulty of test shape on response time. In other words, the greater the difference between the standard and the test shapes, the quicker a "different" judgment was made. Cooper concluded that the more analytic individual uses a process specialized for detecting differences, one in which isolated features of the test and standard shapes are compared. In contrast, *holistic* subjects showed little effect of differences between test and standard on response times. One explanation for this could be that holists look for a match between test and standard rather than seeking distinguishing features, a rapid, parallel comparison of whole stimuli with little analysis into constituent features. Having identified what appeared to be consistent individual differences, Cooper became interested in whether subjects could be induced to adopt a different approach to visual comparison. In other words, were these differences due to consciously adopted strategies or did they have the more inflexible quality of styles? After a series of experiments, Cooper concluded that while holistic subjects were able to switch to a more analytic mode in response to task demands, analytic subjects had more difficulty in switching to an holistic mode. This leaves the question of whether we are dealing with strategies or styles hanging in the air, but, perhaps, the more important point is Cooper's conclusion that "strategy" selection does represent a stable individual difference.

Attention

As mentioned above, attention is the process whereby certain percepts are brought into conscious awareness and subjected to further elaboration. In a review of attentional mechanisms, Davies *et al.* (1984) recognize two that are of interest to us. First, there is the extent to which the person relinquishes one focus of attention and establishes a second. Differences in the extent to which such shifting occurs appear to have been recognized in the cognitive style *scanning*. Second, people also differ in their tendency to establish and maintain a focus of attention despite the presence of distracting stimuli, the relevant cognitive style being *field articulation*.

Scanning. Consistent differences in the breadth of attention deployment have long been recognized at an anecdotal level. For instance, descriptions of the obsessive individual commonly refer to an extreme narrowness of attention, an intensely sharp focus on detail that excludes both incidental information and casual impressions (Claridge, 1985; Shapiro, 1965). On the other hand, obsessives are known to accumulate vast amounts of information, on whatever it is that they are attending to, something that implies breadth of attention. Paradoxes of this kind were common in early studies on the scanning style, where some confusion reigned until it was recognized that the term "breadth" can be used in two senses (Kogan, 1971). If one thinks of attention as a beam of light moving around a field, then breadth can refer to the *extensiveness* of the scan (extent to which the beam moves around) as well as to its *intensity* (extent to which the beam is focused). Presumably various combinations of the two are possible, but "scanning" has been defined as a contrast between extensive/intensive and limited/diffuse styles (Santostefano, 1978). Thus, as Kogan (1971) points out, obsessives are actually broad scanners in that they scan extensively but with an intensely focused beam. Hence, there is attention to large amounts of detail but a tendency to miss links between these details. Messick (1976) speculates that narrow/extensive scanning serves a defensive purpose, an attempt to reduce uncertainty by amassing an excess of information. We shall return to these issues in a later chapter. For the time being, I shall assume that extensive/intensive scanning is typical of an analytic style, while limited/diffuse scanning is holistic.

Field articulation. Earlier, I suggested that the balance between automatic and deliberate perceptual processes might underlie some cognitive style differences. Those with a bias toward deliberate attention may be inclined to focus attention while screening out, or suppressing their reaction to, irrelevant information. In contrast, those who are unable to do this, or who are disinclined to do so, may have difficulty in ignoring informational "noise." If there are stable individual differences involved here, then they are important ones, for one can hardly place much faith, for instance, in an air-traffic controller who cannot, or will not, ignore distraction. Similarly academic work requires one to process large quantities of information, with the fond hope of sorting out the wheat from the chaff. Paradoxically, of course, it is overlooked bits of chaff that usually turn out to be the most interesting, a matter to which we shall return later.

Individual differences of this kind have been identified on a variety of selective attention tasks used in research on selective and dichotic listening, central-incidental learning, and speeded classification (Davies *et al.*, 1984). For instance, in a common task used to study central-incidental learning,

> subjects are shown a series of cards; on each card, there are two stimuli, an animal and a household object, one of which is placed at the top of the card and the other at the bottom. Subjects are instructed to direct their attention to one of the stimulus categories (animals or household objects) during the presentation of the picture arrays and are subsequently asked to recall the location of items in this category; the number of locations correctly recalled constitutes the central-task score. Subjects are also required to indicate the irrelevant stimulus with which items from the relevant stimulus categories were paired; the number of correct pairings constitutes the incidental-task

score. Changes in the degree to which attention can be focused on relevant items are inferred from the relation between central and incidental task scores. (Davies *et al.*, 1984, p. 398)

However, as far as I can determine, there have been no attempts to integrate these various findings of individual differences in selective attention into any conception of broad, stable, individual differences.

In the cognitive style literature, two styles have been identified that appear to reflect individual differences in selective attention: "field dependence–independence" (FDI) (Witkin *et al.*, 1979; Witkin & Goodenough, 1981) and "constricted-flexible control" (Gardner *et al.*, 1959). The empirical relationships found between common measures of this perceptual conception of FDI and the Stroop Color-Word test ("constricted-flexible control") led Gardner *et al.* (1959) to suggest that both styles might be usefully subsumed under the rubric of "field articulation." Subsequent studies have supported this integration (Davies *et al.*, 1984; Santostefano, 1978). Since there is a great deal of research on FDI, I shall focus on this style.

Interest in FDI originated in experiments on a classical problem in perception: the relative importance of inner and outer cues (information) in the perception of the upright (*i.e.* how we judge which way is up). Normally, we rely on two sets of information for this: inner vestibular and kinaesthetic cues (sense of balance) resulting from the effect of gravity on our bodies; and, outer visual information about the orientation of things like floors, ceilings, walls, and so on. Either set of cues will suffice under normal conditions, but there are situations where inner and outer cues present us with conflicting information, such as when a pilot is flying through layers of cloud that look horizontal but actually are not. Over the years, the Witkin group developed a number of experimental situations for studying this perceptual conflict, notably the Body Adjustment Test (BAT) and the more commonly used Rod and Frame Test (RFT). In the latter, the subject sits in a blacked-out room facing a luminous square frame containing a luminous rod, both of which are pivoted about their common centre. The experimenter sets the frame and rod at different angles, while the subject is required to adjust the rod back to the true vertical. This is difficult in the absence of cues from the darkened room other than the tilted frame which conflicts with the person's inner, bodily cues about whether or not they are sitting upright. As with the Body Adjustment Test, Witkin found wide individual differences ranging from those who had little difficulty in finding the true vertical to those who aligned the rod with the angle of the frame. Thus, experimental findings of this kind led Witkin to propose a perceptual style dimension which contrasted those who rely on internal cues (field-independent) with those who are more influenced by the external context (field-dependent).

Subsequent research extended the range of FDI differences to include other perceptual tasks such as the Embedded Figures Test (EFT). In this, a standard figure is surrounded by a more complex one, the idea being to camouflage the standard figure with irrelevant and confusing material. The experimental subject is presented with a large number of these figures and is required to pick out the standard figure as quickly as possible. For the more field-independent person this is relatively easy, the standard or hidden figure seems to leap out of the surrounding camouflage. However, the field-dependent person has great difficulty in disentangling the target figure from its background.

On the basis of what seemed to be substantial correlations between the BAT, RFT, and EFT, Witkin reinterpreted FDI as a perceptual style that reflects differences in *disembedding* "capability." People were said to differ in their ease or difficulty in separating an item from an organized field or overcoming an embedding context. Disembedding was considered to be an analytic tendency characteristic of field independence. Needless to say, there have been criticisms of the FDI concept, especially its development into a broader personality dimension, a matter to be discussed later in the chapter. For the moment, I shall limit the discussion to problems with FDI as a perceptual style.

First, the BAT, RFT, and EFT are tests of correctness and accuracy which really measure ability. Consequently, field dependence–independence is actually a unipolar dimension with field *independence* at the accurate, more virtuous pole. Despite Witkin's attempts to enhance the positive aspects of field *dependence* by attributing to it such qualities as interpersonal competence, field dependence is still measured by default, an inability to avoid error on the defining tests. This has led many commentators to reject FDI as a pervasive style, preferring, instead, to regard it as an ability (McKenna, 1984; Shade, 1984; Widiger *et al.*, 1980). Thus, when one finds that field-independent subjects outperform field-dependent subjects on a wide variety of analytic problem-solving tasks (Henneman & Rouse, 1984; Myer & Hensley, 1984; Roberge & Flexer, 1983; Ronning *et al.*, 1984), it is not clear to what extent one is seeing the effect of an ability or a style.

Second, the stability of the FDI concept has always been questionable, given the relatively low correlations that are found between its defining tests (Missler, 1986; Shipman & Shipman, 1985). As a consequence, the Witkin group has reconsidered the matter, recently redefining FDI in terms of two separate but related factors (Witkin & Goodenough, 1981; Goodenough *et al.*, 1987).

For our purposes, though, we need not become too embroiled in these twists and turns of theory. Rather, it is enough to acknowledge that individual differences in perception have been identified which appear to contrast varying predilections in the separation of relevant from irrelevant information. Whether one considers this to be an ability or a style is not crucial to the argument. When one adds to this, the differences that have been observed in scanning, then there is sufficient reason to believe that one is observing analytic–holistic differences in perceptual mode.

MEMORY STYLES

The cognitive processes involved in memory allow us to maintain a reasonably complete record of our life experiences. Just as in a library or data bank, information is stored in an organized form so that it can be retrieved when we have need of it. To discuss memory, therefore, it is useful to talk about the form in which information is stored (representation), how information is organized (organization), and the processes involved in retrieving that information (retrieval).

Representation

Information is thought to be stored as representations or *codes*, the precise nature of which remains controversial. Advocates of dual-coding (Paivio, 1971) maintain that both verbal and imagery codes occur in memory, while Anderson (1980) argues for a more abstract propositional code as the sole basis of representation. This difference of opinion has been around for some time, to the extent that many in the field are a trifle weary of the debate, preferring, instead, to accept that many codes are involved in memory (Hunt, 1982).

Verbal codes, which take the form of "linguistic units" or words, are thought to be particularly suited to, and facilitate, analysis, which is why Glass *et al.* (1979) refer to them as *analytic* codes. In contrast, the nature of imagery codes is less clear. In some instances, a verbal–visual distinction is drawn, implying the primacy of visual imagery and the storage of images as mental pictures. However, since the congenitally blind are capable of vivid imagery (Howard, 1983), it seems we can and do store images in other sense modalities (such as the sound of thunder, the feel of a cat's fur and the smell of garlic). It is for these reasons that Glass *et al.* (1979) prefer to label such images as *analogue* codes.

Dual-coding theory suggests, therefore, that memory is composed of an integrated system of words and images. Although this view of memory is rejected by some researchers, the notion of dual codes has proved extremely useful in certain areas of research, such as that on hemispheric specialization. For instance, the left hemisphere of the brain is thought to specialize in the use of verbal codes and is therefore heavily involved in analytical thinking. On the other hand, the right hemisphere appears to be organized so as to process imagery (analogue) codes, which involves it in holistic thinking (Benson & Zaidel, 1985). Needless to say, effective thinking requires the involvement of both codes and both hemispheres, a matter to which we shall return at various points in the book.

Although everyone makes use of verbal and analogue codes to some extent, consistent individual differences occur in this regard. For instance, the traditional distinction between verbal and visuo-spatial abilities implies differential facility with memory codes. However, the matter is not as straightforward as it seems since ability tests that, on intuitive grounds, should engage a certain kind of coding may not do so (Katz, 1983). A case in point is the Rod and Frame Test which, one would think, should engage subjects in visuo-spatial imagery. However, while this is true of some subjects, others use a more verbal strategy (Shore & Carey, 1984). It is not surprising to learn, therefore, that consistent individual differences in the use of either verbal or analogue codes have been shown to underlie performance on a variety of ability measures (Rubini & Cornoldi, 1985; Shore *et al.*, 1982).

The most extensive research on individual differences in the use of codes, interpreted as a stylistic preference, has been conducted by Riding and his co-workers. Much of their work is based on a "verbal-imagery ratio test" which attempts to determine the relative preference shown for each code by children. The test is based on a passage taken from the children's classic *The Wind in the Willows*, which is further subdivided into several paragraphs. A question is posed about each paragraph which cannot be answered directly from the information in the passage. Half of the questions can be answered from images which, it is assumed, are generated from information in the paragraphs. For example, one paragraph reads: "It was small wonder, then, that he suddenly flung down his brush on the floor, said 'Bother' and 'O blow' ... and he bolted out of the house without ever waiting to put on his coat." The associated question: "What colour is the brush?" assumes that some children will tend to produce vivid, even colourful, images of the scene. In contrast, the paragraph: "The sunshine struck hot on his fur, soft breezes caressed his brow ... [and] the carol of happy birds fell on his dulled hearing almost like a shout," is followed by the question: "Is a carol the same as a song," a question that taps semantic associations only indirectly related to the story (Riding & Calvey, 1981). The child's response-times to each question are assumed to reflect his or her relative use of verbal or imagery codes in reading each paragraph, and the resulting ratio is used to place children on a verbal–imagery style continuum. These ratio scores have been found to predict the performance of children in a number of learning situations involving such things as prose recall, reading, and spelling attainment. Typically, children appear to learn material most effectively when it is presented in their preferred code. For instance, in a study by Riding and Ashmore (1980), one-half of the children were presented with a long prose passage describing a rural scene, while the other half were shown the same scene in the form of a picture. After studying the material for a short period, all the children were asked a series of questions requiring time to recall details of the scene. It became clear that "verbalizers" recalled more items from the prose description than from the picture, while the opposite was the case for "imagers." As a result of such studies, Riding concludes that:

> While almost all individuals can generate verbal and imagery representations of information if they make a deliberate effort to do so, each person has a preferred mode of representation which is habitually and involuntarily used.... There is a considerable range of these habitual modes from almost entirely verbal to almost completely imaginal, and this style represents a continuum of performance with individuals positioned uniformly along it.... Verbal–imagery learning style should be distinguished from "intelligence" since taken overall, verbalisers do as well as imagers when a variety of different tasks are involved. (Riding & Boardman, 1983, p. 71)

One cannot dismiss an ability interpretation of these findings, however, since it could be argued that individuals use the code with which they are most skilled or, may lack the metastrategies needed to help them match an appropriate code to a particular task. Possibly, research on inducing children to shift their habitual codes might clarify the first question by showing that children have equal facility with both codes but prefer one over the other. Something of this sort is implied in Katz's (1983) examination of metastrategies in adults. He was aware that to distinguish between an encoding preference rather than a metastrategy deficit would require one to demonstrate that, while subjects were sensitive to the coding requirements of different tasks, they still preferred to use only one code. Evidence along these lines was obtained in two of his studies. Thus, consistent individual differences in the use of verbal (analytic) and imagery (analogue) codes have been demonstrated and have been represented by some authors as a stylistic continuum.

Organization

In discussing individual differences in the organization of permanent memory, I shall focus on only one of the three memory systems proposed by Tulving (1985). The reason for this is simple enough—most of the available information on individual differences has to do with *semantic* memory, the memory system that is thought to store conceptual information.

One of the more popular theoretical conceptions of semantic memory depicts it as a conceptual network with each node or concept being composed of the word label for the concept, together with additional semantic and perceptual information that establishes the meaning of the concept. For instance, Fig. 9 shows the way in which a tiny fragment of such a network might be organized (Glass *et al.*, 1979). The various *concept nodes* (or ideas) are represented by the words in small print (cat, dog), while their semantic labels are printed in capital letters and indicated by a double arrow (CAT ⇒ cat). Since a concept is meaningless unless it is associated with some kind of information, you will see that each node (*e.g.*, cat) is linked to perceptual information represented in analogue codes ("meow" and a visual image of a cat). Notice also that the concepts *cat* and *dog* are related to one another by being linked to, or subsumed under, the broader concept *animal*, which in turn is subsumed under the even broader concept *living thing*.

Individual differences in semantic organization arise because people differ both in the number of concepts they develop and the extent to which they integrate them into hierarchical structures. Thus:

> cognitive styles have been described from a systems perspective as *structural properties of the cognitive system.* In this usage, style refers to consistent individual differences in properties of cognitive structure, such as degree of differentiation, of discrimination or articulation, or of hierarchic integration of cognitive units. Together these three dimensions are taken ... to comprise a style of cognitive complexity versus cognitive simplicity. (Messick, 1984, p. 61)

In the traditional view, cognitive complexity results from high levels of differentiation, articulation, and integration, while cognitive simplicity reflects low levels of each component. There are good reasons for disputing this conception of cognitive complexity, but before getting too embroiled in the matter we should examine each structural component further.

Conceptual differentiation. The term "differentiation" refers to the extent to which an homogeneous field is broken down into clearly distinguishable parts. When talking about highly or poorly differentiated conceptual networks, therefore, we are interested in the sheer number of concepts involved. The more distinct concepts a person "possesses" the more differentiated his or her conceptual network is assumed to be—the practical problem being how one determines whether or not someone

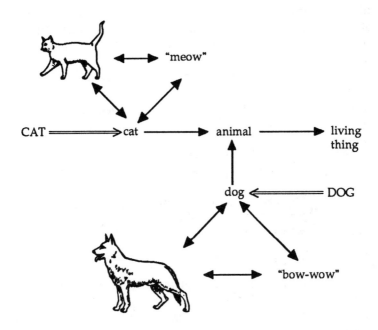

Figure 9. A fragment of a conceptual network, showing how words, concepts, and perceptual information are associated. (From Glass *et al.*, 1979.)

"possesses" a particular concept. Most of the research on this issue assumes that you can infer the number of concepts in a conceptual network from a person's judging and sorting behaviour. Fine-grained, highly discriminating judgments are thought to imply that the person has available a large number of clearly defined concepts.

The most common assessment procedures, therefore, involve some form of object-sorting task derived from either the Repertory Grid of Kelly (1955), as in Bieri *et al.* (1966) and Landfield (1971), or bearing resemblance to object-sorting procedures in experimental psychology, as in Gardner *et al.* (1959) and Scott *et al.* (1979). In grid methods, for example, the subject is required to rate or rank-order a number of target persons known to him or her on the basis of concepts provided by the investigator or elicited from the subject. The *variety* of ratings is used as an index of differentiation. For instance, a subject who is provided with ten distinct concepts but uses them as if they were synonymous is assumed to be relatively undifferentiated.

There are, of course, a number of problems with this procedure (A. Miller & Wilson, 1979). The assumption that variety of judgment reflects differentiation of concepts is dubious for it fails to distinguish orderly differentiation from conceptual fragmentation and confusion. In Bieri's version of the Repertory Grid, for instance, one could obtain a high differentiation score by filling it with random ratings. Indeed Bannister and Fransella (1966) have pursued this very point in constructing their grid test for schizophrenic thought disorder in which it is assumed that variety of ratings between test and retest is a sign of conceptual fragmentation.

More problems arose with this approach to differentiation when efforts were made to establish predictive validity for the various indices derived from grids. Much of the relevant research examined the relationship between differentiation and social acuity, the general hypothesis being that high levels of conceptual differentiation should result in accuracy of social judgment. As Neimeyer *et al.* (1983) point out in their review of this work, however, it was characterized by a number of design faults over and above problems with the differentiation indices themselves. For instance, differentiation by itself is not likely to result in sophistication of social judgment in the absence of conceptual integration. In predicting social acuity, therefore, one would need to take into account both differentiation *and* integration, something that earlier workers failed to do. When one does so, one finds, for instance, that highly differentiated but poorly integrated subjects are prone to exhibit socially inappropriate behaviour, as Neimeyer *et al.* have demonstrated in some of their own research. In addition, the assumption that one should be able to predict social acuity on the basis of the subject's differentiation score alone, in the absence of information about the target person, is untenable in this age of interactionism, according to Neimeyer *et al.* (1983). Once again, they cite evidence in support of the notion that the conceptual structure of the target person is equally as important as that of the judge in person perception experiments. For instance, highly integrated individuals appear to be more understandable than poorly integrated and presumably more inconsistent targets. The disappointing results of early work on the validation of differentiation measures are understandable, therefore, in light of these, and other, design problems.

This failure to establish the validity of differentiation indices, together with additional problems in demonstrating the generality of differentiation across stimulus domains (A. Miller, 1978) has resulted in a fading interest in conceptual differentiation as a broad, stable trait. In its place, cognitive-social psychologists are paying more attention to "schema complexity"—a more limited, domain-specific conception (Fletcher *et al.*, 1986). Their assumption is that it is unreasonable to expect individuals to show the same level of differentiation across all areas of their conceptual network. There is some sense to this. Scorer (1977) implies as much when he refers to professionals as "clever morons," individuals who attain high levels of differentiation (and integration) in decidedly limited areas of their experience.

The case for stylistic differences in conceptual differentiation remains unproven, therefore, and will remain so in the absence of adequate research. Whether the recent work on schema complexity reduces the credibility of the idea of a broader trait is arguable since this same research is conducted within a psychological specialization noted for its disdain for broad dispositional traits (see Chapter 1). Perhaps what we are seeing here, therefore, is not so much doubts about the existence of individual differences in differentiation but rather a debate about the breadth of the disposition(s) involved. Interestingly, the debate itself, reflects individual preferences for broad and narrow categories, a topic to which we now turn.

Conceptual breadth. In addition to the sheer *number* of concepts in a system, the *structure* of the concepts themselves is also important. One approach to this issue has been to talk about *conceptual articulation*, the extent to which the instances of a concept are separated from one another. However, I prefer to look at a related aspect of the structure of individual concepts, namely, *category breadth*, which refers to "consistent preferences for broad inclusiveness as opposed to narrow exclusiveness in establishing the acceptable range for specified categories" (Messick, 1976, p. 15).

Individual differences in category breadth are important because of their implications for intellectual style, particularly the conceptual styles underlying creativity. Messick (1976), for instance, suggests that the narrow categorizer is conceptually more conservative, uses stricter criteria for category membership and is less tolerant of deviant instances than the broad categorizer. Block *et al.* (1981) observed similar differences among children. It is as if the narrow categorizer attempts to impose structure on an intruding environment, using a narrow attentional focus to exclude information. The broad categorizer, on the other hand, appears to be more passive, imposes less structure on the environment and shows a relative inability, or disinclination, to exclude input. We have seen analogous differences in behaviour before, of course, in the section on attentional styles. It is interesting that the personality correlates of broad and narrow categorizing, noticed to occur as early as three years of age by Block *et al.* (1981), were also observed at age seven, suggesting the possibility of a stable cognitive type that develops early and persists. The significance of all this for creativity is that the renowned ability of creative individuals to make links between disparate, often contradictory, ideas requires some tolerance in the use of categories (Bastick, 1982). Too stringent a set of rules for combining instances may preclude the possibility of innovative connections. It is for this reason that broad categorizers may have some advantage, at least in the early stages of the creative process.

A wide variety of tasks has been used to assess category breadth, in all of which the subject is presented with an average or focal value and is required to set the limits of the category. In one widely used instrument, the categories involved are such things as annual rainfall, width of windows, and length of whales, while the upper and lower limits are selected from a set of provided values. Less direction is offered in object-sorting tasks in which subjects are expected to group an array of common objects into the kinds of category with which they are most comfortable (Kogan, 1971, 1976). Although Kogan claims that "consistency" has been demonstrated for both kinds of task, not everyone would agree. Garber and Miller (1986) have recently attempted to clarify doubts about the stability of category breadth as a style by presenting subjects with tasks of the "bandwith" variety. That is, six sets of stimuli (drawings of animals, human faces, photos of butterflies, etc.) were used, with instances varying along a continuum from a central prototype. Subjects were required to decide which instances belonged to the prototype category. The results of the study indicated that there was little consistency in strategy across the six tasks. Even aggregation of strategies for each subject provided only moderate consistency, at best—a similar finding to that of Block *et al.* (1981). Garber and Miller concluded that, while subjects may be consistent over a short period of time, most people appear to use many strategies or criteria of category breadth.

Hierarchic integration. This structural property of semantic memory refers to the degree to which differentiated concepts are linked into a hierarchy or some other meaningful array. A highly integrated system is one that contains many interconnections between concepts, while the concepts of a poorly integrated system would be relatively isolated. Although hierarchic integration is an important conceptual quality, it has received relatively little attention and there is even less research on individual differences in integration. This is very curious, given that the ability to integrate ideas is a crucial element in many walks of life, especially academic life. One would have expected, therefore, a keen interest in the topic, but this is not so. Possibly, the difficulties involved in both conceptualizing and measuring hierarchic integration account for the dearth of interest (see A. Miller & Wilson, 1979, for a review of these problems). For instance, when one talks of "links" between concepts, one is referring to an integration of meaning. At first glance, this may appear to be a perfectly straightforward idea, but in practice it is very difficult to distinguish between concepts that are "linked" and those that are not differentiated (*i.e.*, between integrated and undifferentiated concepts). One of the more interesting attempts to overcome such problems is discussed below.

In an early pair of studies using Repertory Grid methods, Norris *et al.* (1970), and Norris and Norris (1972) compared the conceptual structures of obsessive-compulsive patients with "normals." Three groupings of concepts were found: primary clusters composed of highly correlated concepts; linkage concepts which were significantly correlated with other concepts in two or more primary clusters; and, isolates, *i.e.* concepts showing no relationship to others. In this study, then, integration is conceptualized in terms of the number of superordinate, linkage concepts. Various combinations of these groupings produced the patterns of constructs shown in Fig. 10, two of which (segmented and monolithic) were characteristic of the obsessive-compulsive patients. The segmented pattern is composed of several unrelated primary groups, the implication being that there is no way in which one part of the system can influence any other. A segmented structure may allow the discrete cataloguing of the separate aspects of a person, but the system lacks the cohesive theme that would allow these to be brought together into a single identity (Norris *et al.*, 1970). In other words, the conceptual system is fragmented, lacking hierarchical integration. On the other hand, the monolithic pattern is composed of a large primary cluster, a closely related secondary cluster, and some isolates. Norris *et al.* (1970) suggest that with this type of conceptual organization, a person would find it very difficult to make independent judgments with opposing implications, for the absence of differentiation between concepts means that the use of one concept implicates most of the others in the cluster. Neither the segmented nor the monolithic patterns can be said to be "integrated" in any sense. Rather, they differ in that the former is relatively differentiated, the latter not. In direct contrast is the well-differentiated and integrated "articulated" pattern of the "normal" subjects. Here one sees separate but related groups, with linkage constructs establishing meaningful relationships between them. (I shall return to these three patterns of constructs shortly for they are prototypical examples of analytic, holistic, and integrated memory structures.)

Attempts to replicate these patterns of concepts have been only partially successful. Millar (1980), for instance, was unable to demonstrate more monolithic structures in obsessive-compulsive patients, although he did find the latter to be less integrated than "normals." On the other hand, Ashworth *et al.* (1982) found less articulated (differentiated and integrated) structures amongst a group of disturbed patients when compared with a less disturbed control group. However, these "cognitive

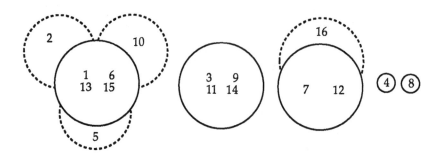

(*a*). The segmented structure found in one obsessional patient. There are three primary clusters with four secondaries, and two isolates, but no linkage constructs.

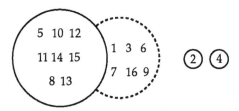

(*b*). The monolithic structure of an obsessional patient. Eight constructs form the primary cluster and six others the secondary cluster. The remaining two constructs are isolates.

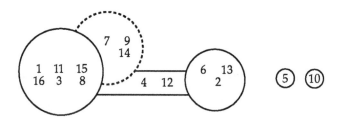

(*c*). The matched control showing an articulated structure. There are two primary clusters, a secondary with a linkage cluster, and two isolates.

Figure 10. Conceptual structures in obsessives and normals. (From Norris *et al.*, 1970.)

abnormalities" seemed to have disappeared when the same patients, now recovered, were retested (Ashworth *et al.*, 1985).

The distinguishing feature of this research is the attempt to identify hierarchic integration directly and independently of level of differentiation, the assumption being that high levels of integration can be associated with varying levels of differentiation. In other words, even though an individual may have but few concepts, they could well be integrated in a complex way. This concept of integration is not well developed, however, either theoretically or empirically. Thus, the existence of stable individual differences remains unproven.

Conceptual complexity. A common assumption in the style literature is that differentiation, articulation (category breadth) and integration are developmentally linked so that a conceptually complex system involves high levels of all three components (Messick, 1976). For instance, Conceptual Systems Theory postulates a developmental sequence in which each stage is characterized by progressively higher levels of differentiation and integration (A. Miller, 1978). In this, and other similar theories (*e.g.*, Loevinger, 1976), the hypothesis linking complexity to high levels of differentiation and integration (category breadth is commonly omitted from discussion) has not been subjected to direct test by, for instance, exploring the conceptual systems of complex and simple individuals. Instead, it is assumed that "complexity" is likely to have certain predictable correlates and it is the latter that are used to assess the individual's standing on the complexity–simplicity dimension. In the case of Conceptual Systems Theory, the most complex stage, variously called "integrative complexity," "conceptual complexity," "conceptual level," and "abstractness," is said to be characterized by the ability to cope well with interpersonal conflict. Thus, in one popular method for assessing this quality, subjects are presented with a sentence completion task composed of sentence stubs which imply interpersonal conflict, such as: "When I am confused...," "When I am in doubt...," "When I am criticized...," and so on. The scoring protocol assesses responses in terms of the conflict resolution strategies used: rejection and denial of conflict (*low* levels of complexity), recognition of conflict but compartmentalization of response (*moderate* levels), and recognition and resolution of conflict (*high* levels of complexity). Clearly some stable quality of the individual is captured by this method of assessment for it shows high levels of reliability and predictive validity (Hunt *et al.*, 1978; A. Miller, 1978). For instance, "conceptual level" is a useful predictor of students' responses to teaching and learning situations (A. Miller, 1981) and patients' therapy preferences (Hesteren *et al.*, 1982; Holloway & Wampold, 1986; Stoppard & Miller, 1985). In all of these studies, "complex" subjects were found to be most comfortable when matched with relatively unstructured situations in which they were allowed some degree of personal control, whereas "simple" subjects preferred highly structured situations controlled, even dominated, by the teacher/therapist.

Although interesting, this research tells you little about conceptual structure, although it does suggest something about conflict resolution styles. Questions about the nature of "complexity" are left hanging. My own sense of the problem is that complexity probably does *not* involve high levels of both differentiation and integration, but rather moderate amounts of the former. I cannot see how a highly differentiated system (the segmented structures of Norris *et al.*, 1970) can be easily integrated. Or to put it in another way, how can a student or scholar who spends an inordinate amount of time obsessively collecting enormous quantities of information then turn around and integrate it in any coherent way? In this sense, excessive differentiation stands in the way of effective integration. Perhaps only moderate levels of differentiation lend themselves to integration.

To my knowledge, no one has explored this possibility, although the potential for doing so exists in the methods used, for example, in research on expert cognition (Arkes & Freedman, 1984; Chi *et al.*, 1982; Fiske *et al.*, 1983; Lesgold, 1984; Voss *et al.*, 1983). Here, an attempt is made to assess conceptual structures directly where, as one might expect, it is found that experts construct more highly differentiated and integrated conceptions of problems than do novices. At present, however, research in this area does not explore which level of differentiation is most conducive to higher forms of integration, although there is no reason why it could not do so. In addition, research on expert cognition assumes that "complexity" is domain-specific, *i.e.* something that is not easily transferable outside one's area of expertise. While common sense suggests that this may well be the case, Voss *et al.* (1983) raise the interesting possibility that distinctive cognitive styles may have been operating amongst the experts they have studied, thus providing a matter for further research.

Once again, therefore, I must conclude that, while individual differences in "complexity" of style have been demonstrated, the precise nature of this "complexity" awaits further elucidation.

Retrieval

Given that semantic memory is organized in the form of a conceptual network, retrieval can be regarded as a search through this network from one node to another, a sort of walk through the hypothetical pathways of the mind (Howard, 1983). Retrieval, therefore, is thought to involve the activation of concept nodes, each of which has a particular threshold level, beyond which the concept enters consciousness. Two distinct processes may be involved (Gitomer & Pellegrino, 1985). *Automatic* retrieval, which is not under conscious control, seems to involve the spreading of activation throughout related areas of the network with the result that ideas may "pop" into awareness for no apparent reason (Mandler, 1985). *Intentional* retrieval involves the conscious effort to restrict attention to a particular concept or group of concepts, thereby maintaining some degree of control over the activation process.

Although I have not been able to find any discussion of the matter, individual differences in retrieval styles could be defined in terms of the relative balance between automatic and intentional processes. Something of the sort is implied by the *scanning* style mentioned in the earlier section on attention. Thus, narrow scanners have a tendency to search in a highly selective manner, as if they were confining their attention to the most direct route to the item being sought, while seeking to activate only one conceptual node at a time. On the other hand, broad scanners seem to search several memory pathways at once, activating not only the conceptual node of immediate concern but also nodes in adjacent areas of the conceptual network. This is a more diffuse search strategy, one that will bring into consciousness a great number of memories, many of which will be irrelevant to, and perhaps may interfere with, attempts to remember a particular idea.

These differences in what might be called *focused* and *diffuse* retrieval strategies reflect differences in the way that the respective memory pathways were encoded in the first place. For instance, there appear to be at least two different styles of encoding. On the one hand, one sees a primarily conscious, intentional process in which there is considerable semantic elaboration of concepts and the development of logical linkages with other concept nodes through the use of denotative meanings. In contrast, one also finds a less intentional, more automatic form of encoding in which contextual cues are stored along with the main item. As a consequence, the conceptual networks that are formed may be less "logical," being more dependent on connotative meanings, situational cues and emotional states (Glass & Holyoak, 1986). One would expect to find, therefore, individual differences in the search strategies used to access these different kinds of conceptual network. One strategy would tend to be a tightly controlled, "logical" search, while the other could be seen as a more diffuse, less controlled search, guided by emotional and situational cues. Although no one in cognitive psychology has attempted to develop empirical support for such differences in retrieval as stable styles, a potential basis for doing so is provided by Bower's (1981) notion of state-dependent memory. In this view, emotional nodes are considered to be important components of semantic networks, becoming linked with conceptual nodes during the encoding of daily events and acting as retrieval cues on subsequent occasions. In reviewing recent work on state-dependent memory, Blaney (1986) draws attention to the apparently automatic tendency of depressed individuals to retrieve unpleasant or self-deprecating memories. Some of the current research on the extent to which such individuals can exert conscious control over these more automatic, state-dependent processes is particularly interesting for, in essence, it is attempting to determine whether subjects can alter the balance between automatic and intentional retrieval strategies.

The cognitive style dimension of relevance to these individual differences in retrieval strategy is "convergence–divergence." Although this style is commonly used to refer to a broader set of differences in cognition, individual differences in retrieval strategies are central to the distinction being made. Thus, Guilford (1967) defines *convergent production* as the revival of information from memory storage in which the search narrows down to one item. *Divergent production*, on the other hand, involves a search for an unspecified number of items, *i.e.*, there is no simple, or correct, end-point for the search. It follows that convergent retrieval strategies can be seen as narrow, deductive, logical, and using sharper search criteria, while divergent strategies are broad and associational, rather than logical, and use vague search criteria.

Differences between these two retrieval strategies become apparent in responses to two different kinds of psychological tests: the conventional intelligence test and the so-called tests of creativity. Conventional intelligence tests set a series of simple problems, each of which has a single correct answer. The person being tested is required to *converge* on the correct solution. For instance, in asking "which two of the following words are opposite in meaning: a) old, b) dry, c) cold, d) young," the only acceptable answer is old–young. Tests of this kind favour those who prefer, and are able, to search their memory quickly and efficiently, using the strategy I have referred to above as being logical and sharp. As the test items become more difficult, those subjects who prefer a more diffuse retrieval strategy will be at a serious disadvantage because of the many interfering memories triggered during their memory search.

In contrast, tests of *divergent* ability, are open-ended in the sense that there is no single correct answer to each item. Rather, the individual is invited to produce many answers without undue concern about being logical or reasonable. For example, in the test Uses of Objects, a standard question is "How many uses can you think of for a brick?" The typical *converger* (one who uses a convergent retrieval strategy) will tend to produce relatively few responses, often of a strictly logical and practical kind, such as: "for building; as a door stop." The *diverger*, however, may release a flood of witty, ingenious but often impractical answers: "to break windows for a robbery; to determine depth of wells; to use as ammunition; as a pendulum; to practice carving; as part of an abstract sculpture; footwiper; to block rabbit hole;" and so on. It is as if the diverger ignores strictly logical connections between ideas and "free associates," spewing forth answers that are only distantly related to the question at hand (Hudson, 1968). Thus ideational fluency (the sheer number of responses produced) has been identified in a number of studies as the central quality that distinguishes between the two forms of retrieval (Kogan, 1983), while, in turn, differences in ideational fluency may result from underlying differences in breadth of attention deployment during retrieval (Wallach, 1970).

As with all styles, the evidence in support of stable individual differences in retrieval style is mixed. Thus, Kogan concludes that, while "the accumulated evidence is in general support of the long-term stability of divergent-thinking performance across the years of middle childhood (approximately age 10) through a substantial portion of adolescence (approximately ages 16 to 17)," the magnitude of stability coefficients "can vary substantially as a function of testing context and sex of subject" (Kogan, 1983, p. 647). Apparently, divergent production is more evident in playful situations as opposed to a more evaluative, critical atmosphere. In addition, Jaquish (1983) has produced evidence in support of the contention that divergent retrieval is a function of stimulus domain. Consequently, a person who is divergent in one sphere may not be so in another. I shall return to these issues at the end of the chapter, where I try to explain why one should not be unduly alarmed about the apparent instability of styles.

THINKING STYLES

The term "thinking" implies something more than simply perceiving and storing information; it suggests the use of such information, if not for some clear purpose, then in a way that goes beyond its original form. As a result, there appear to be many different kinds of thinking ranging from reasoning and problem-solving to dream states. The more directed form of thought, commonly called *secondary process thinking*, is both realistic and logical, whereas *primary process thinking* is less concerned with either reality or logic (Martindale, 1981). As you might already have anticipated, I would suggest that the relative balance between secondary and primary processes could well form the basis of stable individual differences. In trying to support this contention, however, I am faced, once again, with a dearth of suitable evidence. Unfortunately, cognitive psychology has focused almost exclusively on secondary process thinking (Jacoby & Brooks, 1984) and on general processes, rather than individual differences. What I shall do, therefore, is look at the available evidence on individual differences in reasoning, the prototypical secondary process, and try to show how stylistic differences appear to reflect a secondary/primary balance, which by implication is also an analytic/holistic balance. For convenience, I shall discuss inductive reasoning, subdividing it in the conventional way into: classification, analogical reasoning, and judgment (Pellegrino & Goldman, 1983).

Classification

Classification has to do with the learning and acquisition of conceptual categories (concepts). Because the world around us is so complicated, filled with a myriad of objects and events, human beings have learned to organize and to simplify this profusion by forming categories. In this way, we know that the members of a category are likely to behave in the same way and to have similar characteristics. The kind of reasoning involved in the formation of categories has been explored largely in the context of classical categories (see Chapter 1), so that much of the available research on *classification* emphasizes logical, analytic thinking and the role of hypothesis testing in concept formation. However, this research is not without interest for our purposes since the individual differences that occur in hypothesis testing show signs of both analytic and holistic processing.

In the typical early experiments on concept formation, subjects were presented with a series of geometric figures differing in form (triangle or circle), size (small or large), colour (red or green), and number of borders (one or two) and were required to identify the attributes of a concept known to the experimenter (such as a large green triangle with one border). Although one might think that the reasoning involved in successfully completing these tasks would be prototypically "analytic" in the sense of involving the separation of relevant from irrelevant information, subjects actually exhibit a variety of successful strategies (Floyd, 1976). For instance, in the classical experiments by Bruner and his co-workers, focusing and scanning strategies were recognized (not to be confused with the attentional styles discussed earlier). The *focusing* strategy is one in which subjects considered one attribute at a time, eliminating irrelevant attributes in a serial fashion, a form of controlled experimentation where one variable is studied, while the others are held constant. It is as if this kind of individual prefers to concentrate on one thing at a time, wanting to get it absolutely clear before moving on to something else. Thus, those who use the focusing strategy worry away at difficulties until they have been mastered, in preference to leaving loose ends (Floyd, 1976). In contrast, the *scanning* strategy is more holistic, involving the attempt to eliminate whole concepts in one fell swoop by a form of what appears to be template matching. Thus, the hypotheses tested are not about single attributes but, instead, collections of attributes. It follows that scanners seem happy enough juggling several ideas at once, hoping the situation will clarify itself in due course. Although Floyd is of the opinion that focusing and scanning are stable styles, with subjects emphasizing either one or the other, Laughlin (1973) disagrees, arguing that not only is this not so but one cannot even distinguish adequately between the two strategies on either logical or practical grounds. Fortunately, some indication of the generality of hypothesis-testing strategies and the possibility of stable individual differences in categorizing styles comes from a different research tradition. I draw heavily on the reviews by Entwistle (1981) and Floyd (1976) for descriptions of, and comments on, this work by Pask and his co-workers.

In a classical series of experiments (Entwistle, 1981), Pask asked students to find out the way in which two hypothetical species of Martian animals, the Clobbits and Gandlemullers, were classified into subspecies. Subjects were provided with cards containing information about such things as the habitat, physical characteristics, and appearance of these creatures. The experiment required each subject to select one card at a time and give a reason for having chosen that card. This allowed the experimenters to follow the sequence of hypotheses generated about the nature of the classification system involved. Clear differences appeared amongst the experimental subjects. For instance, some students preferred to test simple working hypotheses, such as "Do Gandlemullers have sprongs?" in a systematic, step-by-step sequence. Pask described these subjects as *serialists*, whereas we would refer to them as showing an *analytic* thinking style. A more *holistic* strategy was evident in those students who worked with complex hypotheses which combined several properties simultaneously, such as "Are there more kinds of Gandlers with mounds (dorsal or cranial) than Plongers?" A second kind of holist, *the redundant holist*, was also found by Pask. These individuals used extremely idiosyncratic and personal hypotheses containing imaginary descriptions of the Martian creatures not contained in the information cards: "The ones that were discovered at first are gentle; the other kinds, the aggressive beasts were found later, well they are the ones with less mounds" (Entwistle, 1981, p. 90). Pask concluded that, while redundant holists personalize their learning experiences using subjective impressions of the information at hand, they eventually achieve an understanding of the classification scheme just as well as the serialists or other holists. One might add that redundant holists show clear signs of the "intrusion" of primary process thinking into their efforts to reason in a logical fashion.

The same dichotomy of strategies was also found by Pask when serialists and holists were asked to "teach back" what they had learned about the fictitious animals (Entwistle, 1981). For instance, *serialists* kept to the point, describing the bare essentials in a straightforward manner:

> Zoologists have classified the Gandlemuller on the basis of physical characteristics. The three main types are Gandlers, Plongers and Gandleplongers. Gandlers have no sprongs. Plongers have two sprongs, Gandleplongers have one sprong. There are four subspecies of Gandler: M1, M2, B1 and B2. The M's have one body, the E's have two bodies. The M1 and B1 have a single cranial mound. The M2 and B2 have a double cranial mound.... (Entwistle, 1981, p. 91)

The description by the *redundant holist* was, however, quite different:

> I want to tell you about a funny Martian animal which has been recently discovered and classified by scientists conducting surveys. They are funny sluglike things with various protruberances. These animals are called Gandlemullers, because they churn about in the swamps near the Equator and Gandler is Martian for swampmud, hence the Swampmudmiller ("Müller" is German for "Miller"). These things churn through the mud eating it by some curious process which means they eat and excrete at the same time. (Entwistle, 1981, p. 91)

Thus, the serialist teaches back what he or she learned in a logical, step-by-step manner, exactly as the material was encountered in the first place. On the other hand, the holist teaches back his or her own version, restructured in an idiosyncractic way and replete with additional, redundant impressions that are not strictly part of the exercise. It is as if the holist enjoys looking at things from different perspectives, aiming at ideas from new angles, going off at tangents by elaborating the most interesting points in a very personal way (Floyd, 1976).

A variety of experiments along these lines, led Pask to propose a dichotomy of learning styles which represent stable expressions of his hypothesis-testing strategies in learning situations. However, Messick (1987) argues that the two learning styles, *operation* (serialist) and *comprehension* (holist), are more appropriately regarded as strategies since they appear to be used in response to situational demands rather than being stable across situations. This is an on-going argument, of course, common to all conceptions of styles and traits. Evidence concerning the stability of the learning styles of Pask, and others, has been reviewed by N. Ford (1981), Richardson (1983) and Schmeck (1983), their conclusion being that the debate shows little sign of abating. To my mind, the strongest evidence in support of stable operation and comprehension learning styles comes from research on matching and mismatching styles to teaching methods. In mismatch conditions, subjects previously classified as serialist or holist learners had great difficulty in switching to a more appropriate mode. In particular, a holistic teaching programme "completely defeated the mismatched serialists" (Richardson, 1983, p. 320).

Analogical Reasoning

Analogical reasoning is widely considered to be an important component of effective thinking, not only in everyday life, but also in the more specialized intellectual world of arts and science (Holyoak, 1984; Nickerson *et al.*, 1985). We engage in analogical reasoning whenever we attempt to understand some unknown event or situation by comparing it to a known one. For instance, relatively simple analogical problems, of the form A: B :: C : D are included frequently in intelligence tests where, for example, the question is posed: "Boat is to plank as house is to _____?" You are then given some items to choose from, such as garden, brick, rent, or garage, and you would, of course, choose "brick." In reasoning analogically, what you are doing is using a *known* relationship (between boat and plank) to give you some clues as to the nature of the *unknown* relationship (house and _____). This allows the transfer of knowledge and understanding from a known problem to a novel one, even when the two appear, at first sight, to have little in common. Such a transfer of knowledge is crucial to effective learning and reasoning.

The successful completion of proportional analogies is said to involve four necessary stages (Sternberg, 1977). *Encoding* involves the identification of the attributes of each term in the analogy, after which one *infers* a rule that relates adjacent terms (*i.e.*, between boat and plank). *Mapping* is a more difficult stage in which one must discover a rule relating non-adjacent terms (*i.e.*, between boat and house). Finally, one applies both rules in completing the analogy (Alexander, 1984).

The prevalence of proportional analogies in tests of "intelligence" has contributed to the tendency to regard individual differences in analogical reasoning as abilities, measured in terms of the speed and accuracy of performance (Pellegrino & Goldman, 1983; Sternberg, 1987). The presence of stylistic differences would, presumably, only be observed if subjects were presented with a less structured problem and allowed the time to approach it in their preferred manner. An interesting step in this direction has been taken by Holyoak (1984) who studied a more complex form of analogical problem-solving. The latter differed from the simple analogies of intelligence tests in that the base problem (the known situation), rather than being provided, had to be selected by the subject. In other words, the subject is creating the analogy, rather than simply solving a pre-formed one, a much more demanding and imaginative task.

Although Holyoak does not discuss his findings in terms of stylistic differences, they provide the first glimmerings of a stylistic dimension. He found that at least two different kinds of analogy were generated: *literal* (in which the base analogue is very close to, and shares many obvious elements with, the target problem) and *deep* (an analogue between quite disparate situations in which the base and target problems share only essential attributes).

Evidence in support of a cognitive style contrasting preferences for either literal or deep analogies is circumstantial to say the least. It is also extremely limited. Anecdotal evidence comes from R. Hoffman's (1980) examination of the use of metaphor in science in which clear differences of opinion about the wisdom of using metaphor were apparent. Of particular interest is the rejection of metaphor by logical positivists (analytic style). Similar findings are also reported by Pollio and Smith (1980), whose factor analytic studies of figurative speech led them to conclude that not everyone has the same tendency either to understand or to use figurative expressions. In particular, the frozen (*i.e.* in the lexicon for some time) and novel (*i.e.* unique, surprising, unusual) figures of speech which were identified seem comparable to Holyoak's literal and deep analogies, respectively.

The tentative nature of these formulations is also found in the cognitive style literature, where interest in individual differences in analogical or metaphoric reasoning appears to be recent. Thus, Kogan (1982) notes the recent development of a stylistic dimension that contrasts a literal/analytic style with that of a poetic/synthetic style. Similarly, in discussing the kinds of cognitive processes involved in metaphoric thinking, Kogan (1983) suggests that one would expect to find individual differences amongst children, although the matter has yet to be investigated fully. Research appears to be hampered by difficulty in finding ways of measuring individual differences in the use of metaphor. A more clearly stylistic approach to analogical reasoning is taken by Pask (in N. Ford, 1981) in contrasting the learning behaviour of serialists (operational learners) and holists (comprehension learners). The latter develop a picture of what has to be learned by using analogies in relating one area of knowledge to another. Operational learners, on the other hand, tend not to use analogies and seem not to appreciate how one area of knowledge may be analogous to another. Entwistle (1981) also points to the finding that, not only are comprehension learners more likely to use analogies, but they also develop their own idiosyncratic analogies which may not be formally correct but which help in developing a more complete understanding of the task at hand.

The most one can say, therefore, is that there are intimations of a style contrasting preferences for either "tight," formal, literal analogies, or "loose," informal, deep (metaphoric) analogies. However, the matter awaits further research.

Judgment

In making decisions, often we have to judge the probability of events made uncertain by the absence of adequate information or clear rules about using whatever information is available. Two common examples of such decision situations, in the professional world, are clinical diagnosis and weather forecasting. Ideal, or normative, models of the cognitive processes involved in such judgments suggest that we should sample the available information adequately, treat both negative and positive information impartially, and have some effective way of weighing and combining information so as to arrive at an optimal decision. Under some circumstances (amongst those educated in science, for instance), this ideal may be approached. However, in daily life, ordinary people do not seem to follow such systematic procedures. Instead, heuristic judgments (a form of reasoning that Neimark, 1983, regards as a poor cousin to logical thought, riddled, in her opinion, by cognitive errors) are common. Nickerson *et al.* (1985) have described these errors as biases in drawing a sample (*i.e.* failure to sample enough information in an unbiased, impartial way), biases in relating a sample to a hypothesis (*i.e.* ineffective use of negative, probabilistic, or abstract statistical information, resulting in a failure to discard hypotheses), and biases in forming new hypotheses (*i.e.* considering too few alternatives and basing hypotheses on a misinterpretation of covariance and correlation).

During the 1970s, the use of heuristics (and other departures from the normative ideal) was taken to mean that most people were severely limited in their cognitive capabilities. Indeed, some psychologists seemed to delight in demonstrating how cognitively foolish their experimental subjects could be, seeing them as "faulty computers" or "mental simpletons" (Fletcher *et al.*, 1986; Kenrick & Dantchik, 1983; Sorrentino & Higgins, 1986). More recently, however, the possibility has been raised that, rather than representing a cognitive deficit, these so-called errors in thinking may actually reflect an alternative, legitimate form of reasoning.

Rosch (1983), for instance, distinguishes between what she calls *logical* and *reference-point reasoning*, the former referring to reasoning that approximates the normative ideal, while the latter is characterized by the use of "error-prone" heuristics. Reference-point reasoning involves the use of some vivid, personally relevant instance or event as a standard against which to compare other events. For instance, in deciding to buy a particular model of car, one might base one's judgment on the opinion of a close friend, who has had some experience with that make of car, rather than using base rate information provided in consumer magazines. Thus, specific instances are taken to be representative of the broader picture, a strategy that is said to be in error when it is clearly contrary to the available base rate data. However, Rosch argues that deserting statistics and "facts" in favour of personal experience may not always be inappropriate for the "facts of the matter" are not invariably correct or complete. Thus, reference-point reasoning (which could also be called prototypical reasoning, since prototypes are a form of reference point) could be the most adaptive means of dealing with situations where one is faced with incomplete, ambiguous, or contradictory information. Although Rosch regards these two forms of reasoning as alternative, independent modes, it is interesting that Neimark (1983) takes the additional step of suggesting stylistic preferences in their use. In other words, while all of us make use of both modes, there may be consistent preferences for one or the other in some people. It is also interesting to find that Neimark clearly regards the "logical" mode as being analytic and the "reference-point" mode as holistic. However, in the absence of further research, much of this remains at the level of speculation, albeit useful speculation for our purposes.

Both Bruner (1984) and Zukier (1986) recognize a similar dichotomy in inferential reasoning in their distinction between *paradigmatic* and *narrative* modes of thought, two irreducible modes of reasoning and thinking each characterized by a particular logic for selecting, organizing, and using information. Thus, the paradigmatic mode is logico-scientific in the sense that it seeks to establish general laws of causal relations between events in the world, laws that are context-free and universal. The verification of ideas is through formal and empirical proof, the correspondence of ideas with reality. However, comprehensiveness and richness of ideas are sacrificed in pursuit of rigour; denotation is preferred over connotation. In contrast, the narrative mode is a form of storytelling that seeks to establish, not general laws, but patterns of behaviour, general themes that typify a single human life seen in its full social context. Truth, in this case, is what seems credible, the verisimilitude of the picture that has been constructed. Thus, rigour is sacrificed for idiographic richness and coherence.

Zukier is of the opinion that, while both modes may be deployed at different times by all of us, we may come to favour one over the other, a tendency that may constitute an enduring style. He has explored this possibility in a number of experiments. For instance, in a study of inferential reasoning (Zukier & Pepitone, 1984), a group of first-year medical students and a group of surgery residents were required to estimate the likelihood that a series of stereotypical and neutral statements actually described a target person (an engineer). The authors "hypothesized that a medical education, with its emphasis on diagnostic procedures and the differential likelihood of various etiologies might sensitize people to a paradigmatic orientation and that this orientation would also dominate in other, unrelated tasks" (Zukier, 1986, p. 486). A total of 100 statements were judged after the experimental subjects had been informed that only thirty of these vignettes described engineers, the remaining seventy being descriptions of other professionals. Thus, the base rate probability of any single description being that of an engineer was 0.3. Subjects using a paradigmatic mode would be expected to produce mean probability estimates close to the base rate, whereas those using a narrative mode, being more influenced by the *contents* of each description rather than the overall base rate, would diverge from 0.3. As it turned out, the behaviour of the two experimental groups confirmed expectations. The surgery residents stayed close to the base rate, while the first-year medical students did not. A reasonable conclusion seemed to be that the surgery residents, because of their diagnostic training, were more inclined than the less experienced students to use the paradigmatic mode. While this research demonstrates that training can establish certain habits of thought in diagnostic situations, it does not, of course, demonstrate the existence of a more general stylistic dimension. To do so, one would, presumably, need to examine within-group differences rather than the between-group comparisons made by Zukier. In doing so, one might expect to find stylistic differences that (if one is to believe the views of Hudson, 1968, and Witkin & Goodenough, 1981, on the development of cognitive styles) are well established in the individual prior to the ravages of higher education.

The prospects for such a style, however, have received something of a blow in a study by Wright and Phillips (1984), who were led to postulate "probabilistic" and "non-probablistic" cognitive styles following their cross-cultural studies on judgment under uncertainty. The two styles were characterized in the following way. A probabilistic thinker is said to take a probabilistic rather than a non-probabilistic view when confronted with uncertainty. Such a person values information that could reduce uncertainty, revises probabilities in light of new information, is less prone to violating the normative axioms of decision theory, and shows no bias for certain overly uncertain events. In contrast, the non-probabilistic thinker translates uncertainty into "yes–no, don't know" terms, places little value on fallible information, tends not to revise probabilities in light of fallible information, violates normative axioms, makes plans on the basis of best guesses, and is biased towards opinions with certain consequences. However, their most recent research, using a variety of simulated decision tasks, casts doubt on the stability of these

TABLE 2. RELATIONSHIPS BETWEEN COGNITIVE STYLES

Cognitive Process	Analytic Style	Holistic Style
Pattern Recognition	Analytic	Holistic
Selective Attention	Field Independence	Field Dependence
Representation	Verbal/Analytic	Visual/Analog
Organization	Conceptual Differentiation	Conceptual Holism
Retrieval	Convergence	Divergence
Classification	Serial	Holistic
Analogical Reasoning	Tight	Loose
Judgement	Actuarial	Intuitive

hypothesized styles. They conclude that, while probabilistic and non-probabilistic thinking do not appear to be unidimensional cognitive styles, nothing in their study denies the possibility that an individual could develop a consistent style of probabilistic thinking.

One is left, therefore, with some uncertainty about whether logical/paradigmatic and reference-point/narrative modes are styles or strategies, a dilemma that should not obscure the fact that the two modes do seem to occur and that they reflect analytic and holistic reasoning, respectively.

TOWARD A PROTOTYPIC DIMENSION

What I have demonstrated in the preceding discussion is that each component of the information processing model (Fig. 8) is associated with a particular kind of cognitive style. In turn, each of these styles contrasts an *analytical* with a *holistic* form of perceiving, remembering, and thinking. It follows that all of the eight styles can be grouped together to compose a broad, generic *analytic–holistic* style (Table 2). However, the relative paucity of the available evidence leaves many loose ends, while at the same time raising the possibility that what I have constructed is essentially a house of cards. Two considerations reduce the qualms I have about all this.

First, it is true that a number of the styles in Table 2 have achieved only modest levels of stability, while others are in the early stages of development. However, what surprises me is that any stability has been demonstrated at all for I believe that most research on styles is flawed. As long ago as 1962, Wallach drew attention to the problems created for research methods by variations in stylistic consistency (Wallach, 1962). Some people are consistent; others are not. Thus, when people are lumped together in research, rather than segregating them into sub-groups, there is the possibility that inconsistent subjects mask the stability shown by others. A similar warning came from Berg *et al.* (1981–82), twenty years later:

> [I]n a population many people may not have a particular cognitive prefer-ence or perhaps, more generally, a specific cognitive style. The various cognitive style labels such as field independence ... may each be valid descriptors for a limited proportion of people. The exact proportion depends on the style and on the nature of the population. For such people convergent validity should be found. Other people with weaker preferences on styles would contribute random variation in validation studies and show very situation specific styles. (Berg *et al.*, 1981–82, p. 202)

To my knowledge, both admonitions have been disregarded in virtually all style research. Adequate research on the analytic–holistic dimension would require that four subgroups be recognized: the analytic and holistic specialists, generalists/versatiles, and the non-specific group. I assume that the versatile and the non-specific types would, because of their variability, contribute the "random" variance to experiments that Berg *et al.* (1981–82) mention. How one might separate and then study these subgroups is another matter, although Hudson (1968) appears to have taken a step in the right direction. What all this amounts to is that the available research on styles is a morass. The fact that some consisten-cies have emerged is surprising, suggesting that stable individual differences do exist beneath the welter of "random" variation.

Second, trying to fit together various styles into a broad, generic dimension is a difficult business, the experience of the Witkin group being a case in point. We left the FDI story at the stage where a perceptual style, based on correlations between the BAT, RFT, and EFT had been postulated. This, in itself, was controversial enough because of the instability of relationships between the defining tests (no doubt for the reasons mentioned above). The situation became even more empirical-ly perilous, however, when the perceptual style was incorporated into a broader perceptual–cognitive style, labelled *articulated–global*, following the demonstration of what appeared to be stable correlations between the perceptual tasks and a variety of cognitive measures, including subtests of the WAIS (picture completion, object assembly, block design). This stylistic dimension was, in turn, incorporated into an even broader personality dimension labelled *psychological differentiation*. With each attempt to broaden the style, however, came a growing amount of criticism about the stability of the relationships involved (see, for example, Haaken, 1988, and Missler, 1986). The whole enterprise was viewed, in some eyes, as dubious in the extreme. I suspect that the same arguments and doubts can be applied to the relationships in Table 2. However, my harmony is not disturbed too much by the Witkin experience for what I believe myself to be doing is attempting to identify a prototypical dimension, almost an ideal dimension, one that typifies relatively few people. Clearly, most of us will, over the course of time, show a mixture of analytic and holistic styles. Only a few will exhibit the stable, pure styles implied in Table 2. However, it is these prototypical cases that serve as useful reference points in thinking about styles, as I hope to show in subsequent chapters.

Chapter 3

The Affective Dimension

THE AFFECTIVE (emotional) dimension of my personality model, *emotional stability–instability*, refers to consistent individual differences in the *intensity* of emotional reactions to daily life. At one extreme of the dimension are those who lead lives of vivid intensity, reacting to even mundane events with such strength of feeling as to make life for both themselves and others difficult, if not unbearable. In contrast are those relatively placid souls, slow to anger or excite, whose lives are permeated by a degree of blandness. One senses that they look out onto a world coloured in pastel shades, rather than the extremes of light and dark so characteristic of the more emotionally reactive. The contrast between these two emotional styles, and their consequences, is well illustrated by an incident that took place one day in 1780.

> The proceedings of the Connecticut Assembly were threatened by an outbreak of panic when an unprecedented darkening of the sky suggested the arrival of a much-prophesied Day of Judgment. Then a member made the following ruling, "Either this is the end of the world or it is not. If it is not, our business should proceed. If it is, I prefer to be found doing my duty. Let lights be brought." (Higgins, 1982, p. 278)

Although the emotional calm of this stalwart gentleman won the day, stoicism has its limits. A similar reaction to literary or artistic works, or to "matters of the heart," might well be considered personally and socially inappropriate. I should make it clear at the outset, therefore, that the terms "stability" and "instability" do not imply a value judgment; stability is in no sense "better" than instability. Rather, each emotional

69

style has both advantages and disadvantages depending on the prevailing circumstances.

What I intend to do in this chapter is to review the many ways in which this emotional style dimension, commonly referred to as *emotionality*, has been conceptualized, paying particular attention to recent theoretical developments that portray it in a more positive light. The many differences of opinion over the nature of emotionality have their origins in differing assumptions about emotion itself. This is especially evident in the many disparate views on the nature of, and relationships between, physiological arousal, cognitive appraisal, and emotional "intensity." To begin with, therefore, I review current theories of emotion in the hope that I can illuminate why, for instance, traditional conceptions of emotionality focus on negative emotionality or distress, while ignoring positive emotionality. After discussing both negative and positive emotionality in some detail, I turn to a more recent and alternative conception of emotional intensity which cuts across matters of emotional content and is couched in more purely stylistic terms. This *affect intensity* trait is proposed as the most appropriate way in which to depict the affective dimension of my personality model.

THE NATURE OF "EMOTION"

The concept of emotion has had a chequered career in psychology. In modern times, its importance was recognized during the eighteenth century when it was incorporated, along with reason and desire, into the classical tripartite system. Even then, however, it continued to play an uncertain role in psychological theory, due in part to the persistent difficulty in distinguishing it conceptually from both cognition and conation (Isen, 1984). Despite such definitional problems, certain aspects of emotion, notably the "feeling" component, were recognized as topics of central importance, by both experimental and clinical psychologists, up until the beginning of the present century. Even Watson, a founder of behaviourism, was keenly interested in emotion, although not, of course, as a feeling in consciousness (Campos & Barrett, 1984).

By the late 1920s, however, with the rise of behaviourism/positivism and the consequent discrediting of introspection, the topic of emotion went into serious decline. Not only were emotions difficult to define and measure in ways that satisfied positivists, but emotional concepts seemed largely irrelevant to the kinds of behavioural theory being developed. Such concepts appeared to be too closely linked to what behaviourists considered to be naive, romantic, and unscientific language (Campos & Barrett, 1984). The advent of the cognitive revolution in the 1960s appears to have pushed the study of emotion even further into the doldrums for, even in the late 1970s, relatively few studies on emotion were being published (Pervin, 1985). Even those cognitive psychologists interested in emotion (*e.g.*, Schacter) treated it as an epiphenomenon, something that accompanies cognition and physiological arousal but has no causal impact on events (Campos & Barrett, 1984).

Over the last two decades, however, there has been a quickening of interest in emotion as a respectable research area due, in part, to the advocacy of eminent cognitive psychologists who have argued that the study of "cold" cognition (in the absence of emotion) has led to impoverished theory (Sorrentino & Higgins, 1986). Although there remains, amongst some psychologists, a begrudging attitude to granting emotion independent status (Leventhal & Tomarken, 1986), the topic does appear to have been re-established as one worthy of consideration (Pervin, 1985; Singer & Kolligian, 1987).

This belated recognition of emotion is a mixed blessing, however, for it confronts us with the unresolved task of trying to decide what an "emotion" is and exactly what is involved in emotional processes. William James found this to be an onerous task in the 1890s, one that has changed little in the intervening years—as we shall see.

Problems in Defining Emotion

Most of us seem to have a modicum of skill in identifying and reliably naming the emotional states of ourselves and others. Difficulties arise, however, when we are required to give a formal definition of emotion, a dilemma that is also experienced by psychologists (Fehr & Russell, 1984). In the recent past, attempts have been made to identify emotions with single events, such as feelings, overt behaviours, or certain types of physiological activity. Taken in isolation, however, none of these aspects of emotion seem to capture the full flavour of what is commonly taken to be an "emotion." This has led some psychologists, such as Lazarus (1984), to argue that emotion is multifaceted and that all three of the above "events" must be present if one is to label something as an emotional state (Fehr & Russell, 1984). In other words, an emotion comprises *physiological activity* (usually couched in terms of arousal), *subjective experience* (the conscious and subconscious experience of feeling), and *behavioural expression* (the communication of emotional states through facial and bodily expression). Not everyone agrees with this definition, of course. For example, Averill (1982) and Campos and Barrett (1984) suggest that emotion manifests itself in so many different ways that none of the three components are essential aspects of "emotion," making a precise definition virtually impossible.

This difference of opinion is yet another example of the debate over the use of classical and prototypical categories in psychology. A classical definition of emotion would require that a list of necessary and sufficient conditions or attributes be identified, while a prototypical definition would recognize emotions as fuzzy sets—collections of behaviours bearing a family resemblance to one another. Ordinary or "folk" conceptions of emotions appear to be based on prototypes (Fehr & Russell, 1984; Shaver *et al.*, 1987). For our purposes, however, it is not necessary to become involved in this debate. Rather, I shall simply outline what are commonly considered to be the three basic components of emotion, while recognizing that there is some debate about the way in which they combine to form an "emotion," an issue to which we shall return later.

The Components of Emotion

Neurophysiological activity. It is traditional in western society to link emotion with changes in physiological activity (Averill, 1974). In this way of thinking, emotions are primitive events that are visited upon us, rather than being the products of the more rational, "higher" mental processes. Taken to an extreme, this viewpoint results in the definition of emotions as *patterns of visceral activity* (Wenger, 1950), while a more moderate expression of the same tradition simply states that physiological activity is an essential component of emotion (Schacter, 1964).

Since the 1930s, physiological activity and change have tended to be discussed in terms of *arousal*, a concept that was introduced in response to the confusion surrounding attempts to define emotion. It was hoped that arousal would provide a physiologically based concept (as opposed to a mentalistic one) that was both conceptually unidimensional, as well as being amenable to both quantification and measurement (Neiss, 1988). Such a concept, it was thought, would replace the more antiquated, mentalistic conceptions of emotion which could then be allowed to fade from the scene. Subsequent events have, however, cast doubt both on the unitary nature of arousal and its central role in emotion. I shall discuss the former issue here and leave the question of the role of arousal until a later section.

The fundamental problem with the notion of arousal as a unitary phenomenon is that there is now a great deal of research indicating that various bodily and neural systems can become aroused to varying degrees in response to the same situation, *i.e.*, they do not covary (Farley, 1985; Neiss, 1988; Thayer, 1985). To complicate matters further, patterns of arousal seem to differ across individuals, making it difficult to compare one with another. The debate has now shifted to the question of how best to conceptualize the many forms of arousal and their interactions, with the result that there are numerous multidimensional models of arousal (Farley, 1985). I am drawn to Lacey's (1967) views on the matter in which three kinds of arousal are recognized:

1. *Behavioural arousal.*

In everyday life we are most familiar with behavioral arousal, which varies along a continuum from deep sleep to great excitement. Its most obvious aspect is activity. In deep sleep there is little movement—only the occasional twisting and turning of the body and, rarely, sleep walking.... During the first stage of wakefulness (drowsiness) there is more activity, but movements are sluggish and energy expenditure is small. Activity is moderate during ordinary wakefulness, as we go about the business of dealing with the environment, and it peaks during great excitement or in heavy exercise or work. Thus the higher the level of [behavioural] arousal, the greater the motor activity. (A. H. Buss & Plomin, 1984, p. 32)

Behavioural arousal, therefore, refers to what Lacey (1967) calls skeletal-motor activity and is a function of the amount of activity engendered by the body's voluntary muscles. As we shall see shortly, behavioural arousal is allocated a central role in those theories of emotion that emphasize the importance of feedback from the voluntary muscles, especially the face, in generating emotion.

2. *Autonomic arousal.*

Widespread bodily arousal, involving respiration, heart rate, blood flow, sweating, and the stopping or starting of digestive processes, is mediated by the autonomic nervous system. Of its two well-known divisions, the *parasympathetic* division ... is involved in the low arousal, routine vegetative functions necessary to maintain life. The *sympathetic* division ... is involved in the high arousal necessary for dealing with emergencies. High arousal is especially necessary in the face of threat, when the organism reacts with a fight-or-flight reaction that requires massive physical exertion. (A. H. Buss & Plomin, 1984, p. 33)

The two divisions of the autonomic nervous system act in concert to enable the individual to adapt to circumstances. During uneventful times, the parasympathetic division may dominate, whereas the appearance of threat or emergency causes the sympathetic division to swing into action. Autonomic arousal, therefore, refers to the activation of the *sympathetic* division with all its consequent effects on the visceral and endocrine systems. It is these physiological changes that have been traditionally associated with an emotional experience, so that it is not surprising to find that many theories of emotion afford autonomic arousal a crucial role.

3. *Cortical arousal.* This form of arousal refers to the degree to which the cells of the cerebral cortex are activated. When monitored by EEG recording, low cortical arousal is associated with large, slow brain waves, whereas those resulting from high cortical arousal are small, fast, and irregular.

> The extent to which the cortex is aroused depends on how much input it receives from the reticular formation, which itself receives stimulation. This stimulation can arise from the senses which pass on inputs from the environment; from the cortex itself, which can stimulate the reticular formation with exciting thoughts; and from the limbic system, which conveys the arousal involved in motivation and emotion. The key, however, is the reticular formation, which is believed to regulate the amount of neural input coming from the senses or neural structures and going to the cortex. (A. H. Buss & Plomin, 1984, p. 33)

Traditional theories of emotion do not discuss cortical arousal. While the activity of cortical cells may play some role in intelligence or temperament, it is not normally seen as an aspect of emotion. However, recent theoretical developments on the importance of affective schema in the experience of emotion, as well as new conceptions of "positive emotionality," all of which will be discussed shortly, suggest that cortical arousal should be incorporated into theories of emotion.

There seems to be a reasonable degree of consensus that the three forms of arousal are products of different neurophysiological systems which are, to some extent, independent (Derryberry & Rothbart, 1984; Eysenck & Eysenck, 1985; Thayer, 1985). For instance, it is possible to be intensely involved in thinking through an idea (cortically aroused) while slumped in an armchair (behaviourally and autonomically inert). The precise nature of the interaction between the various forms of arousal remains controversial, however. While Eysenck and Eysenck (1985) argue that cortical and autonomic arousal tend to covary positively when an individual is highly aroused, Thayer (1985) holds the opposite view that a person's energetic (cortical) and tense (autonomic) arousal are negatively correlated at high levels of energy expenditure.

As we shall see, the use of *arousal* in conceptions of emotion and emotionality creates some difficulties for, among other things, it is not always clear to which kind or kinds of "arousal" the author is referring, and how they are supposed to interact.

Behavioural expression. One of the main functions of behavioural expression in social animals, such as humans, is the communication of emotional states. This is achieved through various combinations of facial expression, vocal changes, and bodily postures commonly referred to as non-verbal expressiveness or "body-language." In reading another's emotional condition, therefore, we pay particular attention to changes around the eyes and mouth, variations in the tone and pitch of voice, alternation in speech patterns, and various shrugs, gestures, and other body movements. Many of these movements are spontaneous, a function of the somatic nervous system, particularly the non-pyramidal division, which controls general muscle tone, posture, and motor patterns (Buck, 1984). Indeed, there is a commonly held view that non-verbal expressiveness is involuntary, a form of innate behaviour common to all human beings, which leads to similar patterns of facial expressions across all cultures (Izard & Malatesta, 1987). Each culture, however, has its own *display rules*, which specify the forms of emotional expression considered to be acceptable within that culture. Through socialization we become more or less adept at controlling and/or concealing our "genuine" emotions in favour of those that are more socially approved. Paul Ekman, for instance, notes that facial expression is often a combination of an *involuntary* expression which stems directly from one's emotional state and *voluntary* (conscious) attempts to cover this up with another emotion (Ekman, 1984). Despite our best efforts to create some kind of facade, however, some form of *emotional leakage* occurs. This may be a fleeting facial expression detectable only by slow-motion photography, or hand and feet movements that we forget to control in our preoccupation with maintaining our facial mask. Ekman describes a case in point:

> Mary was a forty-two year-old housewife. The last of her three suicide attempts was quite serious. It was only an accident that someone found her before an overdose of sleeping pills killed her. Her history was not much different from that of many other women who suffer a midlife depression. The children had grown up and didn't need her. Her husband seemed preoccupied with his work. Mary felt useless. By the time she had entered the hospital she no longer could handle the house, could not sleep well, and sat by herself crying much of the time. In her first three weeks in the hospital she received medication and group therapy. She seemed to respond very well: her manner brightened, and she no longer talked of committing suicide. In one of the interviews we filmed, Mary told the doctor how much better she felt and asked for a weekend pass. Before receiving the pass, she confessed that she had been lying to get it. She still desperately wanted to kill herself. After three more months in the hospital Mary had genuinely improved, although there was a relapse a year later. She has been out of the hospital and apparently well for many years.

The filmed interview with Mary fooled most of the young and even many of the experienced psychiatrists and psychologists to whom I showed it. We studied it for hundreds of hours, going over it again and again, inspecting each gesture and expression in slow-motion to uncover any possible clues to deceit. In a moment's pause before replying to her doctor's question about her plans for the future, we saw in slow-motion a fleeting facial expression of despair, so quick that we had missed seeing it the first few times we examined the film. Once we had the idea that concealed feelings might be evident in these very brief *micro expressions*, we searched and found many more, typically covered in an instant by a smile. We also found a *micro gesture*. When telling the doctor how well she was handling her problems Mary sometimes showed a fragment of a shrug—not the whole thing, just a part of it. She would shrug with just one hand, rotating it a bit. Or, her hands would be quiet but there would be a momentary lift of one shoulder. (Ekman, 1984, p. 16)

Behavioural expression is an important component of emotional behaviour, therefore, but its role is complicated by social convention which imbues us with the need to conceal, or at least selectively express, what we are genuinely feeling.

Subjective experience. The subjective experience of emotion is commonly referred to as *feeling*, an aspect of emotion that is represented in conscious awareness. To say that we "feel" something is to imply that we sense, at some level of awareness, that we are in an emotional state. Thus, feelings can occur at all levels of awareness. At the lowest level, we are barely conscious of the feeling and may have difficulty in identifying it or evaluating its significance. Feelings of this sort give rise to notions of the unconscious, barely sensed promptings which, nevertheless, carry with them a sense of urgency. At high levels of awareness, feelings may dominate consciousness making it imperative for us to reflect on them, as well as to take steps either to enhance or to control them (Izard, 1982).

The precise nature of *feeling* is controversial. On the one hand, there are those who prefer to restrict the term to the direct apprehension of emotional states, untrammelled by cognitive evaluation (Izard, 1982, 1984). In contrast, others suggest that feelings should be seen as comprising the products of both perception (apprehension) of emotional states and the various representations, symbols, and labels derived from cognitive appraisal (Epstein, 1984). In other words, some people distinguish between "feelings" and "thoughts-about-feelings," whereas others do not. The advantage of the former position is that it allows you to distinguish more clearly between affect and cognition, thereby maintaining the idea of "emotional" processes as independent entities (Izard, 1984). There is some developmental evidence in support of the latter position. Children, for instance, have a built-in capacity for experiencing feelings directly, *i.e.* in the absence of reflection or labelling. Their "feelings" are sense impressions devoid of symbolic representation. The latter come later, when children develop the capacity to reflect on their feelings and represent them cognitively (Izard *et al.*, 1984).

The origins of feelings, and the processes involved in their appearance in consciousness, are also controversial. Perhaps the difference of opinion in this area is best represented as being between peripheral and central viewpoints. The peripheral position is that feelings result from apprehension of proprioceptive and kinaesthetic feedback from the body which convey information about the degree of behavioural and autonomic arousal that is occurring (Epstein, 1984). The problem with this position, as we shall see later, is that paraplegics with severed spinal cords can experience intense feelings in the apparent absence of bodily feedback (Chwalisz *et al.*, 1988). Clearly, some other mechanism must be involved which, according to the central position, must reside within the brain. One possibility is the "readout" of neurochemical activity from brain structures, such as the limbic system, directly into consciousness (Buck, 1984). Feelings, therefore, depending on the viewpoint to which one subscribes, might be seen as the occurrence in awareness of some combination of peripheral feedback, central readout, and cognitive appraisal.

Having outlined briefly the nature of neurophysiological activity, behavioural expression, and subjective experience, we need to look now at the way in which the three components interact to generate "emotion." Speculation on the matter is incorporated into models of emotion and emotional processes, to which we now turn.

THEORIES OF EMOTION

Two different models can be distinguished among the more commonly held views on the nature of emotional processes, namely, *cognitive-arousal* and *somatic* (Zajonc & Markus, 1984). A third model is in the process of being developed, and, since it has no obvious label, I shall refer to it as *central template* theory. My purpose in discussing all three models is to develop some understanding of the way in which *emotional intensity* has been and might be conceptualized.

Cognitive-Arousal Theory

Cognitive-arousal theory (Schacter & Singer, 1962; Schacter, 1964; Mandler, 1975) is organized around two basic postulates (Leventhal & Tomarken, 1986). First, emotion is said to result from the interaction of autonomic (sympathetic) arousal and the cognitive appraisal of the causes of that arousal. Second, both autonomic arousal and cognitive appraisal are considered to be essential components of all emotional experiences. In other words, without arousal there is no emotion and, in the absence of cognitive appraisal, there is only undifferentiated arousal. Thus, some event may trigger autonomic arousal, and you may well become aware of it but you only experience an "emotion" after cognitive intervention. The situation is scanned, the causes of the arousal are identified, and a suitable "emotional" label is applied to the arousal state. In this way of thinking, *emotional intensity* is a function of the degree of arousal, whereas *emotional quality* is determined by the appraisal process.

Like all psychological models and theories, however, the cognitive-arousal approach has been found wanting in a number of regards. For instance, in focusing on autonomic arousal, it is assumed that the autonomic nervous system contains all the neural tissue needed to account for emotion, an assumption that is inconsistent with the extensive literature implicating the limbic system in emotion (Izard, 1982). In addition, somatic and cortical arousal are ignored. Yet, as we shall see, somatic arousal is afforded a significant role in somatic models of emotion, while Epstein (1984) offers the interesting observation that "all emotions share a general state of increased cortical excitation" (p. 73).

Serious doubts have arisen, however, about the supposed causal role of autonomic arousal. The assumption that heightened arousal is *essential* for emotional experience is not well supported by the available evidence (Cotton, 1981; Leventhal & Tomarken, 1986; Reisenzein, 1983). For instance,

> numerous investigations have tested the prediction that the particular combination of drug-induced arousal and either misinformation or no information about the source of that arousal heightens responsivity to emotionally relevant contextual cues. In turn, this heightened responsivity is expected to result in intensified emotional experience relative to that found in subjects that were similarly drugged but correctly informed or subjects not drugged ... the great majority (of studies) have failed to provide support for the prediction that increased arousal heightens self-reported emotional experience relative to that found in placebo conditions. (Leventhal & Tomarken, 1986, p. 568)

Similarly, research on individuals with injuries to the spinal cord provides only partial support for the role of arousal. Cognitive-arousal theory would predict that the intensity of emotional experience should be proportional to the degree and location of the spinal injury. That is, the more complete the severance of the spinal cord, and the higher it is located up the spinal column, the less autonomic feedback the patient will experience. However, Chwalisz *et al.* (1988) have found that even patients with high, severe lesions are capable of experiencing intense emotions. Indeed, in one case, a patient remembered becoming so angry with an instructor that he wanted to run over him with his wheelchair. Autonomic arousal does not appear to be essential, therefore, for emotional experience. However, Chwalisz *et al.* (1988) did find that higher spinal lesions were related to a decrease in intensity of reported emotion relative to patients with lower spinal lesions. They conclude, therefore, that while autonomic arousal may not be essential, it does seem to play an amplifying role in both sustaining and intensifying emotional feelings that are, presumably, instigated by some mechanism other than that proposed in cognitive-arousal theory. What this might be is not clear, but they do note that their study does not rule out a possible role for somatic/facial feedback, which is unaffected by the kinds of injuries sustained by their subjects.

Turning to the role of cognitive appraisal in emotion, the opposing viewpoints on the matter are exemplified by the debate that took place between Zajonc and Lazarus in the early 1980s. In Zajonc's (1980, 1984) estimation, emotion and cognition are best seen as independent processes, and, further, emotion is not commonly instigated by, nor does it require, cognition. The latter, he argues, is a slower, more analytic process than the rapid, holistic nature of emotion. Lazarus (1984), on the other hand, maintains that, if we are to experience emotion, then we must *comprehend* on-going events as relevant to our personal well-being. Thus, cognition enters the picture in two ways, as *primary appraisal*, a primitive/intuitive evaluation of emotional stimuli, and as *secondary appraisal*, a more reflective, symbolic interpretation of events (Greenberg & Safran, 1987). Since neither form of appraisal necessarily precedes the other, both may play a role in the instigation of emotion. Although the debate generated a great deal of interest, it appears to have been, at least in part, a matter of semantics (Buck, 1985; Epstein, 1984). Both Zajonc and Lazarus agree on the need for some kind of primitive perceptual appraisal of events to determine their emotional significance but differ over the involvement of cognitive (secondary) appraisal, if "cognitive" is taken to mean a higher-order, symbolic, analytic process. Zajonc sees no essential role for the latter, while Lazarus believes that "emotion" stems from the interaction of primary (perceptual) and secondary (cognitive) appraisal. As to which is the more plausible, I am inclined to agree with Epstein's (1984) conclusion on the matter, that "most emotions, by far, are instigated by preconscious appraisal of events, with other influences tending to serve a contextual or ancillary role" (p. 81). In other words, cognitive appraisal, like autonomic arousal, may augment emotional experience by, in this case, reflecting on and elaborating, subjective feelings.

It seems reasonable to conclude, therefore, that cognitive-arousal theory oversimplifies the origins of emotional experiences, focusing excessively on two processes, autonomic arousal and cognitive appraisal, which may, in fact, play only a subsidiary role. It follows that conceptions of emotional intensity couched in terms of this model may be similarly impoverished.

Somatic Theory

In somatic theory, the neural basis of emotion is said to lie in the somatic nervous system with feedback from the facial muscles being paramount in the instigation and regulation of emotion (Izard & Malatesta, 1987; Tomkins, 1962). The perception of an emotional stimulus produces a pattern of neural activity and expressive behaviour that is both innate and specific, in the sense that each emotion in a set of basic emotions is associated with a unique pattern of somatic responses. Feedback from the latter registers in consciousness as the subjective experience of emotion. In this scenario, then, autonomic arousal is not ruled out, but it plays a subsidiary role in emotion, just as cognitive appraisal is seen as relatively unimportant (Greenberg & Safran, 1987). Thus, in somatic theory, an "emotion" is composed of neural activity in the brain and somatic nervous system, facial-postural feedback, and subjective experience—an unmediated and direct product of biological substrates (Izard & Malatesta, 1987).

Support for somatic theory is mixed. The notion of innate and distinctive patterns of response is consistent with such findings as: the universality of emotional expressiveness across cultures, the appearance of discernible facial expressions soon after birth, and similarity in rates of differentiation of facial expression in blind and sighted children (Leventhal & Tomarken, 1986). However, attempts to evaluate the facial feedback hypothesis are complicated by, among other things, the strength of social convention about the expression of emotion. Thus, experiments that examine the effect of direct and indirect manipulation of facial expression on the subjective experience of emotion report only minor changes in the latter (Leventhal & Tomarken, 1986). However, Ekman (1984) has been more successful in this regard perhaps because he used professional actors as subjects, individuals who could, presumably, overcome social taboos on emotional expression. In general, though, evidence in support of the facial feedback hypotheses seems difficult to obtain.

My impression of somatic theory is that, like the cognitive-arousal model, it emphasizes one aspect of what is clearly a multifaceted process. Increasingly, one senses that a major element in emotion is missing in these models, an element that has become the focus of the *central template* models to be discussed below. I should also mention that somatic theories seem not to attend to the question of emotional intensity. Presumably, the latter would be a matter of the degree of *somatic* arousal, but I can find no reference to this possibility.

Central Template Theory

Models of this kind are in the process of being developed by such people as Bower (1981), Fiske and Pavelchak (1986), Lang (1984), and Leventhal (1982). As a consequence of being in such a formative stage, there has been little opportunity for evaluative review. What I shall do here, therefore, is outline the main characteristics of this kind of model, and, in doing so, I shall rely on an integrative summary provided by Greenberg and Safran (1987).

To take Leventhal's model as a typical example, three interdependent mechanisms are said to be involved in the generation of emotion. First, an innate, central neural programme is thought to generate both feelings and expressive actions. This bears some similarity to the central processes postulated in somatic theory but, unlike the latter, sees no crucial role for somatic feedback. Second, a conceptual processing mechanism is involved in the appraisal and analysis of concrete emotional experiences, thereby drawing conclusions about possible causes of emotional reactions, as well as directing attention to salient features of the situation. A cognitive appraisal process of this kind is also an important feature of cognitive-arousal models, as we have just seen. Characteristic of central template models, however, is the recognition of the role of emotional schemata or templates as an important third mechanism. An emotional schema is a representation in memory of the specific emotional experiences that have occurred in a person's life, together with the perceptual features that tend to elicit such experiences. Emotional memories of this kind are likened to associative networks containing information on all aspects of an emotional experience, such as: the eliciting event, associated perceptual images, subjective experiences, and accompanying motor expressive and autonomic responses. What is implied by the notion of an associative network is that any of its components, when activated, can initiate an emotional sequence that draws in some, or all, of the remaining parts of the network (Epstein, 1984). In this view, then, peripheral feedback, which is so important in cognitive-arousal and somatic theory, does not instigate emotional experiences on a regular basis, although it might do so on occasion. Instead, the central emotional schema automatically initiates a variety of responses that prepare individuals for adaptive action, while at the same time feeding information directly into subjective awareness. Thus, emotional schema theories shift the emphasis in emotion models away from peripheral processes toward a more complex central mechanism that integrates the many part-processes emphasized in other models.

To summarize this section on models of emotion, the more recent emotional schema models imply that the origins of emotion (and emotional intensity) are more complex than traditional theories would have it. Proponents of cognitive-arousal theory, for instance, see emotional intensity as a simple function of degree of autonomic arousal, while somatic theorists would, presumably, argue along similar lines for a link between intensity and somatic arousal. However, emotional schema models imply that emotional intensity will be a function of the "intensity" of each component incorporated into an associative network. To my knowledge, this hypothesis has yet to be explored, although there are signs that the first conceptual steps are being taken in this direction. It follows that most conceptions of emotional intensity (and the conceptions of "emotionality" and "emotional stability–instability" derived from them) remain firmly rooted in the more traditional (peripheral) models of emotion. How these latter concepts have been formulated and the way in which they are used to represent individual differences in emotional style is a matter to which we now turn.

EMOTIONAL STYLES

I consider *emotional stability–instability* to be an emotional style dimension reflecting individual differences in emotional intensity. Relatively little attention has been paid to the notion of "emotional style" *per se* by psychologists. Instead, research on stylistic behaviour is conducted under the rubric of both "emotionality" and "temperament." For instance, Thomas (1985) equates temperament with behavioural style, arguing that the former is composed of up to nine *stylistic affective response tendencies*. Commenting on this viewpoint, Bates (1987) maintains that only some of Thomas's temperamental traits are stylistic (*e.g.*, intensity of emotional reaction), the others refer to emotional content (*e.g.*, approach–withdrawal behaviour). Thus, there is little consensus on how emotional styles might be conceptualized or defined. For our purposes, we might begin with the distinction between emotional *style* (*i.e.*, the characteristic *way* in which emotions are experienced or expressed) and emotional *content* (*i.e.*, *which* emotions are experienced/expressed). Consequently, in referring to someone as "frightened" or "angry," one is referring to the *content* of their emotional experience. In contrast, "style" implies a more structural component of emotion, in the sense that someone may be inclined to experience emotions strongly, or show a wide *range* of emotions

(Sommers & Scioli, 1986), or be extremely *variable* in their emotional expression (Diener *et al.*, 1985). Although Lerner and Lerner (1983) suggest that, in practice, it is difficult to distinguish between emotional content and style, I find the contrast useful and shall pursue it here.

Defined as the characteristic way of experiencing emotions, emotional style takes on the properties of a stable personal disposition that generalizes across time and situation. As a consequence, it is subject to all of the criticisms about generality and stability levelled at personality traits. For instance, Derryberry and Rothbart (1984) assert that the generality of emotional styles across response modalities is not strong. However, such arguments do not seem to deter at least some psychologists from working with trait concepts, stylistic or otherwise. I do not intend to re-open the issue of stability yet again but will mention it from time to time in what follows.

Dimensional Conceptions of Emotional Style

In order to discuss, in some rational way, the disparate conceptions of emotional intensity and style contained within the fields of "emotionality" and "temperament," we need some organizing framework. Several such frameworks are provided by research on emotional structure, or the structure of "affective space," which seeks to elucidate the relationships between discrete emotions. In the process, a small number of superordinate dimensions have been identified which purport to represent emotional characteristics that cut across, or are shared by, discrete emotions. Since these dimensions are derived from factor-analytic studies of emotional language, and given the predilection of factor analysts to disagree over method, it follows that the precise number and location of factorial dimensions remain in dispute. Two alternative "rotations" within the same affective space vie for attention: hedonic tone–arousal and positive–negative emotionality (Fig. 11). While different theorists prefer one or the other rotation, each is said to represent "affective space" adequately and to complement the other interpretation (Larsen & Diener, 1987; Watson & Tellegen, 1985).

The hedonic tone–arousal rotation. A number of studies recognize hedonic tone and arousal as basic structural dimensions (Daly *et al.*, 1983; Russell, 1979, 1980; Thayer & Miller, 1988; Watson & Tellegen, 1985). Hedonic tone is formulated as a pleasant–unpleasant dimension contrasting emotional states that are content/happy/kindly/pleased with those that are grouchy/blue/lonely/sad/unhappy. The second dimension has been conceptualized in a number of ways, and, while it is commonly referred to as an "arousal" dimension, it has also been interpreted as a matter of emotional *variability* (Wessman & Ricks, 1966) and *engagement* (Watson &

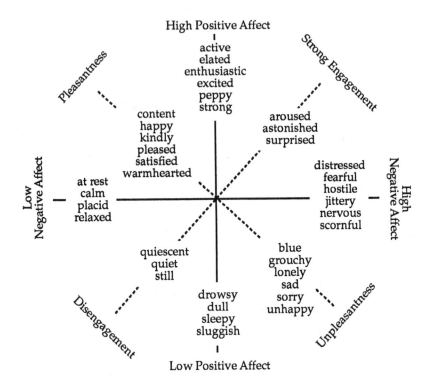

Figure 11. The two-factor structure of affect. (From Watson & Tellegen, 1985.)

Tellegen, 1985). Presumably the reason why this second dimension is commonly labelled "arousal" is because those who do so are working within an implicit model of emotion (such as cognitive-arousal) that affords arousal a central role in emotional processes. As Larsen and Diener (1987) recommend, however, it might be better to view the dimension in question as a matter of *intensity*, one that is defined at the physiological, experiential, and expressive levels. I shall return to this later. As it stands, the arousal dimension is said to contrast active (agitation/frenzy) with passive (sleep/relaxed) states. Of interest to us is the precise nature of this active–passive distinction for it seems to describe cortical and/or behavioural, rather than autonomic, arousal. Perhaps this is why Daly *et al.* (1983) have sought to add to these two-dimensional schemes a third structural dimension, *i.e.* "intensity," which reflects the depth or stength of emotions and is defined as a contrast between the experience of no emotion versus the experience of strong emotions. What this boils down to is that Daly *et al.* are suggesting a three-dimensional model akin to Osgood's (Osgood *et al.*, 1957) well-known trilogy of evaluation (hedonic tone), activity, and potency (intensity). Daly *et al.*'s recognition of what amounts to two arousal dimensions is also consistent with Thayer's (1985) proposal for the existence of energetic (cortical) and tense (autonomic) arousal, respectively. The reasons why we should be concerned with these rather esoteric issues of dimensional structure are twofold. First, structural models link intensity (and hence emotional style) with arousal, and not with hedonic tone, which is seen as emotional quality or content. Second, there is some confusion or uncertainty over the nature of the "arousal" dimension, reflected in the difference of opinion over whether it is best represented by one or two (or more) dimensions. I shall return to these issues as we proceed.

The positive–negative emotionality rotation. By rotating the factorial solution forty-five degrees to the hedonic tone and arousal dimensions, one obtains positive and negative affect, *i.e.* the *state* dimensions underlying the *trait* dimensions of positive and negative emotionality (Fig. 11). Proponents of this rotation consider the resulting dimensions to be more meaningful than the alternative hedonic tone–arousal solution (Clark & Watson, 1988; Tellegen, 1985; Watson & Clark, 1984; Watson & Tellegen, 1985; Watson *et al.*, 1987). There is considerable controversy in this research area over the proposed independence of positive and negative affect, for everyday experience would suggest that it is difficult to be extremely happy and extremely fearful at the same time. However, the independence of these dimensions is justified on the basis of long-term patterns. Over an extended period of time, the experience of positive and negative emotions does not covary (*e.g.*, see Diener *et al.*, 1985). Since positive and negative emotionality are, in this structural representation, a combination of hedonic tone (emotional content) and arousal (emotional style), neither kind of emotionality is a "pure" stylistic concept, although each contains an element of style. However, most of the available research on emotional personality traits has been done on "emotionality," especially negative emotionality. To understand *emotional stability–instability* more fully, therefore, especially how it *has* been construed in personality theory and how it *could* be construed as an emotional style, we need to look more closely at research on negative and positive emotionality. After doing so, we can turn to more "pure" stylistic notions based on the alternative rotation.

Negative Emotionality (NE)

When the term "emotionality" is used in everyday speech, as well as in personality theory, it is commonly taken to mean "negative emotionality." There is seldom any mention of "positive emotionality." Indeed, the very idea that there might be something called "positive emotionality" is quite unusual. By far the greatest amount of attention has been focused, therefore, on the expression of strong negative emotion. Why there is this tradition of concern with what Zuckerman (1985) calls the unhappy triad of fear, anxiety, and depression is not clear. Perhaps it is due to the influence of clinical psychology on personality theory and the practical availability of patients as research subjects—a form of captive audience, as it were. However, I am inclined to the view that there is a more funda-mantal reason rooted in western intellectual tradition, one that treats emotions as irrational states that are "visited" upon us, the unwilling victims of our passions (Averill, 1974). According to Averill, the term "emotion" has etymological roots implying states of agitation, pertur-bation, and disturbance. The antiquity of this view of emotion as distur-bance can be seen in the Galen–Wundt typology which recognizes an emotional–unemotional dimension contrasting anxious/worried/quickly aroused with calm/contented/hopeful states (Eysenck & Eysenck, 1985). Similarly, the same tradition has been continued in the present era by Heymans (Van Der Werff, 1985) who, at the turn of the century, iden-tified an "emotionality" dimension defined as emotional/demonstrative/touchy/violent versus quiet/modest/even-tempered.

Adding to this negative view of emotion is the tradition of linking it with physiological change, hence the tendency to focus on arousal, and other bodily changes, in conceptualizing "emotion." One can observe this tradition in modern theories of "emotionality." A. H. Buss and Plomin (1984), for instance, who distinguish between high arousal (fear/anger) versus low arousal (delight/disgust/love/hate) emotions, define "emotionality" solely in terms of fear and anger, which are their high arousal emotions.

Current conceptions of negative emotionality. As mentioned in Chapter 1, many factorial studies have identified an "emotionality" factor that, more properly, should be labelled "negative emotionality" (Brand, 1984; Digman & Inouye, 1986; McCrae & Costa, 1985, 1987; Noller *et al.*, 1987; Zuckerman *et al.*, 1988). The same factor, which contrasts the tendency to experience strong negative emotions with the relative absence of such emotions, crops up in a number of guises. For instance, in studies of infant temperament, common reference is made to "emotionality" as a dimension involving, at one pole, a tendency to become upset easily and intensely when confronted with the routine stresses of daily life. At the opposite pole are children who are more stable and less distressed by the rough and tumble of life (A. H. Buss & Plomin, 1984).

The study of adult temperament has also produced a similar factor, the conception of which is dominated by the big three personality theorists: Eysenck, Cattell, and Guilford. Until recently, when he changed its label to "emotionality," Eysenck described the factor as *neuroticism* (Eysenck & Eysenck, 1985), a superordinate trait that, at the "strong" pole, comprises: anxiety, depression, guilt feelings, low self-esteem, tension, irrationality, shyness, and moodiness. In other words, there is a strong fearfulness component in *neuroticism*. Similarly, Cattell's conception of negative emotionality (Cattell & Kline, 1977) is incorporated in a third-order factor labelled *trait anxiety* (weak ego strength, timidity, suspiciousness, guilt proneness, tension, low self-sentiment). Guilford (1975) prefers to label the factor *emotional stability–instability* (pessimism, excitability, variability).

A number of empirical analyses support one's intuitive sense that these various conceptions of negative emotionality are virtually identical (Campbell & Reynolds, 1984; Noller *et al.*, 1987; Zuckerman *et al.*, 1988). In addition, Watson and Clark (1984) have conducted an extensive study of the relationships between common conceptions of the tendency to experience aversive emotional states. Going well beyond the conceptions of the "big 3," they intercorrelated a variety of measures of trait anxiety, neuroticism, ego strength, general maladjustment, and repression-sensitization, concluding that, to all intents and purposes, they measure the same thing. Thus, Watson and Clark consider negative emotionality to have as its core feature *trait anxiety* (feelings of tension, worry, guilt, nervousness) together with the more general negative condition associated with such affective states as anger/scorn/revulsion/self-dissatisfaction/rejection.

The apparent similarity between these various conceptions of negative emotionality should not obscure some rather interesting differences, however. For instance, authors differ over the role of anger in emotionality. A. H. Buss and Plomin (1984), McCrae and Costa (1984), Tellegen (1985), and Watson and Clark (1984) include both fear and anger as central constructs, whereas Eysenck and Eysenck (1985) and Zuckerman *et al.* (1988) exclude anger. Perhaps the difference lies in a concern with *neuroticism* (which is essentially fearfulness), compared with a broader view of *emotionality*, seen as a tendency to experience a variety of negative emotions. The latter view seems more reasonable given that both fear and anger are part of the emergency response system of fight (anger) and flight (fear) (Epstein, 1983). The tendency to experience strong fight/flight reactions would, therefore, lead to high levels of negative emotionality. A further difference between conceptions of negative emotionality has to do with the incorporation of non-emotional components. Some authors, (*e.g.*, A. H. Buss and Plomin, 1984) restrict their view of the concept to purely emotional reponses (fear and anger). Others, however, broaden the concept to include not only "dysphoric affect" but also aspects of self-concept, such as low self-esteem. Tellegen (1985) is the most explicit in this regard, defining negative emotionality as a tendency to become anxious, to worry, and to react with anger, coupled with an appraisal of oneself as being unpleasantly engaged in life.

To summarize, negative emotionality (NE) is a widely used bipolar concept that contrasts a tendency to experience aversive emotional states with that of a less reactive, less emotional disposition. In its narrowest version, it is defined primarily in terms of fearfulness, while broader, more inclusive, conceptions include anger as well as aspects of negative self-evaluation. Clearly, "negative emotionality" is a more complex concept than what might be called an "emotional style." The implications of this for formulating the emotional dimension of my personality model will be discussed later.

Physiological correlates of negative emotionality. Given the traditional inclination to explain "emotion" in terms of physiological change, it follows that the physiological correlates of NE have received a great deal of attention. As a result, much is known about the peripheral behaviours associated with the autonomic and somatic nervous systems, largely because they are relatively easy to measure. In contrast, the possible role of brain systems in both emotion and emotionality is less well understood because of the difficulty in studying these systems directly. There are both ethical and technical limitations on what can be attempted. Thus, the role of central brain systems in generating NE remains largely speculative.

Most models of NE focus on the concept of *arousal,* or some version of it, assuming that individual differences result from variability in the ease with which the brain and nervous system, or some specific parts thereof, react to stimulation by becoming aroused. Thus, a general neurophysiological property is proposed, variously labelled as *arousability* (Buck, 1984), *reactivity* (Neblitsyn, in Mangan, 1982), *excitability* (Kagan *et al.*, 1987), and *strength–sensitivity* (Mangan, 1982). There is reason to believe that these terms are synonymous and can be taken to mean the capacity of a neurophysiological substrate to become active (Buck, 1985). The neurophysiological substrate in question is widely believed to be the limbic system. Its role in the generation of emotion and emotionality is championed by Eysenck and Eysenck (1985), Claridge (1985), many eastern European researchers (Mangan, 1982), and a number of scholars interested in infant temperament (A. H. Buss & Plomin, 1984; Kagan *et al.*, 1987; Rothbart, 1986). With one voice, these researchers propose what might be called the *arousability postulate* which states simply that NE is a consequence of individual differences in the arousability of the limbic system. That is, individuals high in NE produce activity in the limbic system more readily than low NE subjects. Activity in the limbic system leads to, among other things, autonomic arousal, particularly of the sympathetic division, the assumption being that high NE is associated with a tendency to excessive sympathetic activation (A. H. Buss & Plomin, 1984).

Most of the attempts to evaluate the arousability postulate in personality research have sought to link questionnaire measures of NE with both objective and subjective measures of autonomic arousal. This is, at best, an indirect strategy but one that is forced on researchers by the technical limitations mentioned earlier.

1. *Objective research.* Activation of the sympathetic nervous system (SNS) results in the contraction of the visceral/peripheral arteries, thereby channelling blood to the brain and voluntary muscles. At the same time, heart and metabolic rates increase, while muscles tighten and pupils dilate. It follows that objective measures of SNS activity would seek to determine changes in such things as heart rate, muscle tension, breathing rate, pupillary dilation and rate of blinking, skin conductance, and blood pressure. In fact, there are literally dozens of indices of SNS activity currently used in this kind of research, the technical complexities (and controversies) of which are reviewed at length by Fahrenberg (1987), Fahrenberg *et al.* (1986), and Myrtek (1984). For my purposes, I am interested primarily in the main conclusion from this research, which is that the association between high NE and high SNS activity remains controversial and difficult to demonstrate. In large part, the reason for this is that the various indices of SNS arousal tend not to covary. Ideally, one would hope that the opposite was the case, but following Lacey's (1967) classic paper on the topic, it has become clear that there is considerable intra- and inter-individual variation in indices of arousal. Thus, one cannot assume that a single index, such as heart rate or galvanic skin response, can serve as a reliable indicator of SNS activity. There remains, however, the possibility that patterns of indices or aggregate measures might overcome this problem of variability in response. Unfortunately, the extensive research conducted by Fahrenberg (1987) and Myrtek (1984) on adults, leads them to the conclusion that it is not possible to demonstrate a consistent pattern of autonomic arousability. Curiously, Kagan *et al.* (1987), working with children, come to quite the opposite conclusion. While recognizing the relatively low intercorrelations between their numerous measures of SNS and endocrine activity, they found that an aggregate index of SNS activity produced reasonably high correlations

with individual measures. Further, when correlated with their measure of NE, Kagan *et al.* (1987) were able to demonstrate a consistent pattern of relationships at three different age levels ranging from twenty-one months to five and a half years of age. Why the two research groups arrive at such diametrically opposed conclusions is not clear, except that SNS activity may be less differentiated in children and more likely to result in covariation of indices. It does seem, therefore, that recent research on the relationship between NE and objective indices of SNS arousal leaves the validity of the arousability postulate in as much doubt as that found by Stelmak (1981) some time ago.

2. *Subjective research.* One alternative to objective indices is the use of self-report measures of arousal states. Thayer is an advocate of this approach, claiming that self-ratings are more sensitive measures of global arousal states than are physiological measures (Thayer *et al.*, 1988). In support of this contention, he argues that his particular self-report test has been validated against both physiological correlates of arousal and behavioural responses predicted from the arousability postulate. For instance, the self-report measure correlates better with aggregate indices of physiological arousal than the individual physiological measures correlate amongst themselves. Using this self-report measure, Thayer *et al.* (1988) found a consistently strong positive correlation between tense (SNS) arousal and NE. They conclude, along with Eysenck and Eysenck (1985), that while high NE may not be associated with *chronic* SNS arousal, it is plausible to argue for individual differences in arousability.

In a similar vein, Rachman *et al.* (1983) were able to demonstrate a significant relationship between NE (using a hypochondriasis scale) and self-reported symptoms of SNS arousal amongst bomb-disposal experts. In particular, a small group of soldiers was identified at the extremely stable pole of the dimension, reporting few signs of SNS arousal under trying circumstances. Interestingly, many of these same men had been decorated for gallantry.

In sum, the arousability postulate has received mixed support. Bearing in mind recent changes in models of emotion, however, perhaps one would not expect any other conclusion. What I mean is that the arousability postulate appears to have been derived from one of the more traditional theories of emotion which overemphasize the role of physiological arousal in the genesis of emotion. In contrast, central template theories suggest that physiological arousal is one of a number of components that may or may not be activated during an emotional experience. Or to put it in another way, the occurrence of physiological activity may be mediated by cognitive processes that are part of the "emotional associative network." Fahrenberg recognizes as much when he says:

> It probably will depend on the researcher's general attitude toward the neuroscience or the cognitive science whether he or she tends to postulate that relatively consistent and stable personality traits like emotionality (NE), assessed by questionnaires, are based on distinct properties of separable subsystems of neural substrate or on diffuse cortical, but essentially semantic, representations. (Fahrenberg, 1987, p. 116)

Behavioural correlates of negative emotionality. Despite these difficulties in establishing a consistent relationship between NE and physiological responsivity, the behavioural correlates of NE are consistent with the notion of a constitutional predisposition to physiological arousal. One can see this in research on personality and physical and "mental" health.

If high NE is, as hypothesized, a matter of excessive physiological reaction to daily life, then one would expect to find a correlation between NE and stress-induced disease. This does seem to be the case. For instance, Friedman and Booth-Kewley (1987) have demonstrated a consistent relationship between trait anxiety, depression and anger, and a variety of psychosomatic illnesses, including: asthma, ulcers, arthritis, and coronary heart disease. Although the correlations involved are low, they are about what one would expect of personality variables, given the complex origins of disease. In a similar vein, Smith observed significant relationships between trait anger, neuroticism, and Type A behaviour, as well as between Type A behaviour and coronary heart disease. The theoretical explanation offered by Smith for these relationships differs little from the arousability postulate: Type A personalities are said to show excessive physiological reactivity (T. Smith, 1984; T. Smith & Anderson, 1986). However, Smith modifies the hypothesis in an interesting way, moving away from the notion of simple reactivity to a more proactive form of behaviour. In this view, the hostile, competitive, impatient behaviour associated with Type A's is not a reaction to a challenging situation but rather a form of behaviour that Type A's seek to exhibit by selecting and prolonging their exposure to challenging situations. If this is so, then the physical problems experienced by Type A's are exacerbated by prolonged stress, and illness is a function of coping style.

This latter point is an important one. Friedman and Booth-Kewley (1987), for instance, suggest that a constitutional predisposition to physiological reactivity will not, by itself, explain illness. Many people are exposed to stressful situations, but only some of these develop physical illness. Indeed, the modest correlations between NE and illness suggest that, while high NE subjects may experience stress, many do not succumb to physical problems. Similarly, not all Type A personalities have heart attacks; those who do, presumably, push themselves beyond tolerable limits. Thus, it is how one copes with one's stressful reactions to events—one's cognitive-coping strategies—that seems to determine the onset of illness. Consequently, in addition to being reactive, how one controls or inhibits this reactivity becomes salient. Wood (1985), for instance, reports a number of studies linking *low NE* to the onset of cancer, a perplexing finding until one starts to think in terms of emotional suppression and inhibition. According to Wood, many cancer patients can be described as "awfully nice," inoffensive individuals who have learned as children not to express strong, especially strong negative, emotions. Their low NE scores on questionnaires, therefore, are achieved through the rigid control of emotional experience and expression, a recipe, it seems, for illness.

Turning to NE and "mental health," one would expect that chronic negative moods and low self-esteem would lead invariably to problems in social adjustment. High NE individuals may not be "fun" to be with and their social lives may suffer accordingly. Evidence in support of this contention is offered by Eysenck and Eysenck (1985), Watson and Clark (1984), and, most especially, Claridge (1985). Rather than reiterating these summaries, I would like to draw your attention to one interesting feature of this research. Watson and Clark (1984), for instance, find that high NE individuals are more inclined to indulge in introspection and rumination, as well as being less defensive than those who are low NE. This suggests that NE is associated with a tendency to be more open and, therefore, more vulnerable to "reality." Smail (1984) has a similar conception of anxiety neurotics whom, he says, are less defended than more "stable" individuals and, as a result, are more devastated by the ruthlessly competitive and emotionally bruising quality of everyday life. At first sight, however, it would seem odd to think of high NE individuals as being less defended than their more "stable" counterparts, quite the opposite in fact. One possible explanation is that the emotional reactivity associated with high NE makes it extremely difficult to establish effective defences; one's reactions simply break through such coping mechanisms. In contrast, the low NE person may have less difficulty in doing so, a point that does not escape Smail's attention.

To summarize this section, negative emotionality is a widely used concept that assumes a variety of guises, all of which refer to chronic negative moods and low self-esteem. The concept has been established as a stable personality trait with consistent behavioural correlates. Most of the controversy surrounding the concept concerns speculation about underlying physiological mechanisms. The current neurophysiological models have yet to be validated, possibly because they are derived from models of emotion that increasingly appear to oversimplify emotional processes.

Positive Emotionality (PE)

The recognition of "positive emotionality" flies in the face of the conventional view that "emotionality" means negative emotionality. However, everyday experience tells us that some people can be "emotional" in a positive, ebullient way, although the occurrence of such euphoria tends to be infrequent. It is possible that we notice NE to a greater degree because chronically frightened and angry people are more difficult to deal with than their cheerful counterparts. Indeed, Sommers (1984) has found that, among students, only a narrow range of mild positive emotions is considered socially acceptable. Given that PE occurs in at least some of us, however, we should look at how it might be defined and its relationships, if any, to emotional intensity and emotional stability–instability.

The nature of positive emotionality. As mentioned earlier, recent work by Clark and Watson (1988), Tellegen (1985), Watson and Clark (1984), Watson and Tellegen (1985), and Watson *et al.* (1987) concludes that PE is a stable personality disposition that reflects, at one pole, a tendency to experience a state of pleasurable arousal (characterized by excited, enthusiastic, delighted, active, energetic, alert, determined moods) together with a sense of social potency, efficacy, and well-being. At the opposite pole is a chronic absence of positive moods and a weak sense of efficacy and well-being. As such, this definition combines reference to emotional style (energetic arousal) with that of emotional content (pleasurable emotions and mood states). Unlike NE, there is no ancient tradition associated with PE, no body of literature that refers to this concept *per se*. However, measures of PE have been found to be highly correlated with measures of social extraversion and other forms of social activity, leading some researchers to the view that PE and social extraversion are equivalent (Clark & Watson, 1988; Meyer & Shack, 1989; Tellegen, 1985). This is an unusual and controversial proposal for one does not normally think of "extraversion" as a form of "emotionality," positive or otherwise. To evaluate this proposition, we need to look more closely at conceptions of extraversion.

To begin with, it is useful to distinguish between two different conceptions of extraversion, classical and non-classical (Ormerod & Billing, 1982). Classical extraversion (the most prevalent interpretation) is equivalent to social extraversion, while the non-classical form derives from Jung's conception of introversion–extraversion as the direction of one's interests toward either the outer or inner worlds (Caine *et al.*, 1981).

Since "direction of interest" is, in my view, a motivational concept, I include it in the discussion of conation in the next chapter. Social extraversion, however, is a different matter.

There has been considerable debate over the most satisfactory way in which to define social extraversion. Most theorists would agree that *sociability* is a core characteristic, but they differ over its remaining features (Brand, 1984; A. H. Buss & Plomin, 1984; Cattell & Kline, 1977, Eysenck & Eysenck, 1985; McCrae & Costa, 1984; Prior *et al.*, 1986; Zuckerman, *et al.*, 1988). Sociability implies a preference for, and enjoyment of, the company of others. As A. H. Buss and Plomin (1984) note, sociable individuals appear to obtain "interaction social rewards" from the presence and responsivity of others. In contrast, the less sociable individuals seem not to experience such rewards and may find prolonged exposure to others aversive. It is the nature of additional components of social extraversion that remains problematic. For many years, Eysenck maintained that an important second factor was *impulsivity* (a tendency to sensation seeking and the absence of inhibitory control; see, *e.g.,* Eysenck & Eysenck, 1985). A lively debate was thus engendered within the field (*e.g.,* Guilford, 1975). However, current opinion appears to be moving toward a reinterpretation of this second factor, not as impulsivity, but as a form of surgency (energy, activity, liveliness, vigour) (A. H. Buss & Plomin, 1984; Hogan, 1983; McCrae & Costa, 1984; Prior *et al.*, 1986; Zuckerman *et al.*, 1988). Evidently, the Eysencks agree with this for, in their recent statements, they have shifted impulsivity over to their third personality dimension, psychoticism. Thus, social extraversion is currently seen as a combination of *sociability* and *surgency*. An important point to bear in mind about this conception is that both components are defined, at least in part, in terms of positive emotions and pleasurable engagement in social life (*e.g.,* McCrae & Costa, 1984). Presumably, this contributes to the significant correlations between measures of social extraversion and PE. Whether this makes the two concepts equivalent is a matter to which I shall return shortly.

The physiological correlates of positive emotionality. The physiological correlates of PE await further elucidation. Indeed, the only speculation about such correlates has been made by Tellegen (1985) who equates the PE dimension with Gray's (1971) behavioural activation system. Unfortunately, this complicates matters somewhat for the latter is thought by Gray to underlie "impulsivity," which, in Gray's system, is a combination of extraversion and neuroticism. It might be better to postpone discussion of this miasma of conflicting opinion until the end of the chapter. What I shall do here, albeit briefly, is mention the physiological correlates of social extraversion, on the assumption that they may have some bearing on the origins of PE.

Eysenck's psychophysiological model dominates speculation about the physiological correlates of social extraversion (Eysenck, 1967; Eysenck & Eysenck, 1985). His central hypothesis is that introverts differ from extraverts in terms of *cortical* arousal. In particular, introverts produce greater increases in cortical arousal than extraverts in response to a given stimulus, and introverts experience chronically higher levels of arousal than do extraverts. Cortical arousal is thought to be a function of ARAS (ascending reticular activating system) stimulation. The ARAS, in turn, responds to sensory input as well as stimulation by the limbic system, thereby acting as a conduit for many kinds of information. Eysenck's version of this model proposes a corticoreticular loop composed of both excitatory and inhibitory circuits. While the ARAS may excite the cortex, the latter has the capacity to feed back to the ARAS, constraining its activity when cortical arousal becomes too high. In this way of thinking, then, introverts are said to have a low ARAS threshold, which results in the rapid generation of cortical arousal. At the same time, Eysenck suggests that introverts may also be slow to generate inhibition, thereby maintaining chronically high levels of cortical arousal. In contrast, while extraverts are said to generate arousal more slowly, they generate more central inhibition. As a result, extraverts function at a chronically low level of cortical arousal. (Note that central inhibition is not the same as behavioural inhibition—in fact, quite the opposite; the chronically low cortical arousal of extraverts is thought to contribute to their socially *uninhibited* behaviour.) Attempts to validate these contentions are bedevilled both by conceptual and technical problems. Extensive reviews of the issues involved are available in Claridge (1986), Eysenck and Eysenck (1985), Gale (1986), Myrtek (1984), and Stelmak (1981). I shall content myself, here, with a few illustrative comments and examples, the latter being derived primarily from the Eysencks.

Although H. Eysenck's model gives the impression of being quite simple, this simplicity is more apparent than real. For instance, it is often difficult to arrive at a testable hypothesis, given the complex interactions between Eysenck's two arousal systems and their accompanying inhibitory circuits. Added to this is the fact that experimental subjects are continuously adjusting their level of arousal in search of some optimal level, despite the requirements of a particular experimental design. Thus, many predictions about cortical arousal are possible depending on baseline levels of cortical arousal of experimental subjects, the possible intrusion of limbic-autonomic arousal, the stressfulness of the experimental situation, and so on (Claridge, 1986). At a technical level, one sees the same kinds of problems experienced in assessing limbic-autonomic arousal, *i.e.*, there are no satisfactory *direct* measures of cortical arousal.

The hypothesis that introverts are more prone to generating cortical arousal than extraverts has been tested by research on the orienting reaction and habituation (Eysenck & Eysenck, 1985). The orienting reaction is of significance because it is an attentional process thought to enhance the selection and processing of novel stimuli, whereas habituation is the decline in orienting response through familiarization with a given stimulus. The difficulty in framing a testable hypothesis, however, is formulated by the Eysencks in this way:

> It has usually been predicted that introverts should have larger orienting reactions than extraverts and should take longer to habituate. These predictions can be based on the putative high level of arousal in introverts or on the notion that extraverts generate more cortical inhibition than introverts. The theoretical problem is that the orienting reaction and its habituation depend on a complex mixture of arousal, inhibition and neuronal model formation, and it is not easy to decide which of these three processes is most important in producing any observed effects of extraversion. (Eysenck & Eysenck, 1985, p. 219)

Consequently, it is not unexpected to find that the usual experimental tests of habituation (which present the same stimulus repeatedly and measure the subject's response to such things as electrodermal tests) are decidedly equivocal in their findings. Of the twenty-five studies mentioned by the Eysencks, only thirteen support the hypothesis that introverts exhibit a larger orienting response and habituate more slowly than extraverts.

Attempts to evaluate the hypothesis that introverts experience chronically higher levels of cortical arousal than extraverts have commonly involved EEG studies, with similarly mixed results. In trying to explain such disappointing findings, the Eysencks raise the issue of problems with the technique itself:

> It has typically been assumed that high levels of arousal are associated with low amplitude, high frequency activity in the alpha frequency range.... However, serious doubts have been expressed about the value of such measures. Although the EEG is regarded as an indicator of brain activity, it is recorded from outside of the skull. A more consequential objection is that the EEG represents a kind of composite or amalgam of electrical energy generated from different parts of the cortex and may thus provide a misleading impression of the actual activity in any specific area of the brain. (Eysenck & Eysenck, 1985, p. 223)

Compounding such difficulties are procedural problems with the typical experimental situation employed in EEG studies. Gale (1986), for instance, has reviewed many such studies, separating them in terms of the level of stress imposed on experimental subjects. His hypothesis is that experimental situations that involve very low or very high levels of stress will militate against the validation of Eysenck's hypothesis. Thus, in low arousal conditions, extraverts will disregard instructions simply to sit there and do nothing, seeking, instead, by various internal manoeuvers to raise their cortical arousal to an acceptable level. Similarly, in high arousal situations, introverts will attempt to reduce their level of cortical arousal to some tolerable level by restricting attention and avoiding further stimulation. In both cases, such arousal-related manoeuvers will alter the arousal baselines that the experimenter is trying to measure. Thus, only those experiments that expose subjects to moderately arousing situations are likely to support Eysenck's hypotheses. Studies that follow this prescription (in Gale, 1986) appear to support the hypotheses of both Gale and Eysenck, as does the more recent work of C. Davis and Cowles (1988).

Thus, attempts to evaluate hypotheses about the neurophysiological bases of social extraversion using physiological indices have run into the same difficulties as, and arrived at similar conclusions to, those involved in evaluating neuroticism. Not only are the available techniques suspect, but an apparently simple neurophysiological model is, in actuality, so complex as to make testable hypotheses difficult to formulate. As Claridge (1986) observes, it is possible that Eysenck has erred in treating cortical and limbic/autonomic arousal as separate systems, since they do seem to be inextricably interwined.

A somewhat more successful strategy for evaluating Eysenck's hypotheses involves the use of behavioural indices of arousal, derived from either self-reports or performance on laboratory tasks. One interesting area of research, for instance, has examined the influence of stimulant and depressant drugs on performance (Powell, 1981). Stimulant drugs, such as dextroamphetamine, are thought to increase activity in the corticoreticular loop. The effect of this on extraverts would be to raise their cortical level above their chronically low baseline and so enhance performance on a variety of tasks, including academic work. In contrast, stimulants may push the cortical arousal of introverts above their already high level, thereby interfering with, and diminishing, performance. Powell reviews a number of studies that demonstrate such effects, including the controversial use of stimulants to improve the vigilance, and decrease the impulsivity, of hyperkinetic (extraverted) children. Depressant drugs, such as alcohol, which decrease activity in the corticoreticular loop, are expected to have an extraverting influence since they would diminish the level of cortical inhibition of behaviour. Thus, under the influence of alcohol, behaviour is "uninhibited" and socially extraverted. Once again, Powell finds some limited evidence in favour of these predictions—evidence which is complicated by the intrusion of neuroticism (N) into the experimental procedures.

Before closing this section, I should add that Thayer's research using self-report measures of cortical (energetic) arousal appears to have been successful in demonstrating hypothesized differences between extraverts and introverts. Thus, Thayer *et al.* (1988) found there to be a significant correlation between introversion and self-reported energetic arousal, with introverts reporting characteristically higher levels than extraverts.

The behavioural correlates of positive emotionality. By definition, extraverts engage in, and appear to enjoy, a much more diverse array of social activities than introverts. Thus, consistent differences between extraverts and introverts in social/sexual and work behaviour are well documented (Eysenck & Eysenck, 1985). What I would like to focus on here are two postulates of Eysenck that are used to account for these differences in social and work behaviour. First, Eysenck argues that, since introverts are more highly aroused than extraverts, the former are more easily *conditioned.* If this is the case, it might help explain why, for instance, introverted children are easier to "socialize" and control. An easily conditioned child may be more prone to learning fear responses to parental demands and so be more easy to control. In contrast, some extremely extraverted children appear fearless, oblivious to the threat of punishment. The early learning of fear responses in social situations, together with a continuing sensitivity to humiliation, may help to explain the introvert's aversion to many kinds of social activity. The evidence on this conditioning postulate, which has been reviewed by Eysenck and Eysenck (1985) and Levey and Martin (1981) is, like much of the evidence reviewed in this section, mixed. Thus, the Eysencks conclude:

> In sum, introverts often show better conditioning performance than extraverts in studies of aversive classical conditioning, but this main effect of extraversion must be interpreted in light of interactions between extraversion and task conditions. As a first approximation, introverts condition better than extraverts under relatively unarousing conditions, whereas the opposite happens under stimulating or arousing conditions.... It remains a matter of controversy whether there is a general factor of conditionability. (Eysenck & Eysenck, 1985, p. 246)

The second postulate is that introverts are more sensitive to external stimulation than extraverts—the assumption being that the chronically high arousal state of introverts serves to augment incoming stimuli to such an extent that introverts reach their optimal level of arousal at a much lower level of stimulation than extraverts. Introverts, therefore, are said to show stimulus aversion, whereas extraverts exhibit stimulus hunger. It follows that introverts would try to limit their level of arousal by avoiding social activity, while extraverts seek it out as a means of increasing their level of arousal. In contrast, the high arousal of introverts is an advantage in some work situations where persistent attention, vigilance, and resistance to boredom are at a premium, as in academic work, for instance. One would expect that the tendency of extraverts to become easily bored, together with their reduced vigilance, might prove to be a handicap in some work situations. All of this changes of course if high levels of stress are introduced into the work environment, a situation in which one would expect extraverts to cope more effectively. The evidence reviewed by Eysenck and Eysenck (1985) appears, generally, to support the postulate that introverts and extraverts differ in sensitivity to stimulation, although the hypothesis that cortical arousal mediates this effect remains controversial.

In summarizing the Eysencks' neurophysiological model of social extraversion, therefore, I am inclined to agree with their own evaluation:

> [T]he simple notion that introverts have a chronically higher level of cortical arousal than extraverts has proved extraordinarily successful in accounting for an enormous variety of findings. Not surprisingly, there are cases in which the theory's fit to the data is imperfect, and a more complex formulation may be needed at some point. However, the general rule in science is that a theory is usually discarded only when a superior theory replaces it, and this has not happened so far. (Eysenck & Eysenck, 1985, p. 288)

Conclusions on NE, PE, and "Emotionality"

"Emotionality," the tendency to be "emotional" and to experience strong emotions has, traditionally, been couched in terms of negative emotionality (NE), and described as neuroticism, anxiety, and emotional stability–instability. Recently, however, the tendency to experience strong positive emotions has been recognized in formulations of positive emotionality (PE) which, in turn, has been linked, somewhat controversially, to social extraversion. The available evidence suggests that, while both forms of emotionality are well established at the behavioural level, speculations about physiological underpinnings remain controversial and difficult to evaluate. Nevertheless, both NE and PE provide interesting frameworks within which to think about individual differences in emotional intensity. A more "pure" approach to the question of "emotional styles," however, would require a somewhat different conception of emotionality, one that emphasizes consistency of emotional experience across both positive and negative emotions. Such a concept is *affect intensity.*

Affect Intensity (AI)

Just as some psychologists prefer to work with the PE/NE rotation, believing it to be the more fundamental, others prefer the alternative rotation of hedonic tone–arousal, equally convinced that the latter identifies significant affective dimensions. Until recently, however, most of the available research on "emotionality" has been conducted within the PE/NE framework. This has changed, in the last few years, through attempts to reformulate the arousal dimension as *affect intensity* (AI), a stable personality disposition that has all the characteristics of a temperamental trait (Diener *et al.*, 1985). Unfortunately, since AI is still in the process of being developed and evaluated, only a limited body of research has developed around it. What is available is incorporated into a comprehensive review by Larsen and Diener (1987), from whom I draw much of the following.

The nature of affect intensity. AI is treated here as an "emotionality" concept that, unlike PE and NE, cuts across emotional content. Thus, it refers to stable individual differences in the strength with which emotions are experienced and, at the high pole, the regular experience of both strong positive and negative emotions over the course of time. This conception of AI is said to have been derived by Diener *et al.* (1985) from early work on affective structure which interpreted the arousal dimension as a matter of emotional variability, the latter referring to fluctuations and swings in mood. Since wide fluctuations in mood convey the impression of strongly felt emotions, "variability" has tended to be associated with emotional "intensity." However, while "variability" and "intensity" may be related phenomena, they are not identical, as we shall see (Larsen & Diener, 1987).

Evidence in support of the contention that those people who experience strong negative emotions also tend to experience strong positive emotions, *over time*, has been obtained in a variety of longitudinal studies (Diener *et al.*, 1985; Larsen *et al.*, 1986). In a typical experiment, subjects were asked to rate their moods daily over a period of ten weeks. A daily "intensity" score was derived from the strength with which subjects experienced their dominant affect on that particular day. In turn, mean intensity scores were obtained for the subject's positive days and for their negative days during the ten-week period. Correlations between mean positive intensity and mean negative intensity scores regularly reached significant levels of approximately 0.7. Larsen and Diener (1985) were able to demonstrate the robustness of this relationship across a number of different subject samples and experimental methods, including the use of parental ratings of their children's moods.

Larsen, Diener and their co-workers are currently in the process of studying the behavioural correlates of AI with a view to understanding and validating the concept further. For illustrative purposes, I shall mention briefly some of this work which is reported at greater length in Larsen and Diener (1987). First, AI is said to be related to *complexity* of life situation in that high AI individuals are involved in less dense social networks and have more goals that are unrelated to one another. My sense of this finding is that it does not relate to complexity as I have defined it in Chapter 2 but rather to a high differentiation–low integration condition. Thus, AI results in less dense (integrated) social networks in the sense that high AI individuals interact with more people who do not know one another; their social world has more independent units (high differentiation). Similarly, the occurrence of many independent goals in high AI individuals is contradicted by other research linking low AI to role and self-complexity, suggesting that various authors may be using different conceptions of "complexity." Larsen and Diener (1987), in arguing for more research to disentangle this situation, make the interesting point that it is not clear whether high AI causes people to seek more complex (differentiated) lives, or whether high AI is a consequence of leading a complex life. This confusion between cause and effect has interesting theoretical implications, which will be discussed shortly.

Second, AI is said to be related to disturbances of mood. There is some conceptual similarity, for instance, between AI and the concept of cyclothymia, a mild form of bipolar affective disorders such as manic-depression. It follows that measures of both AI and cyclothymia correlate significantly. In a similar vein, AI appears to predict the number of somatic disorders that subjects report. For instance, in two separate studies, the total number of symptoms reported (such as headache, nervousness, feeling uneasy, nausea, shortness of breath, etc.) correlated significantly with AI. However, an interesting feature of this research is that, while high AI individuals may report more general somatic problems than low AI, the occurrence of such problems does not distress them unduly. Larsen and Diener (1987) conclude that the high arousal associated with AI must serve some purpose for which high AI individuals are willing to pay the price of somatic disturbance.

Third, AI shares many of the characteristics of, and is related to, various dimensions of temperament. Thus, preliminary data suggest that AI is stable from childhood to young adulthood, a conclusion based on significant correlations between young adults' reports of their emotional intensity and their parents' ratings of their children's emotionality. Temperamental traits, of course, are thought to develop early and show substantial stability over the years. In addition, a significant relationship was found between AI and four temperament traits: sociability, activity, arousability, and emotionality. Further, a factor analysis conducted by Larsen identified two robust factors comprising AI plus sociability/ activity and AI plus emotionality/arousability (Larsen & Diener, 1987). These are intriguing results for, as Larsen and Diener suggest, they imply that AI heightens all types of emotional experience and, consequently, should be significantly related to any personality or temperament trait that contains in its definition reference to heightened levels of either positive or negative affect. In addition, the factorial study suggests that AI is related to, or underlies, both NE (emotionality/arousability) and PE (sociability/activity), precisely the kind of finding one would predict from the relationship between the PE/NE and hedonic tone–arousal rotations.

The underlying causes of affect intensity. A comprehensive causal theory, akin to Eysenck's psychophysiological model, is not yet available for AI, although some preliminary hypotheses have been proposed based on the familiar notions of optimal arousal and homeostasis. The finding that AI is related to a tendency to engage in activities that are emotionally provoking has led Larsen and Diener to speculate that high AI in- dividuals are chronically underaroused at baseline and use emotional responsivity as a way to generate optimal levels of arousal. The process is analogous to augmenting/reducing and the stimulus seeking of extraverts. However, AI does not correlate with "stimulus seeking" (Zuckerman, 1979) and so must differ from these processes in some significant way. Larsen *et al.* (1987) suggest that at least one way in which high AI individuals manipulate emotional responsiveness is to interpret "emotional stimuli in a way that results in more intense affective response" (p. 767). Thus, cognitive manoeuvers, such as personalizing events, so as to make them more self-relevant, generate more ego- involvement and stronger emotional responses. Of course, much of this speculation is tentative, which is just as well, for it creates some major headaches when one tries to link AI with PE and NE, as I shall attempt to do in the final section.

In sum, AI is said to be a stable, temperamental trait that reflects individual differences in emotional intensity at the physiological, experiental, and behavioural levels. As a temperamental trait, it appears to be "extraordinarily stable over time and consistent across varying situations" (Larsen & Diener, 1987, p. 18). Since AI is defined as the experience of both strong positive *and* negative emotions, it is more clearly a *stylistic* concept than other conceptions of emotionality, such as PE and NE. However, there is one problem with the concept that nags at the back of my mind. Not everyone who experiences emotions intensely has the cyclothymic qualities implied by AI; not everyone is inclined to manic-depression. Presumably, therefore, AI refers only to certain kinds of individuals. Precisely whom, is a matter to which we now turn.

The Interrelations Amongst NE, PE, and AI

Any attempt to combine models invariably produces inconsistencies and incompatibilities. However, such an attempt in the area of "emotionality" appears to produce more than its fair share, moving Claridge (1986) to comment: "[T]o the outsider [the area] must seem like a hopeless mess; even to those inside it, trying to re-discover an elegant symmetry comparable to that of Eysenck's original model is proving to be a difficult task" (p. 80). Although I have puzzled for some time now over the inconsistencies I am about to describe, I have not been able to resolve many of them. I suspect that their clarification awaits further conceptual and empirical research.

To begin with, Fig. 12a summarizes the relationship between the two rotations that are commonly used to account for the structure of affective space (Watson & Tellegen, 1985). When the structural dimensions are depicted as mood states, we see that the experience of positive affect is orthogonal to the experience of negative affect. High arousal, as a mood state, implies the occurrence of high levels of arousal in association with particular emotions. However, if Fig. 12a is interpreted in terms of emotionality traits, the positive and negative affect dimensions are replaced by PE and NE, respectively (Meyer & Shack, 1989), while the arousal dimension is used to refer to a tendency to experience differing levels of arousal. It follows that the high NE/high PE quadrant would identify individuals who experience strong emotions and intense arousal. Unfortunately, on the face of it, this would seem to be inconsistent with Larsen and Diener's (1987) speculation (Fig. 12b) that the NE/PE quadrant, which is identified with high AI, should contain individuals who are chronically under-aroused at baseline. Although such individuals would *seek* to intensify their emotional experience, it is difficult to see how the high AI pole (Fig. 12b) can occupy the same affective space as a high arousal pole (Fig. 12a) which implies the *attainment* of high arousal.

When one turns to Eysenck's model of emotionality, a number of problems also arise. His predictions about the variability of emotional moods (Fig. 12c), based on what is known about temperamental types, suggest that the extremes of variability occur in cholerics (high; neurotic extraverts) and phlegmatics (low; stable introverts). The other two types show moderate levels of variability, with stable extraverts experiencing predominantly positive affect and neurotic introverts being plagued by negative affective states. If one accepts Larsen and Deiner's (1987) contention that intensity and variability are related, then Eysenck's

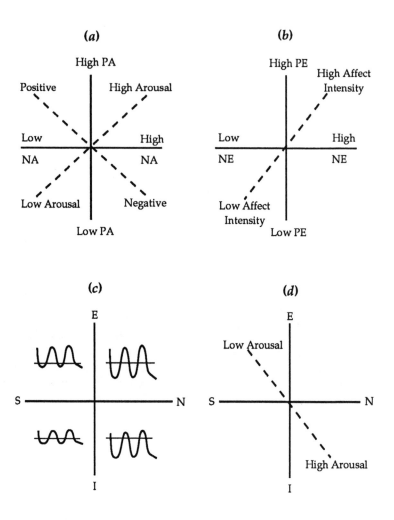

Figure 12. Interrelationships between models of temperament. PA = positive affect; NA = negative affect; PE = positive emotionality; NE = negative emotionality. Each figure summarizes the relationships between temperament, mood, and arousal proposed by various authors. In the case of 12c, fluctuations in mood above (positive) and below (negative) a baseline of indifference are represented by the location and amplitude of the mood curves. (Fig 12c is modified from Eysenck & Eysenck, 1985.)

prediction about the emotional intensity of his four types do not fit one's expectations. Thus, in Eysenck's scheme, extremes of variability involve neurotic extraverts and stable introverts, whereas extremes of intensity lie orthogonally to this dimension, involving neurotic introverts and stable extraverts (Fig. 12d). The orientation of the intensity dimension is consistent with Eysenck's notion that introverts are chronically more aroused at baseline than extraverts, while neurotics are autonomically more reactive than stable individuals, thereby making the neurotic introvert the most prone of all four types to high arousal. To complicate matters further, if you were to superimpose Eysenck's predictions about intensity (Fig. 12d) onto those of Watson and Tellegen (Fig. 12a) and Larsen and Diener (Fig. 12b), one sees that the predictions are orthogonal to one another. That is, Watson and Tellegen's high arousal quadrant is defined as PE/NE (neurotic extravert), whereas Eysenck's is the neurotic introvert. An added ingredient to all this is Claridge's (1986) observation that the empirical evidence available to him suggests that Eysenck's neurotic extravert quadrant, which is predicted as showing moderate levels of arousal, consistently demonstrates the lowest levels of arousal of all four temperamental types.

I could continue listing complications but these few examples are sufficient to convey the apparent confusion in the field. As mentioned earlier, I have little idea how one might disentangle this confusion, other than to await developments at the conceptual and empirical levels. However, at an intuitive level, I suspect that the main problem revolves around the use of the more traditional models of emotion and emotionality, which assume a mechanical relationship between physiological predisposition and behaviour. The need to take cognitive mediation into account is recognized in central template theories, as well as by the Eysencks when they note:

> [T]he crucial difference between the early versions of arousal theory and [more recent versions] is simply that it was originally assumed that an individual's level of arousal determined his behaviour in a direct fashion, whereas it is believed now that the behavioural affects of arousal are usually indirect. The reason for this indirectness is the intervention of cognitive control systems, which are probably responsive to feedback about performance under different levels of arousal. In other words, we are not so completely at the mercy of our internal physiological states as was suggested by the original proponents of arousal theory. (Eysenck & Eysenck, 1985, p. 208)

General Summary

The emphasis on contradiction and inconsistency in the previous section should not obscure the fact that, at the behavioural level, NE, PE, and AI have all been established as relatively stable traits. Most of the controversy associated with these dimensions arises from speculations about underlying neurophysiological causes of observed individual differences in behaviour. These latter difficulties, however, need not detract from the usefulness of all three dimensions as behavioural summaries. No doubt, in time, the neurophysiological models will be refined and incorporated into more satisfactory explanations of individual differences in emotionality that recognize the role of what the Eysencks refer to as cognitive control systems. In the meanwhile, I am faced with the need to select an emotional dimension for my personality model. Since both relations (PE/NE and AI/hedonic tone) have their proponents, the question is how one might choose between them. Meyer and Shack (1989, p. 705) suggest that the research question at hand should determine which dimensions are considered to be the most basic in any particular situation. In other words, selection is a matter of one's interpretation of what is conceptually or experimentally appropriate. Given that the logic of my personality model demands the use of only one affective dimension, I have chosen to represent the *emotional stability–instability* trait as one of individual differences in *affect intensity*. Since AI is couched in more purely "stylistic" terms than PE and NE and cuts across emotional content, it allows one to expand the definition of "emotionality" beyond the traditional preoccupation with NE and the experience of distress. That is, AI combines parsimony with comprehensiveness, an excellent basis on which to select a genotypic trait for inclusion in a personality model.

Chapter 4

The Conative Dimension

THE CONATIVE DIMENSION of my personality model, *objective–subjective*, refers to individual differences in motivational content, *i.e.*, to differences in the things for which people strive. In formulating the dimension, I have been influenced not only by the factor-analytic research discussed in Chapter 1 (particularly Brand's, 1984, will–affection dichotomy), but also by the recognition in scholarly circles of a much broader polarity between two competing value systems. Kimble (1984) observes that this difference in values appears to have been a major element in the conflict between Socratic and Sophistic views on education some 2500 years ago while, in a similar vein, William James sought to interpret "the whole history of philosophy in terms of a constant running battle between two contradictory intellectual styles" (Kimble, 1984, p. 833). In more recent times, both Coan (1979) and Kimble (1984) have characterized psychology as a discipline polarized into two cultures holding conflicting epistemological values and, according to Kimble, engaged in a bitter family feud.

Given my predilection for ancient verities and concepts with lengthy pedigrees, I have set myself the task, in this chapter, of developing a more modern version of this grand polarity. Rather than using James's term *tough-minded versus tender-minded* as a label for the dimension, one that has accumulated an excess of pejorative baggage, I prefer Coan's (1979) more neutral term *objective–subjective*. Since I intend to depict the dimension as a motivational disposition, in contrast to James's view of it as temperamental, we need to begin with a brief discussion of what is meant by "motivation." Thus, the first part of this chapter is concerned with clarifying the nature of *conation*, indicating how it can be viewed as having both unconscious (drives) and conscious (volitions) components.

This allows me to depict *objectivity–subjectivity* as a volitional difference that has its roots in the more primitive conflict between what some authors refer to as *agency* and *communion*, the latter being unconscious drives or core tendencies. Having laid this groundwork, I turn next to a detailed examination of the relevant empirical research as a means of constructing and justifying the proposed dimension. Unfortunately, there is little research on the generic objectivity–subjectivity dimension as I have construed it. Instead, one finds fragments of the dimension being examined in isolation from one another and within the context of different theoretical assumptions. In an attempt to impose some order on this empirical diversity, I have organized the discussion around a model of the dimension that postulates cognitive, affective, and behavioural components. This model is offered as an hypothesis, one that I believe to be plausible in light of the evidence amassed.

WHAT IS MOTIVATION?

One of the characteristic features of human behaviour is that it is not random, at least not all of the time. Each day, whatever we do seems to be more or less organized in pursuit of a variety of goals. Such goal-directed behaviour typically has an intense persistent quality to it, although this varies over time, of course. Thus, *motivated* behaviour can be defined as that which shows *intensity* of effort *directed* to some end. As one might expect, given the differences in values mentioned above, there is considerable disagreement over the most appropriate way in which to depict the origins of motivated behaviour, with the result that there are dozens of motivational theories, which creates a potentially confusing situation. Fortunately, Deci and Ryan's (1985a) distinction between *mechanistic* and *organismic* approaches allows us to simplify the discussion.

Mechanistic Theories of Motivation

Mechanistic approaches to motivation assume that we are passive creatures at the mercy of various internal and external forces which compel us to behave as we do. In other words, behaviour is *determined* by forces over which we have little control or understanding, rather than being freely chosen. This is an old view with roots in such thinkers as Thomas Hobbes (1588–1679) who proposed that behaviour has its origins in the motions of the "vital spirits," the latter being his way of talking about appetites (*i.e.*, for food, sex, etc.) and aversions (avoidance of pain). Human beings, in Hobbes's way of thinking, are helpless animals responding automatically to internal (as well as external) forces in their never-ending pursuit of pleasure and the avoidance of pain (Burnham, 1968). The kind of thinking typified by Hobbes has, over the years, become embodied in what is currently called *drive theory*, the view that behaviour is instigated and directed by innate physiological *drives* (biological motives operating at a mechanical level) that compel us to interact with the environment. All behaviour, in this view, is said to be motivated directly or indirectly by a drive or some derivative of it (Deci & Ryan, 1985a). One of the most widely known drive theories is that of Sigmund Freud, who attempted to account for behaviour in terms of the two fundamental drives of sex and aggression. The physiological energy generated by sexual and aggressive mechanisms is said to be transformed into psychological energy which, taking the form of desires and wishes, creates an inner tension that seeks release. Freud believed that many of humankind's problems arise because of the conflict that ensues between the individual's need to release sexual and aggressive impulses and the restrictions placed on their expression by social convention.

Drive theories assume that the person is largely unaware of the forces that influence his or her behaviour and, as a consequence, has relatively little control over events. In other words, we are robots, pushed around by inner drives which are triggered by bodily conditions and environmental stimuli. People's relative "unawareness" about the origins of their behaviour has been accounted for, in some drive theories, by speculations about an *unconscious* component of the mind, an area of our mental life containing desires, wishes, and thoughts which seldom emerge into conscious awareness but which, nevertheless, have a significant effect on behaviour. Although the "discovery" of the *unconscious* is often attributed to Sigmund Freud, his speculation on, and elaboration of, the concept are actually the culmination of more than 200 years of scholarly thinking on the matter. Whyte (1967), for instance, in describing the "unconscious before Freud" recognizes the work of approximately fifty writers who contributed to the development of the idea during the eighteenth and nineteenth centuries. Despite this long tradition, the *unconscious* has not been a respectable topic in academic psychology, although it has been incorporated into the kind of psychodynamic psychology practised in clinical work. A shift does seem to be occurring in the halls of academe, however, and, with the recent cognitive revolution and the reintroduction of *mind* as an acceptable focus of research, so too has the unconscious crept back into consideration and contention. One sees, for instance, the recognition of unconscious perceptual processes in experimental psychology (Brody, 1986; Shevrin & Dickman, 1980), although the more speculative Freudian view of the unconscious remains highly contentious (Eysenck, 1985).

Organismic Theories of Motivation

Unlike mechanistic theories, which depict human beings as passive robots responding automatically to biologically based promptings, organismic theories assume an active organism, one that is capable of initiating behaviour and acting on the surrounding environment, rather than simply responding to it in a mechanical way. This is not to say that organismic theories ignore the role of drives but that a greater role is afforded the human capacity to control consciously, and to respond to, our biological impulses. This is another way of saying that human beings have some degree of *free will* and that in consciously choosing what we do we exhibit *volition* or conscious striving after freely chosen goals. Modern interest in free will, consciousness, and volition has its roots in the seventeenth century, where one can find, for instance, the introduction of many new "self" words, such as self-knowledge, self-confidence, self-pity, into the English language (Burnham, 1968), the implication being that there is a "self" involved in making choices and responding to the world around us. The subsequent history of European thought suggests that, at least in some circles, there may have been an over-emphasis on free will, an exaggerated belief in our ability to control our personal and collective destinies. This "illusion of control," as it is often called, implies a tendency to down-play the impact of unconscious and situational factors on our lives. Thus, consciousness and will are at the centre of speculation about human motivation in present-day humanistic and existential psychology. Recent existential views on human behaviour stress, for instance, that a truly meaningful and authentic existence involves confronting life's many paradoxes and dilemmas with courageous choices that lead to self-actualization and the development of the self one is meant to be. Clearly, this is a far cry from the pushing and pulling of a passive organism that one sees in mechanistic theories. However, a more widespread interest in free will was stifled in the early part of this century by the rejection of "mind" as a legitimate academic topic. In recent years, though, it is possible to detect the resurgence of research on free will under such names as "intrinsic motivation," "self-determination" (Deci & Ryan, 1985a), and "volition" (G. Howard & Conway, 1986; Westcott, 1985).

In what follows, I shall adopt the organismic view, taking as a self-evident truth that the conscious components of motivation (volition, will, conation) are important and worthy of study. By *volition* is meant the act of *willing* or resolving to do something as a result of conscious choice. *Conation*, in turn, refers to any striving towards a selected goal, with the added implication that such action is voluntary. For convenience, I shall treat all three terms as being synonymous, using *conation* most of the time as a matter of personal preference. In using *conation* to refer to conscious striving, though, I recognize that it takes place within the limits set by our drives and environmental circumstances. Thus, we do have some freedom of choice, but it is decidedly limited.

THE OBJECTIVE–SUBJECTIVE DIMENSION

Up to this point, I have portrayed motivation as a *process*, one in which human striving is determined both by unconscious forces as well as by conscious choice. Since drives are assumed to be innate, it follows that we are "programmed" by forces we cannot turn off. What we *can* do, however, is learn ways of expressing and controlling them, thereby transforming drives into more or less conscious *motives*. Consistent individual differences in these "motives" can, therefore, be viewed as *motivational dispositions* and portrayed as bipolar dimensions. In discussing the objective–subjective dimension as a contrast between opposing motivational dispositions, I shall start by outlining the conceptual roots of the dimension, before moving on to a review of the empirical research on its various components.

Conceptual Roots of Objectivity–Subjectivity

There are many conceptions of personality that imply some fundamental opposition between motivational tendencies analogous to that between objectivity and subjectivity, although they may not be couched in such terms. Maddi (1976) refers to these theories as conflict models of personality, all of which share common assumptions about conflicting *core tendencies* (innate tendencies regarding the overall direction of life):

> In the *conflict* model, it is assumed that the person is continuously and inevitably in the grips of the clash between two great, opposing, unchangeable forces. Life, according to this model, is necessarily a compromise, which at best involves a dynamic balance of the two forces, and at worst involves a foredoomed attempt to deny the existence of one of them. There are two versions of the conflict model. In the *psychosocial version*, the source of one great force is in the person as an individual, and the source of the other great force is in groups or societies. In the *intrapsychic version*, both great forces arise from within the person, regardless of whether he or she is regarded as an individual or as a social entity. (Maddi, 1976, p. 20)

My conception of objectivity–subjectivity is firmly rooted in the *intrapsychic conflict* tradition, the most notable versions of which are associated with Angyal and Bakan (Maddi, 1976). Both theorists consider that we are riven by a persistent conflict between two inherent and opposing sets of drives (what Maddi calls *core tendencies*). On the one hand, we are compelled to assert our individuality, to separate ourselves from others, and to curtail our dependence on them (autonomy, agency). On the other hand, we experience the urge to join with others in cooperative, intimate, and often dependent relationships (surrender, communion). In other words, human behaviour is seen to result from a continuing conflict between innate sets of self-assertive and self-abnegating drives, all of which operate at an unconscious level.

Maddi explains further that, while the two great forces may seem to be irrevocably opposed, psychological health or integrity requires that some compromise be found. The most successful integration would seem to be one in which both core tendencies are represented as much as possible in living one's life. Since this is difficult to achieve, many individuals exhibit an imbalance, one in which either autonomy/agency or surrender/communion dominate. Presumably, that is why, at a different level of analysis, one can observe differences in objectivity and subjectivity among people. It follows, therefore, that one implication of the intrapsychic conflict model is that objectivity and subjectivity represent concrete expressions of these underlying core tendencies.

Similar conceptions of conflict between opposing tendencies, and the need to achieve some judicious compromise between them, are commonly found in stage-sequence theories of personality development (Breger, 1974; Harvey *et al.*, 1961; Kohlberg, 1969; Loevinger, 1976). For instance, in Harvey *et al.*'s Conceptual Systems Theory (A. Miller, 1978), the fundamental opposition in life is that between tendencies to dependence (communion) and independence (agency), different forms of which come into conflict at each of their four stages of development. Essentially, this scheme proposes that development occurs along two parallel lines. On the one hand, there is a shift in the form of dependence expressed, ranging from the submissiveness of children when faced with the absolute control of their parents, through the adolescent's cautious, tentative attempts at forming emotional bonds, to the more mutual, reciprocal bonding of adults. In contrast, independence is said to develop from the crude negativism of the child, through the rebelliousness of adolescents, to a more sophisticated expression of one's self as an independent being, first as autonomous and increasingly, at the highest level of development, as an interdependent individual. The assumption in this theory is that personality development requires the integration of opposing tendencies at each stage into a more sophisticated expression of dependence–independence. The highest form of development, in sympathy with Angyal and Bakan, is one in which both tendencies are present in their most sophisticated (complex, abstract) forms, as seen in the *interdependent* individual.

In sum, intrapsychic conflict theorists recognize joining and separating tendencies at work in personality functioning, with the highest forms of development requiring some optimal integration of the two, as in Harvey *et al.*'s *interdependence* and Loevinger's *integrated* stages. However, not all conflict theorists offer such a balanced view of personality development. As Lykes (1985) notes, the culturally dominant notion of self is rooted in assumptions of autonomy, independence, and separation. One can see this in Erickson's psychosocial developmental theory which, according to Franz and White (1985), fails to deal adequately with the development of "attachment." Feminist critics of developmental theory interpret all of this as representing an androcentric bias in the field, one that overemphasizes male values of agency and devalues the importance of communion in female (and male) development (Gilligan, 1982; Kaplan, 1986; J. B. Miller, 1986). In discussing objectivity–subjectivity, I shall try to avoid this implicit bias.

Empirical Studies of Objectivity–Subjectivity

What I shall assume, therefore, is that objectivity and subjectivity represent concrete expressions of the more abstract tendencies toward agency and communion. There have been many empirical studies of these "concrete expressions," resulting in a profusion of findings under various rubrics. The problem we face in attempting to discuss this information is finding some systematic way of doing so. For instance, among the terms that have been used to label motivational dispositions, one finds: motive, goal, interest, value, expectation, purpose, plan, desire, wish, and intention, to name but a few. Pervin (1983) offers us a way out of this terminological jungle by proposing that motivational structures (goals, he calls them) can be seen as having three components: *cognitive* (the mental representation of the goal and the paths toward it); *affective* (the feelings attached to the goal); and, *behavioural* (the behaviours associated with the plan for attaining the goal). Depending on the emphasis placed on the structure by different researchers, one component is singled out for attention and the motive is labelled accordingly. Thus, when the cognitive component is dominant and the affective component is relatively weak, researchers may claim to be studying *values*. When the reverse is true and affect is dominant, one speaks of *desires* or *impulses*. Finally, when there is a well-developed plan for attaining the goal, research is said to focus on *purposes* and *intentions*. However, all three components are present to some degree in all motivational structures. To simplify matters, I shall use the term *motive* as a generic label for all these various terms, recognizing, as does Pervin, that a "motive" has cognitive, affective, and behavioural properties. Thus, motives can be seen as giving intensity and direction to a person's thoughts, feelings, and actions by indicating what

TABLE 3. COMPONENTS OF THE OBJECTIVE–SUBJECTIVE DIMENSION

	Objective	Subjective
Behavioural	Power	Love
Affective	Emotional Detachment	Empathy
Cognitive	Extraception	Intraception

is important to understand and react to emotionally in this world, as well as prescribing the ways in which one might seek to attain one's goals. Unfortunately, most research on motives is not formulated in this comprehensive fashion. Usually, individual "motives" are dealt with in isolation, with the result that the empirical literature is chaotic to say the least. To provide a modicum of structure, therefore, I propose that objectivity and subjectivity have the components indicated in Table 3.

This taxonomy is based, in part, on A. H. Buss and Finn's (1987) recent discussion of personality dispositions, together with my own interpretation of the literature. Before moving on to discuss each component in turn, it is important to mention the way in which "trait" and "motive" are used in what follows. Some psychologists make a point of distinguishing between the two terms. For instance, Maddi (1976) suggests that we can think of a *trait* as referring to habitual behaviour involving few new choices. Thus, when we call someone an *extravert*, we are referring to his or her habitual behaviour (a trait), usually we are not referring to behaviour that has involved some degree of conscious choice in pursuit of some goal (a motive). However, other psychologists see no reason to attempt such a distinction, being inclined to the view that many "traits" have motivational properties. Clearly, this difference of opinion is a function of the tendency to study the components of "motives" separately. Thus, the behavioural components of "motives" are often referred to as "motivational dispositions," whereas their emotional and cognitive components are called "traits." When I discuss "traits," in what follows, I shall be implying that there are motivational qualities to the behaviours being studied.

The Behavioural Components of Objectivity–Subjectivity

The behavioural components of a motive refer to the actions associated with goal-directed behaviour (Pervin, 1983). A. H. Buss and Finn (1987) refer to these behaviours as instrumental acts which, in turn, can be summarized as personality dispositions within the superordinate categories of *power* (dominance, rebelliousness, aggressiveness, machiavellianism, impression management, excitement seeking, impulsivity, achievement) and *prosocial* behaviour (altruism, nurturance, succorance). Rather than using the term "prosocial," I prefer "love," and see the power (agency, objectivity)–love (communion, subjectivity) dichotomy as a fundamental difference in motivational orientation. Two kinds of empirical research support this distinction: (1) factorial and (2) single-motive studies.

(1) *Factorial studies.* In Chapter 1, I defined objectivity–subjectivity as a will–affection dichotomy, a superordinate dimension derived from factorial studies of personality structure. The behavioural components of *will* include independence, tough autonomy, and masculine dominance, whereas *affection* is associated with affiliation, trust, cooperation, nurturance, and submissiveness. Clearly, these conceptions are similar to A. H. Buss and Finn's (1987) power and prosocial categories. However, American research on the "Big 5" personality factors is less than clear on the occurrence of a "will" or "power" factor. For instance, the "conscientiousness" factor has been referred to as "will to achieve" by Digman and Inouye (1986) in the sense that it involves planning, persistence and a purposeful striving toward carefully selected goals. However, this is a far cry from the tough, masculine, independence of Brand's "will." Elements of the latter appear to be incorporated into the antagonism pole of the "agreeableness" dimension by McCrae and Costa (1987), who see it as a contrast between dependent fawning and more stubborn, uncooperative, narcissistic, arrogant, vindictive, aggressive, and manipulative behaviours.

Although a "power" category has not been clearly identified in recent American research, some of the older factor analysts, such as Cattell, Eysenck, and Guilford have proposed a superordinate category that is relevant. Thus, Eysenck's (Eysenck & Eysenck, 1985) *psychoticism* (aggressive, cold, egocentric, impersonal, impulsive, antisocial, unempathic, creative, tough-minded) connotes the sense of tough, self-centred assertiveness that is implied in a "power" orientation. Claridge catches the flavour of psychoticism in referring to high scorers on the dimension in the following way:

> [B]eing solitary, not caring for people, he is often troublesome, not fitting in anywhere. He may be cruel and inhumane, lacking in feeling and empathy, and altogether insensitive. He is hostile to others, even his own kith and kin, and aggressive, even to loved ones. He has a liking for odd and unusual things, and a disregard for danger; he likes to make fools of other people and to upset them.... Socialization is a concept which is relatively alien to

both adults and children; empathy, feelings of guilt, sensitivity to other people are notions which are strange and unfamiliar to them. (Claridge, 1985, p. 139)

There is some controversy over the precise composition of the psychoticism dimension, as well as its relationship to mental illness (Claridge, 1986). However, such issues are not really germane here, for the point I wish to make is the simple one that factorial studies do seem to throw up conceptions of behaviour centred around a power–love dichotomy. Conceptual clarity might be improved, however, if there was some way in which the relationships between "agreeableness," "conscientiousness," "will" and "psychoticism" might be more firmly established. Fortunately, Zuckerman *et al.* (1988) have undertaken this task in a factor analysis of eight commonly used personality tests. The sequential extraction of seven, five, and, finally, three factors resulted in a factor solution remarkably similar to Eysenck's E, N and P superfactors. It is Zuckerman *et al.*'s (1988) P factor, or PImpUSS as they call it, that is of interest to us. As the label implies, this superordinate factor is composed of elements of psychoticism, impulsivity, unsocialized sensation seeking, and aggressiveness, all of which imply the kind of self-centred assertiveness and hostility that are involved in at least some kinds of powerful behaviour. When one looks more closely at the composition of this factor, it is interesting to note that aspects of what others call "conscientiousness," and "will" are incorporated into the "USS" component, while "agreeableness" is seen as one pole of the psychoticism dimension. Thus, Zuckerman's scheme offers a convenient way in which to integrate a number of rather disparate views.

In sum, two points remain unclear in this research. The "Big 5" research on personality structure, typified by McCrae and Costa (1987), identifies orthogonal factors, whereas Brand (1984) and Zuckerman *et al.* (1988) conclude that their versions of power–love are bipolar. This difference of opinion runs throughout factorial research. For instance, those who approach the problem of classification using cluster analysis produce *hierarchical* conceptions of motives. Thus, Wicker *et al.* (1984) identified two broad sets of goals which they described as *individual striving* and *harmony seeking*. If you were to look more closely at the components of each of these categories you would find that they bear a strong resemblance to agency–communion. Thus, *individual striving* is composed of goals having to do with manipulation, control, achieving superiority, success, and novelty seeking. In contrast, *harmony seeking* involves attaining harmony with, understanding of, and adjusting to, the world around us. In contrast, the research technique known as "smallest space analysis" has been used by Schwartz and Bilsky (1987) to identify what they call *value domains*, which are groups of personal values that seem to fall within a small number of categories. For instance, values that concern individual self-satisfaction are included in the domains of *enjoyment, achievement,* and *self-direction.* In contrast, domains that reflect one's concern for others, and one's relationship to them, include *prosocial, security,* and *conformity* values. Once again, you can see the apparent contrast between agency (self-direction, achievement) and communion (prosocial, conformity). One also sees that different analytical techniques appear to result in either orthogonal or bipolar solutions. We shall return to this matter later.

The second unresolved issue stems from the development of what might be called positive and negative conceptions of "power." Digman and Inouye's (1986) "will to achieve" implies a socialized form of striving, in contrast to the unsocialized aggressive self-seeking of Eysenck's "P" and Zuckerman *et al.*'s (1988) "PImpUSS." The two forms of behaviour would appear to share some interest in power and control but differ in their emotional tone and, presumably, underlying dynamics. The question is how one might develop a better understanding of the similarities and differences involved. Of some use in this regard is the factorial research carried out on *interpersonal circumplexes,* to which we now turn.

Research on interpersonal circumplexes suggests that the relationships between motives (and traits) can be represented as a system of oblique dimensions (Fig. 13). The more prominent circumplex models are based on Sullivan's (1953) personality theory, which stressed the notion of social exchange and a cost–benefit analysis of interpersonal relationships. Since two of the more common psychological commodities exchanged between people are said to be status/power and love, leading circumplex theorists have been inclined to organize their models accordingly, around the two orthogonal dimensions of status (power/agency/dominance) and love (solidarity/communion/affiliation). For instance, Wiggins and Broughton (1985) have organized their interpersonal traits as shown in Fig. 13a, while providing evidence in support of their contention that well-known conceptions of needs (such as those of Murray, 1938) can be organized in comparable ways (Fig. 13b). Circumplex models have been criticized as merely representing an individual's language structure rather than actually depicting "real" behaviour. However, Gifford and O'Connor (1987) and Paulhus and Martin (1987) have addressed this issue, concluding that Wiggins' circumplex is a valid representation of both language *and* behaviour.

In addition to stressing the significance of power (dominance–submission) and love (hostility–nurturance) dimensions, circumplex models also provide for the identification of two forms of power striving, represented by the hostile power and nurturing power quadrants. Perhaps it is this

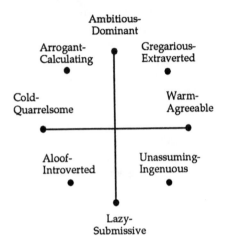

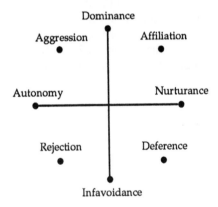

Figure 13. Interpersonal circumplexes. (From Wiggins & Broughton, 1985.)

distinction that is implicit in the "Big 5" factorial studies mentioned above. Thus, "will," "psychoticism," and "PImpUSS" reflect hostile dominance, while "will to achieve," and the more socialized forms of assertion, are located in the nurturing power quadrant. This is a hypothesis that we shall explore further in the next section.

(2) *Single motive studies*. Rather than developing taxonomies of motivational structures, some researchers prefer to examine individual motives in more depth, looking at behavioural correlates as well as origins and dynamics. As a result, a bewildering array of motives fills the literature. For our purposes, we need some way of organizing this profusion. Veroff and Veroff (1980), for instance, suggest that it is common to observe a polarity between two broad sets of self-assertive (achievement, aggression, power, competence) and social relatedness (affiliation, intimacy, love, belongingness) motives. While useful, and consistent with the power-love theme I am developing here, this distinction appears to miss an important point—one that runs something like the following.

The concept of *agency* implies that we are imbued with sets of drives that compel us to assert ourselves as independent human beings. Since we are social creatures, these drives invariably bring us into contact with others who, in turn, are attempting to assert *themselves*. We are embedded, therefore, in various social networks composed of individuals who are trying to cope with one another's agentic tendencies. If we are to develop a sense of self under these circumstances, a sense of being an individual in control of one's own life, then we have the dual task of learning how to *exert* an influence on the world around us, as well as *resisting* control by that world and the people in it. As a result, we achieve varying degrees of independence from both social and physical constraints.

In contrast to agency, which implies a tendency toward self-assertion and self-protection, *communion* refers to the urge toward *self-abnegation*, a wish to *selflessness* by merging with the other. Rather than seeking to further the separation of self and other, communion is the urge to reduce that distinction through fusion between self and other. Thus, rather than seeking to exert power, we are also inclined to *empower* others by offering love and nurturance. Similarly, in contrast to resisting control by others, we may also seek to become *dependent* within the context of a loving relationship.

The intrapsychic conflict between agency and communion, therefore, appears to take the form of an unending tension between self-assertion and self-abnegation. This tension can be depicted as the conflict between seeking (exerting) power and seeking love, and between resisting the power of others, while seeking to empower others through giving love. In other words, two dimensions of intrapsychic conflict can be identified:

seeking power —— seeking love
resisting other —— empowering other.
(giving love)

It is no coincidence, I believe, that the first of these dimensions is referred to in interpersonal circumplexes as dominance–submission and the second as autonomy (hostility)–nurturance. In what follows, I shall review the way in which each dimension has been investigated by those with a more "dynamic" orientation, starting with the "power" motives.

(a) *Seeking power.* A variety of personality concepts has been proposed to account for the different ways in which we exert our influence over other people and the world around us. In addition to *dominance,* one sees reference to *assertiveness, aggressiveness, authoritarianism,* and so on—a profusion of terms referring to manifestations of powerful behaviour. As is often the case in psychology, there is little consistency in the way in which these terms are used. Ray (1981), however, offers a way out of this confusion by focusing on the degree of force involved in the behaviour in question. Thus, when excessive force is used to prevail over others, we tend to describe the behaviour as *aggressive* or *authoritarian.* If a "normal," or socially acceptable, amount of force is used, the behaviour may be seen as being *dominant,* while the use of minimal force is a matter of *assertion.* Ray's scheme provides us with a convenient way in which to discuss variations in the expression of power, for it implies a range from relatively mild or benign assertion to more aggressive forms of behaviour.

Benign expressions of power have been explored in academic psychology under the rubric of *intrinsic motivation* (Deci & Ryan, 1985a,b). As I mentioned earlier, this research tradition grew out of dissatisfaction with traditional drive theories which were unable to account for such ubiquitous behaviours as exploration, curiosity, and play in children. Proponents of intrinsic motivation, therefore, argue that human beings actively seek to *master* both themselves and the world around them and, what is more, that this is a natural tendency. Deci and Ryan recognize two such motives: mastery and self-determination. The *mastery* (or competence) motive involves striving to deal competently with one's environment by exercising and extending one's capabilities, while the *self-determination* motive reflects attempts to achieve freedom from control. While the two motives are so closely related that it is at times difficult to distinguish between them, it is convenient to discuss mastery behaviour as an example of the benign *exertion* of power, while self-determination appears to involve benign attempts to *resist* power.

As children grow older, their innate tendency to exhibit mastery/competence behaviour becomes incorporated within, or develops into, a complex set of motives commonly referred to as "achievement motivation." Spence and Helmreich (1983), for instance, recognize three relatively independent aspects of achievement: work, mastery, and competition. *Work motivation,* defined as a desire to work hard and to do a good job of what one does, is part of a more general pattern of highly socialized life activities found amongst high achievers. Drawing on a national survey conducted in the United States, Veroff (1982) has found, for instance, that male high achievers experience their greatest sense of efficacy and satisfaction in work—the major focus of their lives. In the same sample, female high achievers obtained similar feelings, not from work, but from social and parenting activity. Veroff does note, however, that this latter finding may be undergoing change, along with the changing role of women in society. Spence and Helmreich define *mastery motivation* as a preference for difficult, challenging tasks, as well as for meeting internally prescribed standards of excellence. One can observe this kind of behaviour in the so-called Type A personalities, whose inclination to stretch themselves, to seek out daunting tasks, has been mentioned earlier. Although Type A's are often depicted as hostile, aggressive, and ruthless, Yarnold *et al.* (1987) found that at least half of their male and all of their female Type A's exhibited a relatively benign form of mastery behaviour, one that combined dominance with nurturance. *Competition motivation*, the enjoyment of interpersonal competition and the desire to be better than others, is, I believe, an underlying theme in behaviours such as impression management and self-monitoring. In the latter case, for instance, people are thought to differ in the extent to which they can, and do, observe and control their self-presentation. High self-monitors are sensitive to situational demands and therefore are inclined to affect an appropriate performance for the sake of public appearance. In other words, they dissemble in order to create a good impression. Low self-monitors, on the other hand, lack either the skill or the inclination to dissemble, and, as a result, their behaviour is a more direct expression of their inner states (Snyder & Gangestad, 1986). In sum, benign power striving results in a form of mastery behaviour that may or may not be competitive. In either case, hostility is noticeable by its absence.

Psychologists from various research traditions have explored what has been referred to above as *dominance* behaviour, the somewhat more forceful expression of power striving. For instance, Small *et al.* (1983) define *dominance* behaviour in terms of the following indices: *verbal directiveness* (giving direct orders to others), *verbal ridicule* (putting oneself in a good light at the expense of others), *verbal threat* (verbal challenge with accompanying threat), *verbal control* (struggles to monopolize conversation), *physical assertiveness with contact* ("playful" fighting), *physical challenge* (glaring), and *physical displacement* (controlling another's environment). As a result of their research, these same authors concluded that individual differences in dominance show stable trait-like qualities. When one looks for relevant conceptions of dominance *motivation*, one well-known concept stands out, the so-called power motive (*cf.* McClelland, 1975; D. G. Winter, 1973, and D. G. Winter & Stewart, 1978). After an exhaustive account of the complexities of "power," D. G. Winter (1973) settles for simplicity in defining his concept as a disposition to strive for power. Within this generic power motive, a further, and extremely important, distinction is made between *Hope of Power* (the active seeking after power) and *Fear of Power* (the avoidance of power, particularly that wielded by others). While both forms involve an interest in power, the former might be seen as approach, and the latter as avoidance, behaviour. Winter recognizes that both aspects are significant features of the overall power motive. However, fear of others' power and the attempts to achieve independence that derive from this motive are best dealt with in the following section on autonomy. *Hope of Power*, on the other hand, clearly reflects the kind of dominance behaviour of interest to us here.

In elaborating his conception of *Hope of Power*, D. G. Winter (1987) suggests that it involves strong, vigorous actions that have an impact on others, both intellectually and emotionally. The net result is an array of interpersonal, social, political, and military dominance behaviours, all of which are thought to originate in the same power motive. Indeed D. G. Winter and Stewart (1978) argue that "all the major themes that ... are so characteristic of Western civilization—conquest, organization, prestige, dissipation, and exploitative sex—can be seen as manifestations of a single motive to acquire power" (p. 412). One would have thought that this generalization should be applied more accurately to men, but, in a recent study, D. G. Winter (1988) concludes that the power motive functions much the same way in women. Gender differences in power behaviour, he believes, are less a function of underlying differences in motivation than they are of situational constraints and opportunities. One might also question whether such a wide sweep of human endeavour can be accounted for solely on the basis of a single motive. However, the power motive continues to be of use in understanding various forms of *dominance* behaviour, such as Type A personality (Hooker *et al.*, 1987), interpersonal dominance (Mason & Blankenship, 1987) and nuclear brinkmanship (J. Frank, 1987).

There is a tradition among some personologists to distinguish between normal and neurotic power striving. *Normal* expressions of power are said to reflect one's natural assertiveness and self-expression, whereas *neurotic* striving for power is described in a more negative way as a result of weakness and fear. In the latter case, power is exerted, avoided, or resisted to overcome feelings of inferiority and helplessness (Adler, 1964; Horney, 1950). Thus, neurotic power strivings take a harsher, more extreme form, such as in the aggressive dominance of the authoritarian and the malevolent cruelty of the sadist. For example, Fromm (1973) characterizes *sadism* as a form of malignant *aggression*, one that involves a love of cruelty and destructiveness. Although sadism is commonly used to refer to sexual cruelty, Fromm suggests that nonsexual sadism, the infliction of physical and mental pain, is widespread in human societies. It can be seen, for instance, in wife and child abuse, as well as in cruelty to animals. Smail describes the way in which sadistic men subject their wives and daughters to such humiliating and cruel treatment that the latter are eventually driven to mental health clinics in an attempt to cope with their fractured lives:

> Because of her parents'—particularly her father's—brutality towards her, June was taken into care at the age of seven. At sixteen, she is a sweetly pretty, somewhat overweight girl who goes out of her way to charm those she meets.... And yet her inarticulate conception of herself is as rotten through and through.... Despite sometimes desperate efforts to make people love her, she is convinced that nobody could.... There is little in her life other than pain, veiled self-indulgence, secrecy, deceit and guilt. Her body she regards with loathing. (Smail, 1984, p. 43)

In a similar vein, feminist critics of science and technology point to themes of power, sadism, and machismo in both the behaviour and language of many scientific and technical experts (Cohn, 1987; Keller, 1985). Keller writes, for instance:

> In an effort to "master" nature, to "storm her strongholds and castles," science can come to sound like a battlefield. Sometimes such imagery becomes quite extreme, exceeding even the conventional imagery of the warrior or hunter. Note, for example, the language in which one scientist describes his pursuit: "I liked to follow the workings of another mind through these minute, teasing investigations to see a relentless observer get hold of Nature and squeeze her until the sweat broke out all over her and her sphincters loosened." (Keller, 1985, p. 123)

(b) Resisting power. Resistance has to do with thwarting the power and influence of others over oneself. Henry Murray, the eminent personality theorist (Murray, 1938), caught the flavour of such behaviour in talking about people's need for *Autonomy*, *i.e.*, resisting influence or coercion, defying authority, striving for independence, and *Contrarience*, *i.e.*, acting differently from others, being unique, taking the opposite side, holding unconventional views (Murray, 1938). Thus, terms like *autonomy, independence, rebelliousness*, and *negativism* are used to imply a tendency toward self-protection, warding off attempts by others to define who you are and how you should behave. Just as with the seeking of power, there are some socially acceptable and some socially unacceptable ways of

resisting power. When we do so in relatively benign ways, we are said to show "autonomy/independence." More disagreeable or difficult behaviour is labelled as "rebellious/negative," while clearly neurotic striving to avoid control by others is seen as evidence of paranoia.

As mentioned earlier, relatively benign forms of resistance have been studied under the label of *"self-determination,"* the tendency to seek freedom from control by inner drives or external pressures. In their research on the matter, Deci and Ryan (1985b) have identified what they call *causality orientations*, which are individual differences in the way that people understand the origins of their behaviour. Of relevance to us is the *autonomy orientation* in which one experiences a high degree of choice in the initiation and regulation of one's own behaviour. As Deci and Ryan put it:

> [A] strong autonomy orientation leads people to select jobs that allow greater initiative, to interpret their existing situations as more autonomy promoting ... and to organize their actions on the basis of personal goals and interests rather than controls and constraints. With a high level of autonomy orientation, people are more often intrinsically motivated ... they will be less controlled by extrinsic rewards and will tend to experience them more as affirmations of their competence or expectance. (Deci & Ryan, 1985b, p. 111)

Thus, the achievement of autonomy or self-reliance promotes a sense of well-being in those with an autonomy orientation (R. Davis, 1986). It is not surprising to find, therefore, that McClelland (1975) depicts those who seek autonomy (his Stage II of development) as people for whom *voluntary* control of their own behaviour is extremely important. It follows that, the loss of voluntary control over their fate would be extremely distressing. Strenuous efforts must be taken to avoid this calamity, efforts that are commonly viewed, in adults, as being neurotic or pathological. In children, however, the attempt to be autonomous is accepted as a normal part of growth. Thus, Stage II in Harvey *et al.*'s (1961) developmental scheme is described as a negativistic stage, one that is essential for the development of a sense of identity. McClelland describes this rather benign self-assertion well when he says:

> As a child grows older, he soon learns that he can be powerful simply by saying "No." His mother tries to feed him, and he turns his head aside. She urges him to urinate at a particular time and place, and he refuses. Freudians have associated this willfulness, or assertion of the self, with the anal stage of development, with learning to control defecation, which provides a major opportunity for learning self-assertiveness and self-control. If a child could summarize his feelings with words, he might say something like, "I can control, that is, strengthen myself. I don't need to depend on others for strength." The focus of attention may at first be on controlling

one's own body and mind. A child learns soon enough that while his mother may make him do something, she cannot control what he thinks.... (McClelland, 1975, p. 15)

A conception of resisting power that occupies a position midway between the relatively benign forms of self-determination discussed above and the overtly neurotic that will be dealt with shortly is Winter's *Fear of Power* (D. G. Winter, 1973; D. G. Winter & Stewart, 1978). An individual who is high in Fear of Power is said to be interested in power in order to avoid the power of others—the implication of the label for this behaviour being that it has its origins in *fear* rather than a more "natural" tendency toward self-assertion. Fear of Power has been shown by Winter to be related to a suspicion of authority, an unbending commitment to one's own independence and autonomy, and the valuing of the mind as opposed to the emotions. For instance, students high in Fear of Power protect their autonomy by avoiding highly structured situations (lectures, objective tests, etc.), by disregarding structure when faced with it (resisting deadlines) and by seeking opportunities to be autonomous (as in writing a thesis). D. G. Winter and Stewart (1978) speculate that Fear of Power has its origins in the experience of oppression as a child, presumably in a family setting where excessive adult or sibling control engenders feelings of helplessness and creates a lifelong sensitivity to similar situations.

It is interesting that Winter has found a significant relationship between Fear of Power and paranoia. In commenting on this, he notes:

[I]t appears that ... Fear of Power is related to a somewhat exaggerated disposition to view all power or authority with suspicion and distrust; among individuals classified as schizophrenic this distrust ... becomes pathological or paranoid. (D. G. Winter & Stewart, 1978, p. 423)

Thus, paranoia (the display of excessive suspiciousness and distrust) can be seen as the neurotic extreme of autonomy-seeking and self-determination.

In his exposition on neurotic styles, Shapiro (1965) offers a similar viewpoint in arguing that the paranoid style is basically a pathology of autonomy. A defensive vigilance and a readiness to counterattack characterizes the paranoid's defensive/antagonistic relationship to the external world. This edgy alertness reflects a preoccupation with the threat of being subjugated by the whims of others, a mindset that, in turn, stems from a fragile sense of autonomy. Unlike relatively normal individuals who develop a sense of competence and self-efficacy, the paranoid is said to be deficient in this regard, uncertain and unsure of his or her competence. Such delicate autonomy can only be maintained, Shapiro argues,

TABLE 4. TERMS RELATED TO "SEEKING LOVE"

Abasement	to surrender, to comply, to accept punishment, masochism; self-depreciation
Infavoidance	to avoid failure, shame; to refrain from attempting something beyond one's power
Ingratiation	to seek to win favour; to make oneself agreeable
Obedience	submission; willingness to obey
Submission	meek, humble, compliant
Succorance	to seek aid, protection, sympathy; to be dependent

The terms "abasement," "infavoidance," and "succorance" are derived from Murray (1938).

by a sustained vigilance. It follows that the paranoid person is terrified of "giving in" either to his or her impulses or to the demands of others. The result is a world view characterized by suspicion and hostility, together with a bitter resentment over pressures to submit.

(c) Seeking love. The urge to seek love and care is, according to Bakan and others, both ubiquitous and innate—a healthy expression of the *communion* tendency. The behaviours associated with this urge can be seen most clearly in children. Mussen *et al.* (1979), for instance, define what they call the *dependency motive* as "the wish to be nurtured, aided, comforted, and protected by others or to be emotionally close to or accepted by other people" (p. 211). In preschool children, this motive is expressed as "seeking assistance, attention, recognition, approval, reassurance, contact; clinging to adults or other children; resisting separation from adults; soliciting affection and support from a teacher" (p. 211). In western societies, however, excessive displays of dependency are soon discouraged, at least by some parents, so that "many young children experience considerable conflict between their desires to ask for help and comfort and their desire to please their parents, who are demanding independence" (Mussen *et al.*, 1979, p. 212).

The resulting ambivalence about seeking love and caring is reflected, I believe, in the many labels used in psychology to characterize this kind of behaviour in adults (Table 4). Terms like *"abasement," "ingratiation,"* and *"submissiveness"* have negative connotations, conveying an unacceptable image of grovelling weakness. Why these signs of "communion" should be seen in such a light is a matter to which I shall return shortly.

Birtchnell (1984) has suggested that many of the terms listed in Table 4 can be subsumed under the more generic term *"dependency."* Although this term fails to convey the more positive, constructive aspects of seeking love and care, it is the most convenient of the available labels. Thus, Birtchnell identifies several kinds of dependence, notably *emotional dependence* (equivalent to Murray's *succorance*) and *deferential dependence* (Murray's *deference* and *abasement*). An attempt to link concepts in this way is supported by Wiggins and Broughton's (1985) finding of a positive correlation between succorance, abasement, submissiveness, and lack of self-confidence. Why emotional dependence should be related to deferential dependence in not hard to see. One might agree with Horney (1950) that one way of achieving one's goal of love and caring is to take steps to ensure that one does not anger or "turn off" others.

The dubious feelings about dependent behaviour in adults can be seen in a number of ways. Birtchnell (1984), for instance, discusses the relationship between dependence and childishness, citing a recent study of Scottish psychiatric patients in which there was a significant association between being described as immature and being described as dependent. Birtchnell concludes that it is not unreasonable to consider *excessive* levels of dependence in adults as childish. In a similar vein, Orlofsky and Frank (1986) depict the process of achieving a firm identity in both men and women as the blending of *"less mature* themes involving nurturance and security with *more mature* themes of mastery, competition and independent activity" (p. 580). Thus, seeking nurturance and security is seen as a form of childishness. Dependency behaviour also has been depicted as a form of pathology. In the DSM–III, for instance, submissive patterns of behaviour are said to typify dependent personality disorders (Millon, 1981), a theme that has been criticized extensively by Caplan (1984, 1987).

There is reason to believe, therefore, that many of the current psychological descriptions of dependency behaviour overemphasize its negative aspects, while downplaying the more constructive features of communion. Thus, Gilligan (1982) suggests that, while separation and individuation are crucial issues in the development of male identities, female identity formation is more closely concerned with maintaining attachment and relationship, although Sayers (1986) would disagree with this. In describing women's "search for attachment," Jean Baker Miller points out how difficult it is for them to achieve this goal in a society which, being dominated by male values, so prizes individuality and detachment (J. B. Miller, 1986).

One might be inclined to conclude, therefore, that the treatment of "seeking love and caring" in psychology reflects a certain androcentric bias (Wine, 1982), with the male values of separation and individuation carrying the day. However, this may be an oversimplification for, as Smail (1984) argues, many men who seek to express their more tender aspects experience great difficulty in coping with the tough, objective reality of their more agentic peers. It seems more appropriate, therefore, to speculate that the disparagement of "dependency" may reflect individual differences on the tough–tender or objective–subjective dimension, rather than some pervasive gender difference.

Of the many conceptions of "love seeking" that are extant, I shall concentrate on only one, the *intimacy* motive of McAdams (1982, 1984, 1985). The primary reason for this is that, on the face of it, the intimacy motive conveys the core meaning of communion with greater verity than any other conception. At the same time, I wish to avoid the confusion surrounding another motive system that might be considered relevant to this section, namely the *affiliation* motive. Veroff (1986) and Hill (1987), for instance, talk about a family of motives that have to do with a concern about maintaining close relationships. This same cluster of motives can be traced back to Murray's (1938) suggestion that affiliation (need to form friendships), nurturance (need to nourish others), and succorance (need to seek help) cluster together into a group of needs having to do with affection between people: seeking it, exchanging it, giving it, and withholding it. The problem with this is that, while nurturance and succorance are closely related in such schemes as the interpersonal circumplex (Wiggins & Broughton, 1985), affiliation is thought to include a large dominance component (McAdams, 1982). In other words, affiliative behaviour can be both active and manipulative—not the qualities involved in communion. To simplify matters, therefore, I shall avoid this issue and return to the question of intimacy.

For McAdams (1982), the theoretical roots of intimacy lie in the writings of scholars such as Bakan, Maslow, and Buber, all of whom describe a certain quality of interpersonal experience involving "egalitarian exchange." For instance, the themes used to describe such relationships are: the occurrence of joy and mutual delight, a reciprocal dialogue, openness and receptivity, perceived harmony, a concern for the well-being of the other, surrender of manipulative control and the desire to master the other, and being in an encounter which is an end in itself, rather than striving to attain a relationship or some extrinsic reward. Central to intimacy is the willingness to sacrifice self-control thereby blurring the boundaries of self in the process of relating. He or she is open to the interpersonal surroundings, ready for merger. This communal pose, however, is one of attentive waiting, not active striving. And the merger—the interaction with another as it spontaneously unfolds—is not conditional nor is it a means to an end. (McAdams, 1982, p. 135)

In a similar vein, Maslow (in McAdams, 1982) distinguishes *Being-love* (the tone of which is gentle, delicate, unintruding, and undemanding, much as water gently soaks into crevices) from *Deficiency-love* (the more active striving to fill a void, to satisfy a lack in the individual's interpersonal world).

The intimacy motive, then, would seem to be an interesting way of conceptualizing the kind of motive that might be derived from the core tendency of *communion*, as well as a useful way of operationalizing "seeking love." However, there are some conceptual points that need to be clarified before proceeding. The picture of "intimacy" developed by McAdams implies an egalitarian sharing between two individuals sure enough of their identities to sacrifice a degree of self-control in the process of merging with another. One can see this in his subcategories of "psychological growth" and "harmony," each of which implies the coming together of two equals who grow in the company of each other. Now it is possible that McAdams means to say that there are degrees of intimacy, along the lines of a developmental sequence, but my sense of his "intimacy motive" is that it is a sophisticated achievement, a far cry from what is implied in abasement, obedience, ingratiation, infavoidance, and all the other terms commonly seen as the bipolar opposite of dominance (power). Perhaps I might refer again to Maslow's contrast between Being-love and Deficiency-love to throw light on this conceptual distinction. Intimacy motivation is clearly akin to Being-love, whereas Deficiency-love (*i.e.*, the seeking to fill a void by extracting emotional rewards from others) is more closely related to the dependence motives. It would appear, therefore, that "intimacy" is a mature form of "seeking love."

(d) Empowering others/giving love. By sharing oneself with another, in the sense of giving up control and replacing it with love, one empowers others, enabling them to cope more adequately with the demands of life (J. B. Miller, 1986). Giving love, therefore, is a form of prosocial behaviour, one that is commonly labelled as *"nurturance,"* i.e., helping others without the implication of cost to self, or *"altruism,"* i.e., helping others at some cost to self (A. H. Buss & Finn, 1987). As a matter of convenience, I shall focus on altruism as a prototypical example of prosocial behaviour. It is clear from the literature that two controversies swirl around the concept. First, is the question of the stability of altruistic behaviour and whether or not it can be regarded as a personality trait.

Second, opinions differ over the role of emotional and cognitive factors in altruism, particularly the occurrence of selfless or selfish "motives" at the root of what would, on the surface, appear to be genuinely empathetic behaviour. This latter issue is more conveniently dealt with in the following sections on the affective and cognitive components of conation. I shall, for the moment, therefore, confine myself to the question of the *stability* of altruistic behaviour.

Although altruism can take many forms, Small *et al.* (1983) concluded from a survey of the literature that five acts typify altruistic and prosocial behaviour: (*i*) *physical assistance* (helping another to accomplish a definite end), (*ii*) *physical serving* (doing something *for* someone without their assistance), (*iii*) *sharing* (physically giving some of one's possessions to another), (*iv*) *verbal assistance* (giving verbal help in assisting someone to complete a task), and (*v*) *verbal support* (verbally expressing concern for another's plight in the form of sympathy, praise or encouragement). The question is, whether people show some or all of these behaviours consistently across disparate situations. In other words, is there an altruistic trait? Small *et al.* (1983) and Zeldin *et al.* (1984) examined this question within the context of a wilderness camping trip involving groups of young people. Both studies led to the conclusion that, over time, "participants demonstrated consistent rates of prosocial behaviour" (Zeldin *et al.*, 1984, p. 159), with some adolescents initiating many prosocial acts, while others rarely helped. These findings, together with the high intercorrelations between the five forms of prosocial behaviour noted above, provide strong support for viewing altruism as a stable disposition.

Perhaps the most persistent champion of the altruistic trait is Rushton (1980, 1981, 1984), who notes:

> Despite this voluminous literature [on prosocial behavior] there is as yet no systematic program of research into "consistent patterns of individual differences" in altruistic behaviour. This is because most researchers do not believe there is a trait of altruism—or at least, not one broadly based enough to warrant major research attention. (Rushton, 1984, p. 271)

In seeking to correct what he sees as an erroneous belief, Rushton offers three sets of evidence in support of an altruistic trait. First, he harks back to the classical Hartshorne and May studies of "character" in children, which were published in the late 1920s. In this enormous project,

> investigators gave eleven thousand elementary and high school students some thirty-three different behavioral tests of their altruism, self-control, and honesty in home, classroom, church, play and athletic contexts. At the same time, extensive ratings of the children's reputations with their teachers and their classmates were made in all these areas. By intercorrelating the children's scores on all these tests it was possible to discover whether the

children's behavior was specific to situations or generalizable across them. If the children's behavior is specific to situations then the correlations across situations should be extremely low or even nonexistent. If the children's behavior is generalizable across situations, then the correlations should be substantial. (Rushton, 1980, p. 59)

Essentially, what Hartshorne and May found was that the various behavioural indices of altruism showed low correlations with one another, in the order of 0.23. However, when these five indices where combined into an aggregate score, they were found to exhibit a much higher correlation with ratings of altruistic behaviour obtained from teachers and peers (0.6 or higher). For reasons that are not clear, Hartshorne and May, together with more modern "situationists" (see Chapter 1), have preferred to focus on the correlations derived from single indices in support of their arguments in favour of behavioural specificity. Rushton, however (along with other personologists such as Epstein and O'Brien, 1985), considers this to be an error of interpretation, favouring, instead, the use of aggregate data to support their assumption of behavioural generality and the existence of an altruistic trait. Further support for this latter contention comes from Rushton's (1984) review of studies on the personality of community volunteers. When compared to non-volunteers, on a variety of paper–pencil measures, volunteers have been found to exhibit more empathy and higher standards of social responsibility. Further, self-report measures of altruism, which purport to measure trait altruism, have been found to correlate significantly with aggregate indices of altruistic behaviours reflecting a variety of helping behaviours (Rushton, 1984).

In sum, factorial studies have identified two sets of power–love behaviours that I have chosen to label seeking power (dominance)–seeking love (submission) and avoiding power (autonomy)–giving love (nurturance). Single motive studies appear to offer considerable support for each pole of the dimensions. There are differences of opinion over the most appropriate way in which to depict the relationships between the two dimensions. In research on interpersonal complexes, they are seen as being orthogonal, whereas others working on single motives see natural groupings between dominance and autonomy (in Winter's power motive) and succorance and nurturance (as in Murray's natural groupings). We have met this kind of issue before in discussing the analytic–holistic dimension. Some authors prefer an orthogonal representation of the concepts, whereas others favour a bipolar contrast. For my purposes, I shall collapse the two dimensions into one, recognizing, in doing so, that I may be focusing attention on the circumplex quadrants of hostile/ power versus submissive/nurturance (Fig. 13).

The Affective Components of Objectivity–Subjectivity

Despite their importance, the affective components of motives in general, and objectivity–subjectivity in particular, have received relatively little attention in the research literature. Why this is so is not clear. One possibility is that the neglect reflects the widespread lack of interest in emotion that has plagued psychological theory over recent decades (see Chapter 3). The net result is that I have had great difficulty in finding relevant and interesting empirical information on the affective components of objectivity–subjectivity, with the one exception of research on *empathy*, which is quite extensive. What follows, therefore, is a rather impoverished discussion of the feeling component of objectivity–subjectivity.

Power feelings. While power *behaviour* is what people are willing to do in pursuit of power, power *feelings* are the emotions associated with such a goal. Another way of looking at this is that the urge to experience feelings of power underlies and instigates our efforts to be powerful. In formulating his conception of competence motivation, for instance, White (1959) proposed that there is an inherent satisfaction in extending and exercising one's capabilities. This feeling of competence has also been called "feelings of power" by others (*e.g.*, McClelland, 1975) who suggest that it is these feelings that are the *real* goal of power motivation. Thus, we are thought to achieve feelings of satisfaction at being a *cause*, being able to have an effect on the world around us, and seeing ourselves as *potent* beings.

Many of those who study power motivation, in its various forms, have identified a link between high need for power and an apparent need for excitement. For instance, Deci and Ryan (1985a) report a number of studies which conclude that random samples of college students and children tend to select activities that provide challenges. This seems to suggest that for an activity to be interesting it must be optimally challenging. In a similar vein, McClelland (1975) reports that power motivated men are attracted to extreme risk and, presumably, the feelings of excitement that are engendered by risk. Veroff also links high levels of Hope of Power with the need for stimulation and challenge, concluding that:

> In many ways I think of [the Hope of Power] as a concern about boredom, reflecting a need for excitement in life. Having impact or producing change in the environment is a way of vesting interest in a world that if left unchanged might be uninteresting and even cause anxiety. (Veroff, 1982, p. 126)

The relationship between power motivation and feelings of excitement can be accounted for by reference to theories of optimal arousal (Cofer and Appley, 1984). Over the years, psychologists have proposed a number of concepts such as *optimal arousal, optimal arousal potential,* and *optimal incongruity*—all of which imply that human beings need to experience optimal levels of stimulation and excitement in order to maintain a feeling of well-being. It appears that those who are high in power motivation may need somewhat more excitement than the rest of us in order to achieve this optimal condition. Zuckerman's (1985) work on stimulation seeking is relevant here, as is the so-called thrill-seeking personality (Farley, 1986).

What one might conclude from all this is that power seeking is a means of achieving a *feeling* of potency or mastery. In turn, such feelings arise when one is able to act as a *cause*, the capacity to control one's world in such a way as to maintain optimal arousal. It is the self-perceived inability to be a cause, to have an effect on the world around one that, in some individuals, leads to the extreme forms of power seeking described earlier. Veroff (1982), for instance, characterizes Fear of Weakness as being rooted in feelings of sexual inadequacy. Men who experience these feelings tend, among other things, to have alcohol and drug problems, behaviours that may start out as a "masculine compensatory device," a way of masking one's feelings of impotence, but then get out of control.

More extreme efforts to deal with the same root problem have also been suggested as the origins of sadism. Both Fromm (1973) and Keller (1985), for instance, argue that the sadist suffers from an unbearable feeling of boredom and impotence. While fears of sexual impotence may help to explain the sadistic treatment of women by some men, Fromm suggests that non-sexual sadism stems from a more pervasive feeling of impotence. The incapacity to have others respond in a loving way, or in any way at all, leads the sadist, Fromm believes, to do virtually anything to get a reaction from others and end the grinding monotony of daily life. Thus, the sadist seeks feelings of power, the feeling that one can cause an effect. In the process, sadists may kill and mutilate others or subject others to mental cruelty and humiliation. As Fromm (1973) notes, sadists love power and despise the weak, for the latter are like themselves. In addition, sadists appear to be afraid of uncertainty and unpredictability, presumably because it is more difficult to attain optimal levels of arousal under such circumstances. The same satisfactions and pleasures in attaining one's power goals, described above, can also be seen in resisting the power of others. Achieving self-determination and autonomy seems to result in a positive emotional state. For example, R. Davis (1986) has demonstrated that a high-school curriculum that encourages self-reliance promotes a feeling of well-being among students. Similarly, Ryan (1982) conducted a study in which the types of emotions reported by subjects in experimental settings were related to their causality orientations. Of relevance here is the finding that *autonomy orientation* was positively related to interest and negatively related to hostility toward the experimenter and experimental situation. In other words, the more autonomous individuals, those who felt in control of the situation, responded with feelings of interest.

When one turns to the more extreme forms of resisting power, the emotional substrate of power behaviour becomes more complex. Just as the sadist fears weakness and impotence, so too do the extreme resisters fear being overwhelmed either by the power of others or their own uncontrollable inner urges. In describing the origins of Fear of Power, for instance, both Keller (1985) and D. G. Winter (1973) offer similar scenarios. The experience of powerlessness as a child in the face of overpowering adults leads to an uncertainty about oneself, who one is supposed to be. One way to protect oneself against this uncertainty is to resist the other's will, a strategy that becomes imbued with *feelings of fear* when one's autonomy is threatened—a fear of being controlled by others or by one's own drives. Loss of self-control is avoided, therefore, by attempts to maintain autonomy. For the paranoid person, vigilance against external threats to his or her independence becomes a central feature of daily life. Thus, the extreme resister seems to spend much of his or her time avoiding feelings of fear associated with the power of others.

While the more objective person experiences feelings of potency and satisfaction at being a cause, he or she may, at the same time, show few signs of emotional sensitivity or empathy. Thus, those who seek power may be capable of a wide range of emotional experiences, including such emotions as excitement, fear, and anger, but their more compassionate, empathic ties to others seem to be sorely diminished. Since this topic will be discussed at greater length in the next section, for the time being I shall simply raise a few salient points.

Smail (1984) describes the emotional insensitivity of the objective consciousness as one that suffers from "emotional anaesthesia," the lack of sensitivity to, or concern about, the "finer" feelings of oneself or others. Although objective individuals can recognize such feelings, they quickly discount them or use such information in pursuit of power and control. In so-called "normal" society, this "objectified" response to others is, according to Smail, considered to be adaptive:

> The fact that we must relate to each other as objects ... means that real intimacy is almost impossible to achieve.... Instead, the characteristic and familiar way we relate to one another in our objectified interpersonal space

is to bristle with suspicion and hostility.... Most conversations between two people are double monologues in which each party seeks to ... project our safely established objective evaluations over each other.... (Smail, 1984, p. 57)

To achieve these skills of self-control and self-presentation, we must learn to "dissociate ourselves from our subjectivity" (Smail, 1984, p. 50). In other words, we engage in emotional dissociation, the separation of thoughts from feelings and the suppression of those feelings that may cause anxiety (Nandy, 1983). In return, the status of objectivity:

releases us from some of the terrors attendant on subjectivity—for example, from some forms of psychological pain, loneliness and responsibility, fragility and the threat of fundamental failure [as a human being]. (Smail, 1984, p. 51)

In its most extreme manifestation, such as in the sadistic scientist mentioned earlier, emotional detachment appears to be rooted in Fear of Power (Keller, 1985). Children who develop a fragile sense of self are fearful of losing control of themselves, as a result of either the whims of others or the inexorable pressure from their own impulses and desires. A characteristic reaction among those who ultimately become scientists is, according to Keller, to seek control of these pressures. One strategy is to suppress one's own emotional reactions to events, thereby ensuring that one is not open to emotional manipulation by others. The prevalence of emotional detachment in science has led a number of observers, such as Keller (1985), Nandy (1983), and Roszak (1973), to conclude that "normal" science is pathological. Be that as it may, the main point of interest here is that power seeking appears to be associated with certain kinds of emotional control and detachment.

Love feelings. In seeking communion with another, one seeks both to give and to receive love. The joy and satisfaction that may ensue from the achievement of this goal is seen in such experiences as romantic love or religious ecstasy, and in the existential sense of unity that some individuals develop in relation to the natural environment. In a similar vein, a sense of belonging to, or depending on, a group or movement can bring intense satisfaction (Becker, 1973). The converse of these feelings of joy and satisfaction are the fears generated by separation—the breaking of attachment, which, in its most devastating form, can be seen in separation anxiety in children (Breger, 1974).

As mentioned earlier, a crucial element in the attainment of communion is a capacity for intimacy which, in turn, depends on one's ability to empathize both with oneself and others. What I shall argue here, therefore, is that the most important feelings associated with loving *behaviour* are feelings of empathy.

Modern conceptions of empathy, which are derived from early research in the study of aesthetics, were introduced into the psychological lexicon in the early part of the current century to convey a sense of feeling one's way into the consciousness of another (Wispe, 1987). The term "empathy," therefore, implies an attempt to make contact with the subjective experience of another person. The precise nature of this "contact" is a contentious matter, however. For instance, one can make contact with the feelings of others on either a cognitive or an emotional level. One can *understand* what others feel as well as *feeling* what others feel, which suggests the possibility of distinguishing between two forms of empathy: cognitive and emotional (M. Davis, 1983; M. Davis *et al.*, 1987). Some authors (*e.g.*, Wispe, 1987) emphasize the cognitive aspects of empathy, while others prefer to limit "empathy" to its emotional component, labelling the cognitive aspect as "role- or perspective-taking" and "social acuity" (Funder & Harris, 1986; Moore, 1987). Emotional empathy, on the other hand, is more clearly an emotional reaction—one that is said to reflect the feelings of the other (Moore, 1987) or is characterized by feelings of sympathy and compassion for another's distress (M. Davis, 1983).

The relationship between cognitive and emotional empathy remains controversial, echoing the debates over cognitive–affective interactions in theories of emotion (see Chapter 3). As one might expect, the central issue is "whether the term empathy ought to be restricted to emotion directly engendered by the affect of another ... [that is] whether affect can occur without prior cognitive mediation" (Moore, 1987, p. 340). Opinions differ on the matter and, just as in the debate between Lazarus and Zajonc, one camp argues that empathy is possible in the absence of cognitive mediation, whereas the other insists on the need for role taking (cognitive empathy) as a precursor of emotional empathy (Strayer, 1987). Both viewpoints are plausible and can be supported by the available evidence. For instance, the occurrence of "emotional contagion" in infants (the reactive crying to another infant's distress) is consistent with the notion of a direct emotional response to others (Strayer, 1987). On the other hand, there is considerable evidence in support of the conclusion that "taking another's perspective increases emotional reactions to that person's pleasure or pain" (Batson *et al.*, 1987, p. 172). I suspect that the resolution of this debate would require one to accept that an initial empathetic response, on a preconscious level, could subsequently be augmented by role taking.

A second definitional controversy revolves around the precise nature of the emotional experience involved in emotional empathy and involves the distinction between "empathy," "sympathy," and "personal distress" (Eisenberg & Strayer, 1987). In this debate, "empathy" is characterized as feeling *with* others, "sympathy" as feeling *for*, and "personal distress" is seen as an emotional reaction leading to egotistical responses to alleviate one's own state. Not everyone is interested in making these fine-grained distinctions (*e.g.*, Batson *et al.*, 1987), but Moore makes a case for doing so in the following example:

> When I listen to the plight of an acquaintance who is undergoing a painful divorce, even though I experience concern and sympathy, it does not have the affective kick of a true empathic response. What is missing is the affect; the true experiencing of the affect of the other. When I compare this to the wrenching affect I experience as I watch my son bumble his way through his lines in a school play, the important difference in experience is salient. (Moore, 1987, p. 340)

I shall not bother with the distinction here, however, preferring, instead, M. Davis's (1983) more comprehensive view of emotional empathy as feelings of sympathy and compassion for another.

The interesting question for personality theorists is whether there are stable individual differences in empathy, *i.e.*, can one talk of *dispositional empathy*? I shall discuss emotional empathy here, deferring cognitive empathy (perspective taking) to the next section on the cognitive components of motivation. The available evidence on the matter is rather skimpy but Davis believes that he has demonstrated such a disposition (M. Davis, 1983; M. Davis *et al.*, 1987). For instance, in one study, subjects were pretested on a measure of emotional empathy and then exposed to an experimental situation in which they heard a tape-recorded appeal for help from a young woman. The appeal was highly emotional and involved the plight of an elder sister who, after the tragic death of her parents needed help in looking after her younger siblings. It was relatively easy for the experimental subjects to "escape" from the appeal since their responses were given in writing and sealed in an envelope prior to their leaving the experimental situation. The mood induced by these manipulations was assessed in terms of empathetic emotion and personal distress. What Davis found was that his empathic concern scale (a dispositional measure) correlated significantly with the state measures of empathy and personal distress, but that the relationship between dispositional empathy and actual helping behaviour was less clear. In a follow-up study, the emotional reactions of subjects to two films, likely to induce either sadness or anger, were assessed (M. Davis *et al.*, 1987). Interestingly, it was the subjects' negative emotional reactions that were influenced most strongly by, and related most strongly to, Davis's dispositional measure of emotional empathy.

Clearly, studies of this kind are attempts to develop construct validity for the particular measure used by Davis. As such, they are only illustrative of a possible empathy disposition. In this connection, it might be useful to bear in mind Batson *et al.*'s (1987) criticism of Davis's measure on the grounds that it may simply reflect a form of social desirability. In other words, experimental procedures that rely heavily on self-reported empathy (and altruism) are prone to biases in self-presentation. Unfortunately, the only other common measure of dispositional empathy (Mehrabian & Epstein, 1972) is considered by Batson *et al.* to be more a reflection of general emotional reactivity than a specific measure of empathic reaction. Thus, clarification of the status of dispositional empathy awaits further research. Although it would be useful for my general argument if the expression of empathy could be seen as a stable disposition, it is not crucial. More important is the relationship between empathic feelings and the expression of tendencies to communion and love. In other words, is there a clear link between empathy and behaviours such as altruism? As a matter of convenience, I shall postpone discussion of this issue until the final summary of this chapter.

The Cognitive Components of Objectivity–Subjectivity

The cognitive component of motives includes a person's conceptualization of their goals in life, together with their plans for attaining them (Pervin, 1983). The more central of these goal images are incorporated into our self-concept, providing us with stable pictures of who we are and who we would like to become.

McAdams (1984) is one of the few researchers to have studied individual differences in self-image from the perspective of the intrapsychic conflict model. A content analysis of the life stories of middle-aged subjects enabled McAdams to identify what he refers to as "imagoes" or prototypical characters that capture the individual's idealized image of himself or herself. In a gesture of conceptual elegance, McAdams was moved to identify these imagoes with figures from ancient mythology. Thus, his *power* imagoes included Zeus (the omnipotent), Hermes (the swift traveller) and Ares (the warrior), while the "purest" *love* imagoes were those that personified Demeter (the caregiver), Hera (the friend) and Aphrodite (the lover). The centrality of power motivation is evident in the case of "Tom," a forty-three-year-old police department employee:

> All of Tom's heroes in childhood were war heroes.... Tom described the glory years of high school when he attended a military academy and his subsequent "first big failure" at Notre Dame University where he repeatedly battled a host of authority figures, unwittingly cultivating the role of "rebel." Soon after dropping out of college, Tom enlisted in the Air Force and began

another glory chapter as the good soldier. His life story since then is a roller-coaster ride from periods of glory when he is the good warrior ... to times of depravity and shame when he fails to live up to the warrior code ... and falls into heavy drinking and generally irresponsible behavior.... In sum, Tom's life story is a saga of warfare in which the noble warrior is victorious when he is strong enough to keep the internal forces of dereliction and depravity under raps while channeling aggressive impulses into the arts of preparing for war. (McAdams, 1984, p. 172)

One of the more disturbing features of Tom's life is that it is unmitigated by signs of communion (love), leaving his agentic (power) striving free to ravage his relationships with the world around him.

In contrast, McAdams describes "Sara," a Catholic nun, who epitomized the imago of *lover*:

The lover imago has its roots in Sara's relationship with her grandmother before the age of nine. Never very close to her parents ... Sara considered her grandmother her first heroine.... After joining the religious order, Sara joined her faith and her passion to become, in the eyes of others as well as her own, the "earthy one"—the nun steeped in the world and people rather than abstractions and the dogma of the church. Sara described many very close friendships in unabashedly passionate terms and states that these serve as the greatest source of satisfaction in her life.... Sara's dream for the distant future is to set up a religious community in Wyoming where people can live in peace with each other and with God. She speaks of ministering to others ... enabling people to grow and be who they are. (McAdams, 1984, p. 170)

In addition to illustrating agentic (power motivation) and communion-like (love motivation) themes in people's lives, the imagoes of Tom and Sara are useful in another sense. They reflect what I consider to be one of the more important individual differences in the cognitive aspect of motivation: an orientation to the external world of "objective" reality, as opposed to the internal world of subjective experience. In Tom's case, his conception of both himself and life takes the form of a world of externals, of behaviours and action. In contrast, Sara's world is more concerned with interiors—the establishing of contact with the subjective experiences of others through fostering personal growth. Thus, individual differences in the degree to which one orients either to the external world of behaviours or to the internal world of experience, underlie the cognitive composition of one's self-concept, as well as influencing the nature of one's goals. Or, to put it another way, it is possible that those who orient themselves to the external world are likely to develop conceptions of their life-goals in terms of behaviours and actions, while those who focus on interiors may conceptualize their goals in terms of subjective experiences. For convenience, I shall refer to these two cognitive orientations as *extraceptive* and *intraceptive*, respectively.

These two terms are derived from Murray's (1938) analysis of the Jungian conception of *extraversion–introversion*. As you may recollect from a previous discussion (Chapter 3), modern research on extraversion–introversion has tended to focus on the "social extraversion" aspect of Jung's concept, shifting away from his more central distinction between external and internal orientations—what Caine *et al.* (1981) call the *"direction-of-interest"* component. The fragmentation of Jung's concept is due, in large part, to the rambling nature of his writing, something recognized by Murray in his effort to identify the core meaning of extraversion–introversion. Murray (1938) extracted a number of dimensions from Jung's writings, one of the more important of which was *extraception–intraception*. According to Levinson *et al.* (1966), however, even this attempt at clarifying Jung's ideas left a conceptual muddle, riddled with Murray's own biases—a situation that called for further pruning. Levinson *et al.*, therefore, proposed that *intraception* be seen as a disposition to emphasize and differentiate the psychological aspects of oneself and others. By "psychological aspects," they mean the "most personal qualities of human experience," one's feelings, wishes, private meanings and fantasies. Thus, the central aim of intraception is *to know oneself and others* in an elemental sense. In contrast, the *extraceptive* individual is less concerned with the psychological world than with such matters as physical appearance, social status, and behavioural characteristics.

One of the features of Levinson *et al.*'s description of intraception is that they see it as a relatively stable disposition which shows itself in a variety of modalities, including thought, feeling, and action. This is too broad a conception for my purposes here, I intend to limit my use of *extraception–intraception* to that of a cognitive dimension—one that is akin to M. Davis's (1983) perspective-taking or cognitive empathy. The latter, for instance, is defined as a spontaneous tendency to adopt the psychological perspective of other people, *i.e.* to *entertain* the point of view of others. In recent years, this distinction between an inner versus outer direction of interest has appeared in a number of guises, all of which underscore what I believe to be its fundamental importance. In support of this contention, I shall discuss its use in three areas: epistemological beliefs, attribution theory, and conceptions of moral behaviour.

Rychlak believes that one of the more important manifestations of extraception (extraspection) and intraception (introspection) lies in the contrasting epistemological beliefs that underlie psychological theory and practice:

> The perspective a theorist adopts is a function of his attitude toward the object of his study.... If a theorist takes an introspective attitude and perspective, his constructs will be formulated from the point of view of the *object of study*.... If the theorist takes an extraspective perspective ... he defines his abstractions from his vantage point as an observer, regardless of the point of view of the objective of study. (Rychlak, 1968, p. 27)

Or to put it another way, one kind of theorist acts as an *observer*, imposing his or her own conceptual structure on events, whereas the other acts more like a *participant*, seeking to establish conceptual contact with the other. The consequence of these different orientations in such matters as psychological therapy is that two broadly different kinds of therapy can be distinguished. The more extraceptive treatments, such as behaviour therapy, "are those which do not concern themselves with the personal meaning of the client's complaints but instead try to explain them in terms of a framework imposed by the therapist" (D. A. Winter, 1985, p. 130). On the other hand, intraceptive treatments, such as group psychotherapy, "do attempt to consider complaints within the client's own frame of reference, and generally put more emphasis on the client's autonomy and on the therapeutic relationship" (D. A. Winter, 1985, p. 130). It is interesting, in this regard, that some form of intuitive matching seems to occur in clinical settings between patients and therapies:

> [I]nner-directed [intraceptive] clients tended to present with interpersonal difficulties, which resulted in their being referred for group psychotherapy, whereas the outer-directed [extraceptive] tended to present much more focused, structured symptoms—such as phobias, obsessions, or somatic complaints—which they did not relate to other areas of their life and which resulted in their referral for behaviour therapy. Rather than being passive victims of some disease process, clients were therefore expressing their psychological distress in ways which reflected their [cognitive orientations]. (D. A. Winter, 1985, p. 131)

Not surprisingly, this kind of matching actually results in greater improvements for the client, compared to a mismatch condition (Caine et al., 1981; D. A. Winter, 1985).

Turning to attribution theory, in which attempts are made to model how individuals explain the causes of interpersonal behaviour, theorists commonly use some form of internal–external dimension, one that contrasts a focus on internal causes within the individual with one on external causes in the environment (Fiske & Taylor, 1984). This same difference in orientation is apparent in the person–situation debate in personality theory (Chapter 1). Fiske and Taylor (1984), however, suggest that there is little justification for the importance accorded the dimension since there are a number of conceptual problems with it. For instance, early attribution models assumed that the internal–external polarity operates in an hydraulic fashion, *i.e.*, the more one pole is exhibited, the less likely one is to see the other (M. Ross & Fletcher, 1985). The problem with this assertion is that correlations between perception of internal and perception of external causality, measured independently, typically are nonsignificant or show a weak negative relationship (Fletcher *et al.*, 1986). In attempting to account for this finding, Fletcher *et al.* suggest that causal attributions may be mediated by what they call "attributional complexity," a concept that closely resembles the "conceptual complexity" mentioned in Chapter 2. Less complex individuals may generate relatively simple causal attributions of either an internal or external kind, whereas more "complex people do not concentrate on external attributions to the exclusion of the internal determinants of behaviour, rather they are more complex at both ends of the internal–external dimension" (Fletcher *et al.*, 1986, p. 883). Be that as it may, the point of interest here is that the internal (intraceptive)–external (extraceptive) dimension continues to play a major role in causal explanations.

Finally, a controversy has arisen, in recent years, over the possibility of gender differences in moral reasoning. The debate has been stimulated by Gilligan's (1982) assertion that there are two different conceptions of morality, a *justice* orientation, on which Kohlberg's scheme is based, and a *caring* orientation, which, according to Gilligan, more clearly depicts female reasoning about moral dilemmas (M. Ford & Lowery, 1986). In Kohlberg's cognitive-developmental theory, the morality of justice, defined as the preservation of human rights and life, is considered to be the universal principle underlying all moral judgments. Gilligan, on the other hand, considers caring, defined as the preservation of fair and mutual relationships, to be a second, complementary principle (Lifton, 1985). Empirical support for gender differences along these lines is mixed. While Lifton (1985) and M. Ford and Lowery (1986) offer qualified support for Gilligan's position, Walker (1984) does not. However, for our purposes, the important point is that the *justice* orientation is couched in terms of an extraceptive perspective, whereas the *caring* orientation is intraceptive. That is to say, the justice orientation is one that imposes an abstract ethical principle on behaviour, a collection of rights and rules that form a picture of idealized moral behaviour. In contrast to this, caring emphasizes the maintenance of relationship and responsibility, in the pursuit of which one must, of necessity, engage the "subjectivity" of the other.

In sum, the extraception–intraception dimension is a useful way of drawing attention to individual differences in what might be called *"cognitive values,"* the preferred cognitive relationship one attempts to establish with others. The extraceptive orientation is one in which cognitive detachment is maintained. One acts as an observer, imposing one's own conceptual structure on the other. However, cognitive engagement typifies the intraceptive orientation in that some effort is made to establish contact with the phenomenal world of the other.

The Relationships Between Behavioural, Affective, and Cognitive Components of Objectivity–Subjectivity

In this chapter, I have presented some views on the way in which individual differences in conation can be depicted as an *objective–subjective* dimension, one that contrasts differing predilections toward power (objective) and love (subjective). At the objective pole, there is a preoccupation with agentic behaviour, the seeking of power and control not only over others but also over oneself. It might be reasonable to say that one achieves this power and control at some cost, for it may be possible to exert power only in the context of some degree of emotional and cognitive detachment from both the people and the world around one. By this, I do not mean that extremely objective individuals lack feeling, for such is not the case. They may have strong feelings attached to the goal of power, but their feelings do not include empathy for those around them nor do their images of power include the perspectives of those over whom they seek power. At the subjective pole, one sees communion—an orientation to life that emphasizes love, cooperation, and non-intrusive joining with others. The goal of strongly subjective individuals is to establish relatedness at all levels: behaviourally, emotionally, and cognitively. Thus one sees a moving toward others, the presence of empathy and satisfaction in making contact with others, as well as a meeting of minds at the cognitive level.

Evidence in support of this conception of objectivity–subjectivity is available but scattered and, in some cases, is circumstantial. Since my particular formulation draws together previously disparate areas of research, which usually do not recognize the existence of one another, it follows that there is little integrative research that attempts to explore the relationships between these diverse concepts. As one might expect, therefore, the most interesting evidence in support of these ideas is to be found in psychopathology and clinical anecdote. The co-occurrence of power, emotional detachment, and extraception is well-documented in such personality disorders as psychopathy (anti-social), narcissism, and hysteria, whereas love, empathy, and intraception are associated with such disorders as excessive dependence (Millon, 1981). Since I shall discuss these issues more fully in Chapter 5, perhaps we can leave further details until then. However, before closing, I would like to mention the on-going controversy about the proposed link between altruism (a behavioural component of subjectivity) and empathy (an affective component). This is one area that has received a great deal of experimental attention (Batson *et al.*, 1986, 1987; Cialdini *et al.*, 1987). At issue is the question whether altruism is always based on empathetic emotion, or whether there can be other more egotistic origins. To be brief, it appears that both empathic and egotistic motives can result in altruistic behaviour, depending on the individual and the circumstances. What this implies for my model of objectivity–subjectivity, of course, is that it should be seen as a prototypical dimension. The proposed links between components are typical relationships found in some (prototypical) kinds of individuals. Not everyone will show either objectivity or subjectivity as I have depicted them.

Chapter 5

Personality Types

IN THIS CHAPTER I describe the way in which the three generic dimensions interact to create different types of personality. Of necessity, this chapter will be more speculative than the previous ones. Although there is a great deal of information in support of the individual dimensions themselves, little information is available on the specific combinations proposed in my model. I begin by explaining how the generic dimensions combine to form (type structure) and to interact within (type dynamics) each personality prototype. Four main prototypes are described by means of detailed case studies, while a fifth, versatile type is offered as an example of that relatively rare individual who combines many of the qualities seen in the more specialized and limited types. I then turn to an evaluation of the conceptual and empirical evidence which, while limited, does allow me to build what I believe to be a plausible case for the model. The chapter closes with several illustrations of the way in which the typology can be used to understand differences in normal and abnormal behaviour.

A PSYCHODYNAMIC TYPOLOGY

The terms "dynamic psychology" and "psychodynamics" have often been used to refer to a kind of psychological theorizing that emphasizes the role of motives and drives in determining behaviour. In particular, the psychoanalytic (and analytic) schools of thought created by Freud and Jung are usually said to represent dynamic or psychodynamic theories. However, there is no reason why these latter views should monopolize the term, since "psychodynamics" can be used in the general sense of referring to the way in which personality structures interact with one another. Thus, *personality structure* deals with the more or less stable arrangement of the parts or components of personality, while *personality dynamics* have to do with the functions carried out by these parts (Lazarus, 1971).

Type Structure

Although a three-dimensional model allows one to define eight types, such a large number is cumbersome in practice. It would be convenient, therefore, if there was some way to simplify the description of types without losing essential information about them. Many typologists have been inclined to use two-trait combinations in identifying types (A. H. Buss, 1989). Thus, prior to his development of a psychoticism dimension, Eysenck used the Neuroticism and Extraversion dimensions to great effect (*cf.* Eysenck & Eysenck, 1985). In a similar vein, Wiggins (1980) advocates selecting and combining pairs of traits from his circumplex for particular research purposes. Millon (1986b,c) takes this a step further by using a two-stage process in which he combines two of his dimensions to produce "preliminary" types and completes the picture by adding a third dimension. It seems, therefore, that typologists are inclined to seek simplicity by juxtaposing a few dimensions in search of formulations that suit their purposes or predilections. In following this honourable tradition, I use two of the three genotypic dimensions to delineate four "main" types, within each of which two subtypes are recognized using the remaining dimension. I justify this decision on the basis of mnemonic convenience and also in light of research on scientific and intellectual types. As mentioned earlier, my interest in typologies arose, in large part, from a desire to understand the behaviour of scientists and other professionals with whom I have had contact in my daily life and work. Other typologists with similar interests have tended to emphasize the cognitive and conative aspects of professional behaviour (Cotgrove, 1982; Mitroff & Kilmann, 1978). The work of Cotgrove is particularly intriguing and I have sought to extend and elaborate his insights about intellectual types in the present work. It follows that the "main" types in my model are defined in terms of the *analytic–holistic* and *objective–subjective* dimensions, while *emotional stability–instability* is used to recognize stable and unstable variants within each of the main types (Fig. 14). Details of each type will be discussed shortly.

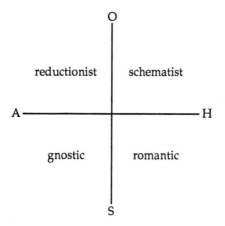

Figure 14. The four main types: A = analytic, H = holistic, O = objective, S = subjective. (From A. Miller, 1988.)

Type Dynamics

As outlined in Chapter 4, the central dynamic underlying my personality model is that of a conflict between two innate, ubiquitous core tendencies commonly referred to as "agency" and "communion." The primary motivational task for each of us, therefore, is to achieve some balance between these conflicting forces, a task that is mediated by the cognitive and emotional styles that we adopt. Or to put it another way, I assume that the conflict between agency and communion (objectivity–subjectivity) is the driving force of personality, while cognitive (analytic–holistic) and emotional (stable–unstable) styles act as mediators in shaping and channelling the individual's characteristic resolution. While some fortunate souls may achieve a working compromise between the two conflicting drives, thereby maintaining a judicious balance in their lives, the implication of my typology is that, for some people, the only solution is to "specialize." One drive is emphasized, the other denied. The conflict model of personality assumes, therefore, that much of life is a struggle to maintain one's existential compromise, to arrange one's daily round in such a way as to protect the fragile truce between competing tendencies. Any threat to this compromise must be deflected so as to allow one to maintain an intact self-concept. How this takes place is a matter to which we now turn. In what follows, I shall draw heavily on Goleman's (1985) views on psychodynamics.

When an event is appraised as a threat to the self-concept, habitual coping mechanisms are triggered. One view of the processes involved suggests that primary appraisal (orienting response) is rapid, holistic, and automatic, resulting in an initial estimation of the level of threat. If further attention is warranted, a more analytic secondary appraisal (threat appraisal) is brought to bear which, in turn, may result in the generation of feelings of stress/fear and a physiological preparedness for action. While theorists differ over the relative importance of primary and secondary appraisal (Chapter 3), the important point is that all "events" in one's daily life are continuously appraised for their "threat-value." Since much of this appraisal is automatic, we simply do not notice that we are engaged in such an activity. If, however, stress/fear reaches uncomfortable levels, coping mechanisms are activated. These include acting on the situation in an attempt to remove the threat (instrumental coping) or acting on one's feelings to calm them (emotional coping). Although both forms of coping are used by most individuals (Folkman, 1984; Folkman & Lazarus, 1985), I intend to focus on the latter. The reason for this is simple enough. Given the difficulties involved in identifying the sources of one's fears and the practical problems involved in instrumental coping, we tend to fall back on emotional coping to save the day. Indeed, many personality theorists argue that the particular form taken by one's emotional (or *"defensive,"* as I prefer to call it) coping plays a major role in shaping personality (Becker, 1973).

Defensive coping. The essence of defensive coping is *avoidance,* a highly selective interaction with oneself and others, aimed at avoiding threat to one's self-concept. The human predilection to avoid "unpleasantness" is aided and abetted by the mechanics of the mind itself (Goleman, 1985). Given the limited channel capacity of working memory (conscious awareness), the effectiveness of our daily functioning depends on our ability to process much of what happens to us outside of our awareness. Without this capability of selective attention, we would become overloaded and immobilized. Selective attention, of course, also provides us with the opportunity to avoid whatever upsets us, a useful coping strategy provided one does not take it too far.

As mentioned in Chapter 2, there is some consensus in psychology that incoming information is screened for meaning at an early stage by a set of filters stored in long-term memory. Only selected aspects of this information finds its way into awareness (*i.e.,* is attended to). By far the major portion of incoming information either decays and is lost, or is processed outside of awareness by automatic or unconscious processes. In other words, parallel conscious and unconscious processing occurs. Evidence for parallel processing comes, for example, from research on subliminal perception and perceptual defence. Kihlstrom (1984) is confident about the quality of this research, noting that "despite shortcomings in the early demonstration of these effects, the case for them seems now to have been made" (p. 164). Thus, it is convenient to think of memory in terms of zones of activation in which conceptual nodes may be highly activated (conscious), partially activated (preconscious), and relatively inactive (unconscious).

It follows that the screening process which controls selective attention is extremely important. Conceptualization of what might be involved has always troubled psychologists for it implies an homunculus, a mind within a mind. However, current opinion is that one can account for selective attention in terms of the controlling effect of salient concepts (or "schema" as Goleman calls them) in long-term memory (Bargh, 1984; Srull & Wyer, 1986; Zukier, 1986), the most important of which coalesce into what we refer to as the self-concept (Goleman, 1985).

Needless to say, emotion plays an important role in screening, since all concepts (schema) are, to a greater or lesser extent, emotionally charged (M. Hoffman, 1986). Attempts to depict this state of affairs can be seen in network models of memory (Blaney, 1986; Bower, 1981), especially those employed in central template theories of emotion (Chapter 3). In these theories, emotional nodes are depicted as being part of the conceptual network and are triggered when a particular concept node is activated. Goleman (1985) suggests that conceptual nodes associated with intense negative emotion (*e.g.*, fear) are unlikely to be retrieved as easily as those associated with positive emotion. In other words, negatively valenced memories are less likely than positively valenced ones to be brought into awareness. Clearly, this could provide a basis for understanding defensive coping, a contention for which there is considerable support. Research on perceptual defence, for instance, suggests that, while events having the potential to upset us are not attended to, they are nevertheless processed unconsciously (Kihlstrom, 1984). Similarly, Isen has demonstrated the "asymmetry" between the recall of positively and negatively valenced memories (Isen, 1984; Isen *et al.*, 1987). That is, while positive memories are easily recalled, stimuli that should elicit negative memories do not always succeed in doing so. Isen explains the latter effect in terms of our preference for maintaining a good mood whenever possible. Some psychologists call this the "Pollyanna Principle" (Matlin, 1983). One exception, though, is to be found among the chronically depressed who seem unable to avoid negative evaluations of themselves and their world (Isen, 1984; Turk & Salovey, 1985). Interestingly, current opinion on the nature of the depressed is beginning to shift toward a sense that their cognitions, rather than being askew, are, in fact, more veridical than those of the so-called "normal" person (Smail, 1984).

Defensive coping is depicted in this psychodynamic model, therefore, as a form of selective inattention, the traditional "defence mechanisms" differing only in the degree of inattention involved. Thus, in repression and denial, attention is diverted from whole events, whereas emotional isolation allows the recall of the cognitive but not the emotional component of a distressing event. Similarly, in projection and reaction formation, attention is diverted from the fact that one is misconstruing the behaviour of oneself, and others (Goleman, 1985).

Finally, we need to look at the role of the three generic dimensions in this psychodynamic model. Clearly, all three may be construed as components of the schema that screen information for meaning and threat-value. Their specific roles can be clarified by using Kihlstrom's (1984) distinction between procedural and declarative knowledge. Conative predilections toward either objectivity or subjectivity play an important part in influencing *what* is attended to, thereby determining the substantive content of declarative memory. On the other hand, *analytic–holistic* skills can be seen as a major procedural element in these same schema, thereby determining *how* declarative information is processed. In turn, the characteristic level of *emotionality* experienced by a person determines the intensity of the emotional nodes in a conceptual network. I assume that the more unstable (emotionally intense) an individual is, the more likely it is that he or she will experience fear and, therefore, initiate defensive coping.

Although this psychodynamic model indicates how the three generic dimensions might interact with one another in a general way, it tells us nothing about the specific interactions within different personality types. To explore this matter further we need to look more closely at the types proposed in my model.

Type Descriptions

In this section I outline the way in which the three generic dimensions interact within each type and illustrate these interactions by means of a case study.

The objective–analytic type (OA). The *objective* aspect of this type is reflected in the adoption of a tough-minded orientation to life in which the central concern is the achievement of a sense of *agency*, a sense of control over oneself and one's immediate environment. This goal may be pursued by seeking power over others, or by resisting the attempts by others to exert power over oneself. In either case, the attainment of power is facilitated by establishing a degree of control over one's emotional and cognitive interactions with other people. Typically, the OA type achieves this by a process of distancing. Thus, emotional control is attained by maintaining *emotional detachment*, the advantage of which is that limited emotional involvement reduces the likelihood that one will be bothered by the vagaries of one's own emotions or by emotional pressure exerted by others. Similarly, cognitive control is sought through an *extraceptive* stance. The potential confusion engendered by taking another person's viewpoint into account is thereby avoided, as are the upsetting consequences of introspection, the exploration of one's subjective world. An illusion of control is sustained, therefore, by focusing on the exterior world of objective certainty, the world of outward appearance and physical reality. As a consequence, a mechanistic world view is developed in which simple cause–effect relationships are sought as a means of understanding and control.

The *analytic* component of the OA type can be viewed as a strategy for achieving objective ends. If one holds a mechanistic view of life, in which both people and things are subject to simple rules of physical causality, then one way to ensure the control of events is to pay painstaking attention to the minutiae of external experience. This goal is facilitated by an analytical style in which factual detail is sought in a relatively circumscribed field. Thus, "objective" facts are thought to provide the key to understanding and control, whereas intuitions and impressions are not.

When these emotional and cognitive control strategies show signs of failing, and the emotional/subjective world begins to intrude, then defensive coping is brought to bear. Typically, the OA type would be inclined toward the use of articulated defences, after the fashion of a surgeon's scalpel, carefully separating unruly emotions from thoughts, so that disturbing events are made emotionally bland, while remaining cognitively amenable. Characteristic forms of defence are, therefore, emotional isolation, intellectualization, and rationalization. I assume that the more *emotionally unstable* the individual, the more he or she would find recourse to defensive coping in everyday life. Thus, the emotionally unstable variant of this type, in contrast to the more stable subtype, would be more driven toward compulsive behaviour, less able to break away from the excesses of analytical and objective tendencies. In sum, the OA type is empirical, reductionist, impersonal, and obsessive. It follows that members of this category might be labelled *"reductionists,"* a prototypical example being the analytical scientist, one who seeks understanding and control through the collection of "objective data" in a narrowly defined segment of the external, physical world. A case in point is Dr. Rita Levi-Montalcini who was awarded the Nobel Prize in medicine in 1986 for her discovery of the role of the Nerve Growth Factor in the differentiation of the nervous system.

In her autobiography (Levi-Montalcini, 1988), she describes her early life in an upper-middle class Jewish family in prewar Italy, a period that saw the rise of fascism and anti-semitism. Despite the perilous position of her family during these turbulent times, however, she seems to have led a curiously detached life. Even when her family was in hiding from the Nazis, she continued her research in a makeshift laboratory—her convent cell, as she called it. The latter phrase is significant, of course, for there was an almost religious zeal about her attitude to research. Indeed, much of her life seems to have involved resisting the power of others, by detaching herself socially and emotionally, thereby freeing herself to explore the intricacies of the mammalion nervous system. Her success, she claims, can be attributed to her single-minded pursuit of her chosen path with a remarkable tenacity in the face of daunting odds. One might say that she was obsessed with her research to the exclusion of all else.

Rita Levi-Montalcini's capacity to encapsulate herself both socially and emotionally began early. As a child, she had a natural reluctance to make physical contact with others, turning away from her father's kiss and her nanny's rough hands. Even at this early age, her inclination was to seek solitude, fleeing contact with other children and adults, with the result that she never made friends during her school days. This pattern of social isolation continued throughout college, where her peers found her rather like, as one put it, a squid ready to squirt ink at anyone who approached. A few young men tried to broach this self-imposed barrier but were either spurned or kept at a comfortable distance, her friendships, such as they were, remaining at an intellectual and platonic level throughout her life. Later, during her lengthy stay in the United States, she spared little time for recreation; an occasional trip on a river boat, during which she would maintain a discrete distance from the other passengers, or a discussion with friends, seemed to have satisfied her need for social contact. Thus, the picture she draws of her life is one that appears to have been devoid of emotional intimacy, with the possible exception of her twin sister and mother. Even in these cases, however, contact remained unspoken and restrained. Rita Levi-Montalcini's capacity for detachment is further exemplified by her apparent willingness to tolerate the dissection of rotting corpses during her medical training and by her interest in research on foetal brains. The latter appears to have produced few qualms, even though the sight of dead foetuses, which were delivered to her wrapped in newspaper, may have given some personality types reason for pause. Similarly, during medical school, lunch often was taken on the roof of the anatomy building where human bones, not yet free of rotting flesh, were spread out to bleach in the sun. However, human beings are never quite without contradiction. At a later point in her life, Rita Levi-Montalcini found it difficult to help refugees in war-torn Italy because she became too involved with her patients. What this implies, of course, is that her emotional detachment must have been a carefully crafted facade, one that helped her maintain the emotional serenity conducive to a life of intellectual endeavour.

Rita Levi-Montalcini's *extraceptive* orientation is evident in her choice of career, as well as in her extraordinary claim that her success in life was due, in large part, to being free of "emotional complexes" and the guilt that often accompanies them. In other words, she was not plagued by emotional conflict. I suspect that this equanimity could only be achieved by an unwillingness to introspect, a personal disinclination that may have helped her to accept her solitary existence in the belief that she was "carrying out one's assigned task in life." Indeed, her discussion of the ideal life, one that combines what Freud would call Love and Work, and her decision to pursue a life of imperfection through work, lacks any sense that she was deeply troubled by her choice.

Her analytic intellect may have had its origins in her father's heretical, freethinking attitudes, something he freely encouraged in his children. As a child, however, Rita Levi-Montalcini was not obviously gifted. There was a long period before medical school during which she drifted aimlessly, due, it seems, to the uncertain position of intellectually inclined young women in a conservative society. One possibility was for her to study philosophy, but she appears to have doubted her power of logical thought, by which I understand her to mean that she felt deficient in the rational, abstract capabilities so necessary in that discipline. At the same time, her early attempts to conduct empirical research, as a research assistant under a famous professor, were disastrous—she had no obvious empirical skills. She also envied the intuitive insight of her co-recipient of the Nobel Prize, something that she believed herself to be without. If one bears in mind that her account of her intellectual capabilities is suitably understated, one wonders what did lead to her scientific eminence. Her own account suggests that it has something to do with the sustained intensity of empirical observation and her capacity, on whatever psychological ability this may have been based, to understand the significance of one crucial series of observations.

As for her level of emotionality, she describes herself as a timid, fearful child, with a natural inclination to avoid other people. On the other hand, she was able later to tolerate the rigours of medical training without undue distress, although her dealings with real, live patients appear to have created some strain. However, her own comments on the detachment she achieved during the war years reveal a great deal about her emotional state. She accounts for this detachment as a form of defence against the unpleasantness of everyday events, a "desperate ... desire of human beings to ignore what is happening in situations where full awareness might lead one to self destruction" (p. 94). I conclude that she has a relatively emotional (unstable) temperament which was kept under control by the use of emotional isolation and intellectualization. This suggests that Rita Levi-Montalcini is a prototypical example of the unstable variant of the objective–analytic or *reductionist* type.

The objective-holistic type (OH). The OH and OA types share the same objective, impersonal manipulative orientation, but power/control is achieved using different strategies. Rather than an attempt to understand and control reality by seeking detailed, factual information (as one finds in the OA type), the illusion of control is achieved by the development of schemes, theories, systems of thought and/or fantasies, all of which serve to organize and control "reality." In contrast to the OA type who seeks to document reality, therefore, the OH type may seek to impose a system of order onto it or to force the surrounding environment to comply with and fit into his or her model of how things should be. When the mismatch between fantasy and reality becomes too great and the OH type's conceptual schemes are threatened, defences of a global nature, such as denial and repression, are used to suppress this unpleasant truth. As with the OA type, I would suggest that the more emotionally unstable the individual, the more he or she would have recourse to such defensive strategies and the less able they would be to adopt alternative approaches to life. Hence the apparent aversion to, and flight from, reality of the histrionic personality—a typically unstable OH type.

Prototypical examples of this *schematist* category, therefore, are the intellectual model builders, rationalists and philosophers who weave speculative tales about physical reality. A case in point is the philosopher–novelist Ayn Rand, famous for her philosophical system of "objectivism," a homage to the power of will, striving, and personal accomplishment. Yet, in her private life, Ayn Rand was, apparently, either incapable of, or unwilling to engage in, introspection with the result that she understood little of her own behaviour and its effects on others. Nor was she sensitive to the emotional states of others, unless these were brought to her attention forcibly (Branden, 1986).

Ayn Rand was born in pre-revolutionary Russia and grew up during the years of upheaval that preceded and followed the communist revolution, an experience that had a great impact on her adult personality. For instance, she is described by Branden (1986) as being fundamentally alienated from, and frightened of, nature and the physical world. Perhaps to compensate for this, she was enamoured of the world of technology, presumably because the latter offered the promise of control over the ravages of nature. I suspect that this pattern of feelings can be traced back to her harrowing experience of dislocation, starvation, and disease in her early years. Secondly, her life appears to have been dedicated to the primacy of reason in all things, with reason and intelligence as absolute goods. Her philosophical position lauds reason and its products, seeing "man as an heroic being, with his own happiness as *the* moral purpose of his life, with productive achievement as his noblest activity and reason his only absolute" (Branden, 1986, p. 52). While this preoccupation with reason may have stemmed, in part, from her father's influence, her philosophical position, or fantasy, could also be interpreted as an expression of her intense need for control—with the advocacy of rationality rather than empiricism as a means of achieving it. It is as if the frightened child, starving in the wastes of Russia had decided that she could overcome all problems by using her formidable intelligence. Hence her early fascination with heroic tales and a lifelong predilection for sunny, optimistic stories that ended with the inevitable triumph of the hero in the face of insurmountable odds. This fantasy world, one that served her personal needs, became the basis for her philosophical writing.

It follows from her philosophical position that Ayn Rand would value power in its various manifestations, as well as the tough-minded masculine attitudes that are associated with powerful behaviour. Indeed, she was openly contemptuous of the more tender, "feminine," qualities such as dependence, empathy, and altruism. These attitudes developed early in her life for she was a bright but *emotionally detached* child who made other children uncomfortable with her searching and insensitive questions. Matters seem not to have improved as she grew older. For example, on emigrating to the United States, she stayed temporarily with some relatives in Chicago who found her impossible to live with. She was, it seems, indifferent to the needs of others, her own need to write taking precedence over the daily household routine, despite the inconvenience this caused to others. Similarly, she was unable to understand the emotional bonds between people since, in her eyes, the only basis on which to judge someone was their intellectual quality. As a result, she bruised the sensibilities of others unintentionally and thoughtlessly. Needless to say, this inability to empathize, and her belief that relationships should be based solely on intellectual values and "philosophical mutuality," wrought a great deal of havoc in her personal life.

In describing Ayn Rand's *extraceptive* orientation, Branden comments: "There is something I never saw in Ayn Rand's eyes. They never held an inward look—a look of turning inside to learn one's own spirit and consciousness. They gazed only and always outwards" (Branden, 1986, p. xi). In other words, Ayn Rand avoided introspection and the disturbing knowledge that this might have engendered. In addition, she spent little time trying to make contact with the subjective world of others, simply dismissing those who did not agree with her as if she knew everything about them that was important and there was no further need to explore their thoughts. Despite her splendid intellect, therefore, she lacked not only self-insight but also missed the nuances in other people's behaviour; too intent was she on imposing her reality on others to pause for a moment to listen either to her inner self or to the concerns of others (Branden, 1986).

As a child, Ayn Rand was encouraged to develop and to display her intellectual skills. The school subjects of greatest interest to her were mathematics and logic, both highly rational, non-empirical endeavours. At the same time, her private world was filled with heroic fantasy and story writing. Both sets of qualities, the intense, rational intelligence and the predilection for fantasy imply an underlying *holistic* thinking style. This appears to have been put to good effect for, by the age of eighteen, she had already developed the essentials of her objectivist philosophy using what she would later call the unsentimental methods of the mathematician. Branden suggests that she was pre-eminently a rationalist and moralist, something one would expect of an objective–holistic intellectual.

Ayn Rand was without question an intensely emotional woman but one who professed "objectivity" and sought to focus her life, and that of other people, on the rational world. Indeed, she claimed to have total control over her emotions and was openly contemptuous of those who were not so blessed, admonishing them for what she saw as their willful disobedience of her instructions. Much of this control was illusory, however. For example, so intensely committed to her ideas was she that any heresy or faltering among her followers resulted in their being purged, literally becoming non-persons. This lack of self-insight seems to have been coupled with an inclination to repress those of her qualities that were inconsistent with "objectivism." Branden suggests that emotional repression was a continuing feature of her life, linked presumably to her need to control the more unpredictable aspects of herself and the natural world. However, her insistence on the primacy of intellectual values and the importance of emotional control proved difficult to sustain in the long run. At the height of her fame and influence, the breakdown of an affair with one of her disciples unleashed such uncontrollable fury that it tore apart the very intellectual network of friends and followers that she had taken so long to cultivate. In sum, therefore, Ayn Rand might be typified as an unstable variant of the objective–holistic, *schematist* type.

The subjective–holistic type (SH). The *subjective* aspect of this type is reflected in a primary concern with establishing *communion* through intimate, nurturing relationships with other people and with the surrounding environment. Given this urge to blend and to join, and the implication that the self of the SH type is relatively "permeable," there is less concern with protecting the self from the influence of others. Indeed, SH types seek to establish a sense of self by joining with others in what the more objective types derisively refer to as "dependent" relationships. Regardless of how one might label this behaviour, it does seem that SH types, rather than seeking power over others, strive to *empower* others through nurturing behaviour. This is facilitated by a well-developed cognitive and emotional empathy, which implies a main interest in subjective experience, be that of one's own inner reality or the inner, psychological world of others. Feelings and personal impressions are given priority over the details of "objective reality."

When subjectivity is coupled with an *holistic* style, then one finds a lack of interest in the analysis of personal experience, and a concomitant preference for *experiencing* subjective reality intuitively or globally. It is possible that SH types view analysis as another form of separation, an alienating experience that they prefer to avoid. As a result, *introspection* (in the sense of analysis of subjective experience) is kept to a minimum, although *intraception* remains a major value orientation. The absence of analysis and the lack of concern about emotional control results in personal reactions intruding into thought, making the latter evaluative, emotionally tinged, and intensely subjective. Thus, the *romantic* lives in an impressionistic, often imaginative, world of personal anecdote and unanalysed subjective experience.

Given this interest in communion and the dislike of separation, it follows that the primary fear for the SH type would be separation anxiety which, in adults, would be generated by an inability to establish intimate contact with others, especially loved ones. The defensive reaction to separation anxiety, and the unwarranted intrusion of the impersonal objective world, would be massive repression and denial, the use of unarticulated defences so characteristic of all *holistic* types. It follows that the *emotionally unstable* subtype, who reacts to the loss, or threatened loss, of intimacy with fearful intensity, would be more prone to the use of defences in an attempt to control mounting feelings of panic.

Rather than using an eminent person as the prototype for this quadrant, I would prefer instead to select one of the legion of women who, as wives and mothers, fill what developmental psychologists call the *expressive role* in family dynamics. They toil to create an atmosphere of emotional warmth, providing emotional support and endeavouring to foster a capacity for intimacy in their children and, often, their husbands.

A case in point is that of Laura who laboured for seventeen years to sustain her marriage to a husband whom she, and others, depict as ambitious, controlling and, at times, violent.[1]

---

[1] Laura is not the real name of the woman in this case. I've changed such details so as to protect the privacy of those involved.

Laura was raised in a family of five girls in those rather bland years immediately following World War II. As the daughter of a self-made, ambitious physician, she experienced a privileged but strict Catholic upbringing. Family life revolved around the demands of her father's career, but this influence on the family was balanced by a patient, nurturing wife who managed to cater to her husband's needs, while at the same time providing the emotional support needed by her daughters.

Thus, at an early age, Laura was exposed to a form of family dynamic and sex-role modelling that she was to emulate in later life. There was no reason for her to think otherwise since her experience of family life was a happy one in which she learned to defer to the family's dominant but kindly male and to model herself on her beloved nurturing mother. A cloistered education in Catholic schools reinforced the virtues of womanly obedience and service, so that she grew up with the unexceptional idea that what she wanted most of all in life was to be a wife and mother, to love and to nurture someone who would love her in return and provide her with a life filled with as little strife as possible. Nothing in her sheltered upbringing, however, prepared her for the rude awakening of married life.

During her training as a nurse, she met and was swept away by an ambitious, intelligent, and handsome law student. Never confident about her attractiveness, she was overwhelmed by her good fortune in attracting someone who appeared to meet her own and her parents' criteria for an ideal beau. As the possibility of marriage drew closer, Laura appeared to ignore aspects of the young man's behaviour that her friends considered to be quite objectionable. She believed, it seems, like so many women, that she would be able to change him with love by becoming a gentle teacher. Yet, her account of their marriage is that of an almost classical confrontation between an empathetic woman and an emotionally distant man.

Laura was, according to those around her, an affectionate girl, quick to become immersed in the trials and tribulations of her friends, sympathetic and understanding in her work as a nurse, and a gentle caring neighbour. However, she was faced with a husband who was, on his own admission, obsessed with neatness and discipline. Life in Laura's household, therefore, was organized according to her husband's wishes, with an almost military precison and a preoccupation with cleanliness and order. Violence towards here began, he recollects, when she finally tried to assert herself, his response being to hit her with such force as to shatter her eardrum.

Although their marriage was not without its moments of happiness, the couple appeared to have had great difficulty in sustaining cognitive and emotional intimacy. The marriage lasted as long as it did, Laura maintains, because of, amongst other things, her beliefs about the subservient role of women in marriage. In addition, her *intraceptive* nature meant that she always tried to understand and to accommodate her husband's point of view. As a result, she was inclined to conclude that the problems they were experiencing were due to her own shortcomings and inadequacies. She prayed that she might understand her husband better so that she might please him.

This self-effacing behaviour was facilitated by her *holistic* style and the tendency to *deny* unpleasantness. Until the marriage drew to a close, both tendencies limited any "realistic" appraisal of her situation. Yet, the signs of potential problems were there if she had been willing to see them. The fact that her husband ground a piece of wedding cake into her face at their wedding reception should have given her reason for apprehension. Later, watching a film of the incident, she comments sadly, "I know now, it's a sign of power and control." At the time, however, it appears that such thoughts were repressed, as they were in similar incidents that followed. As long as there was reconciliation, there was hope. Eventually, however, after many false starts, she could no longer tolerate the situation and filed for divorce.

In many ways, Laura's story is a morality play revolving around the incompatibility of different personality types. As we shall see later, the SH (Laura) and OA (her husband?) types have great difficulty in establishing communication because of their radically different values and styles. Such a marriage, therefore, may have been doomed from the start.

The subjective–analytic type (SA). The SA type shares with the preceding SH type a primary concern with establishing *communion*, a focus on subjective experience and a lack of interest in, or distaste for, the objectified, impersonal world. The difference between the two types lies, however, in the strategy used to achieve communion and in their level of tolerance of separation anxiety.

Thus, the adoption of an *analytical* style by the SA type appears to presume that contact with others is best achieved through understanding and knowledge. It is as if the subjective-holist emphasizes emotional empathy while the subjective-analyst emphasizes cognitive empathy.

It follows that the SA type engages in the analysis of personal experience, a psychologically minded search for the source of one's inner life and that of others. As a consequence, there is a tendency to withdraw into a reflective, narrowly preoccupied world of introspective thought at the expense of engagement in the broader reality.

Since analysis has the effect of distancing oneself from the thing being analysed, I would presume that the SA type has a greater tolerance of separation anxiety than one would find in the SH type, although such tolerance would be much less than that found in objective individuals. Where intimacy is frustrated and objective reality intrudes into the introspective landscape of the mind, the SA type has a particular problem.

Of all four types, the SA person has the greatest difficulty in summoning effective defensive coping. Their commitment to communion, with its implication for the integration of parts of the self into an homogeneous unit, mitigates against the deployment of articulated defences, while their inclination to introspective analysis prevents the use of global defences. Thus, the SA type has difficulty in protecting himself or herself from what Smail (1984) calls the horrors of psychological honesty. As one might expect, it is the *emotionally unstable* variant of this type who would experience these horrors to their fullest intensity. It is no coincidence, therefore, that Sylvia Plath, the prototypical example used to illustrate the SA type, committed suicide at an early age (Plath, 1982; Wagner-Martin, 1987).

As a student, in high school and college, Sylvia Plath was exuberant, overpowering and extremely competitive, altogether too overwhelming a companion for her peers, especially young men. They found her too intelligent, too apparently self-assured, too challenging. Much of this behaviour seems to have been a facade, however, a ploy to cover up an inner core riddled with self-doubt and cursed with an intense fear of abandonment (Wagner-Martin, 1987). In part, these anxieties may have stemmed from the early loss of security following her father's death and the uncertainty of life with an ailing mother.

Thus, a consistent theme in her life (one that she never satisfactorily resolved) was the need to be taken care of, to find someone who could provide the intimacy and security she so desired. In terms of the concepts discussed in Chapter 4, she had a high need for succorance. Any signs of abandonment by those close to her resulted in an intense, often vicious, negative reaction. During her college years, her twofold strategy for gaining acceptance from those around her was to achieve academically and to seek dates with young men. Despite these efforts, however, she never seemed to overcome the intense loneliness that plagued her. This is typical of the *gnostic* type, who is too mercilessly self-critical, too psychologically astute, to be comfortable with the inanities of traditional social intercourse.

In marrying Ted Hughes, an English poet, she seems to have believed that here was someone with whom she could establish the intimacy she sought, someone who also had the vitality and forcefulness necessary to protect her. Unfortunately, however, marriage proved to be intellectually stifling, while her anxieties over money and the future refused to abate.

Sylvia Plath was an *empathetic* woman, who reacted painfully to troubled friends. Indeed, she believed herself to be psychic, so sensitive was she to the emotions and thoughts of others. On one occasion, she broke out in an unsightly rash at the precise moment that the notorious spies, the Rosenbergs, were being executed. A friend with her at the time was shocked to see the rash enlarging and spreading before her very eyes. Her *intraceptive* nature was also evident in her willingness to talk about her innermost thoughts and feelings, including those surrounding her first suicide attempt. This was brought on by her perception of herself as having failed as a guest editor for a well-known national magazine (*Mademoiselle*), a prestigious appointment offered only to outstanding undergraduates from across the country. This supposed failure, made worse by her tendency to excessive self-criticism and doubt, struck at the core of her being, her capacity to write, with the result that she slid into depression and an attempted suicide.

As a child of intellectually minded parents, Sylvia Plath's abundant energy and curiosity were channelled toward literature and scholarly pursuits. She is described by her teachers as skilled at selecting and correlating details, as well as having a remarkable capacity to "understand" literature, *i.e.*, to get to the root of things. After she developed the habit of keeping a journal of her thoughts, she spent a great deal of time scrupulously *analysing* everything in it. However, her ever-present self-criticism appears to have kept her from recognizing these skills. As Wagner-Martin (1987) notes, it was only later that she came to realize that "her kind of intellect—the penetrating and seemingly unsystematic insight of the poet—was as valuable as the more scientific ability" (p. 83). Even this recognition provided little solace for she also worried about the "depersonalizing" effect of analysis. To analyse one's own feelings one had to, in a sense, disengage from them. Similarly, using one's relationships with others as a source of material for writing could be a form of exploitation, she thought, adding further to the load of worry that bore down on her.

Needless to say, Sylvia Plath was an extremely emotional woman, exuberant and lively as a child, prone to worry and depression as a adult. Sleeping pills were a constant companion. Described as "difficult" in her relationships, her reaction to events was, at times, extreme. For instance, her first reaction to her "failure" at *Mademoiselle* was to throw some recently acquired and very expensive clothes out of her office window. Similarly, her attempts to work as a lecturer at Smith College, her alma mater, proved too draining. Plagued by self-doubts, an inability to discipline wayward students, indecisiveness, and a host of other worries, she became physically exhausted.

Thus, one has the picture of a sensitive, introspective young woman seeking, but not finding, the intimacy and security that she hoped might come from others. Constantly troubled by self-doubts and fears of abandonment, she became exhausted by a burden of worry that she was unable to support. Marriage and children seemed only to have increased the demands on her dwindling energies until, finally, she was unable to continue. She gassed herself at the age of thirty-one.

Versatile types. The present typology allows us to recognize what might be called *versatile* types, individuals who have achieved some harmonious balance between the conflicting core tendencies, who are neither emotionally stable nor unstable, and who are capable of employing both analytic and holistic styles where appropriate. I suspect that such monsters of psychic efficiency (as Hudson, 1968, wryly puts it) are few and far between. However, some fortunate souls appear to achieve a rough approximation of this happy state, a noteworthy example being that of Rachel Carson, the eminent natural historian. In what follows, I draw heavily on Briggs (1987) and Gartner (1983).

Born the youngest of three children in 1907 and raised in a splendidly rustic setting in Pennsylvania, Rachel Carson developed an early and abiding love of the natural world. Given to isolated play, she was happiest, both as a child and as an adult, in the woods and fields, indulging her endless fascination with all things living. Bird-watching during the spring migrations was her greatest pleasure, followed, perhaps, by her passion for cats, her closest nonhuman friends. Her closest human friend undoubtedly was her mother, an influential figure in her life, fostering not only a reverence for life, but a broad artistic sensibility and the ambition to write. The latter led her to the Pennsylvania College for Women and a brief foray as an English major before settling down into biology, much to the consternation of those around her who saw little future for a woman in science. Rachel, however, was sufficiently prescient to realize that by studying biology she would be giving herself something to write about. As a dedicated, hard-working student she prospered, winning a fellowship to the famous Woods Hole Marine Laboratory and a scholarship to the Johns Hopkins University from whence she graduated with an M.Sc. in marine biology. Following several years as a teaching assistant, the death of her father brought on the responsibility of supporting her mother, and so she sought and obtained a position with the U.S. Bureau of Fisheries, where she worked for some time in relative obscurity as a science writer. All this began to change, however, as the result of her extracurricular nature writing. Beginning with articles, and then three books, she developed a national reputation as a gifted writer on the sea, with a rare capacity to engage both the feelings and the mind of the reader. During this period, she enjoyed widespread approval from both the scientific community and the reading public. Indeed, her literary success allowed her, in 1952, to resign her position with the Bureau and to devote herself full time to writing. However, this period of relative calm changed in 1958 when, through the trials and tribulations of a friend, she became interested in the effect of DDT on the environment. When her attempts to publish articles on the subject were rebuffed, she realized that she would have to write a book on pesticides. Four arduous years later, in 1962, she published *Silent Spring* and was thrust into a storm of controversy. Vilified by sectors of the chemical industries as an over-emotional female who wrote sloppy science, and championed by the emerging environmental lobby, she was subjected to the full brunt of public clamour. For a very private person, this must have been an exhausting experience, made more stressful by the knowledge that a tumour that had been removed recently from her breast was malignant. Faced with this ominous cloud and despite worsening health, she continued to assert her views on preservation and cruelty to animals. (Two years later, in 1964, she succumbed to her illness.)

In terms of my model, Rachel Carson clearly exhibited both analytical and holistic capabilities. She is described by those who knew and worked with her as possessing an acuity of observation, an eye for detail, a keen mind, and a verbatim memory—all qualities associated with an analytic cognitive style. Perhaps this is why she took so readily to, and had the patience for, the detailed empirical work conducted at Woods Hole and for her M.Sc. degree in embryology. Paul Brooks, her editor and biographer, records that her preparation for her books, especially *Silent Spring*, was meticulous (Brooks, 1972). In the latter case, she felt the need to know everything about pesticides, to the extent that she was almost overwhelmed by the volume of data collected. In the process, she worked herself into a state of exhaustion in an effort to be accurate and responsible. Contrary to the claim of her critics that she was a sloppy writer, one could argue quite the opposite that she was almost compulsive in her data collection.

The analytic/reductive aspect of Rachel Carson's cognitive style was, it seems, counter-balanced by a more holistic capability, one that made use of poetic imagination and fantasy. One sees this fertile imagination at work in her early books where we are transported beneath the sea to become involved, not only in the submarine world, but also in the very existence of the sea creatures themselves. Thus, she sought to develop "sense impressions" in an attempt to convey to the reader some of her own awe and wonder in the face of the natural world.

Rachel Carson's cognitive versatility is evident, therefore, in her ability to pull together a diffuse and confusing body of data and to shape it into a clear picture of (in the case of *Silent Spring*) pesticides and nature. Thus, she was able to work on detail without losing the broader picture, combining factual matter with personal, sometimes poetic, interpretation. Briggs (1987) argues that Carson's strength is that she worked from a solid empirical base in writing *Silent Spring*, building a case by going from the particular to the general, thereby grounding her interpretations in "fact." However, her skill in combining analytical detail and interpretation was questioned by many critics soon after publication. The most common complaint, despite vindication of *Silent Spring* by a Presidential Commission, was that she exaggerated and made mistakes. Interestingly, the same comments can be heard today from writers like Wilkinson (1987), who argues that the book contains numerous scientific inaccuracies and unsubstantiated conclusions.

The apparently effortless blending of science and the humanities in both her work and life suggests the presence of both objective and subjective values. Thus, one way of interpreting her enthusiastic delight in the diversity of nature, her satisfaction in doing empirical research, and her insatiable curiosity about all things ecological is that she maintained a childlike (in the best sense) desire simply to know about things, about how the world *is*. As such, one might label this orientation as benign mastery. Yet, this search for knowledge was unobtrusive and respectful of what she was studying. Gartner (1983) comments that Carson neither interfered nor conquered but simply reacted. Thus, she took pains, for instance, to return specimens to their original habitats, was inclined to remove household pests to the outdoors rather than to kill them, and detested blood sports or any cruelty to animals. Similarly, in her relationships with people, there was the same attempt to temper self-assertiveness with love. Encouraged to develop a sense of independence by her mother, Rachel Carson was not diligent in seeking intimate relationships. She did not make friends readily or carelessly and apparently did not contemplate marriage. A shy, reserved person, she spent much of her life living with her mother. However, there was no lack of altruism and concern in her life for, in addition to supporting her mother, she cared for her two orphaned nieces and later adopted her grandnephew. All of this was in addition to her ambitions as a writer. It is no wonder, therefore (as Gartner, 1983, points out), that she experienced a conflict common to many professional women between the demands of her work and the need to give of oneself in relationships. We would recognize this as the agency–communion conflict.

Although her critics claimed a lack of scientific detachment in some of her work, it is evident from her success as a scientist in her early years that she was capable of emotional detachment and objectivity. However, much of the literary impact of her writing derives from the way in which it fosters emotional empathy in the reader. Thus, Rachel Carson saw little value in an intellectual understanding detached from emotional empathy and as consequence sought to develop *both* in her writing. Similarly, there seems no doubt that she was able to use *extraceptive* frames of reference in her scientific work, while retaining a sensitivity (*intraceptive*) to the personal worlds of others. There is the story, for instance, of a young Rachel Carson encouraging fellow students to be more responsive to a teacher whose distant behaviour (Rachel pointed out) was the result of short-sightedness, not aloofness. Other than this, there is a dearth of information on the personal world of this reserved woman.

Turning to the *emotionality* dimension, detractors of Rachel Carson labelled her as an over-emotional, even hysterical, writer who played on the reader's emotions to make a point. Those who knew her personally, however, regard these claims as ludicrous. They saw a meticulous researcher with a calm, reserved demeanour. In fact, she appears to have handled stress quite well. Toward the end of her life, the death of her mother and her continuing responsibilities for her young dependents, coupled with writing deadlines and other professional demands, were met with stoic resolve (Brooks, 1972). There is no indication of the distress-prone behaviour of someone high on the emotionality dimension. However, throughout her life, she suffered from a number of complaints such as arthritis, ulcers, and heart disease, all of which are thought to have a psychosomatic component. There is the possibility, therefore, that Rachel Carson struggled to maintain a calm outer facade over an underlying emotionality.

In sum, Gartner (1983) suggests that the organizing principle of Rachel Carson's life was *integration*. One can see this in the way in which she sought to reconcile the two major themes that characterized her life. First, she was possessed of a definite sense of mission which involved, not only awakening in others something of her own sense of wonder about nature, but also alerting them to the dangers of arrogant and uninformed interference with the natural balance. This benign self-assertion is a prototypical example of the *agency* theme in life history. On the other hand, there was a pervasive sense of *communion* with nature, a cosmic feeling that the individual is less important than life itself, of which one is an integral point. In this perspective, death is part of life, a notion from which she took great comfort as her own drew near. Rachel Carson, therefore, succeeded in combining the many disparate threads of personality into a fulfilling and caring life.

EVALUATION OF THE TYPOLOGY

In seeking to evaluate the typology, I am faced with the more general question of how one goes about evaluating any psychological theory. Despite the voluminous literature on the topic, there is no well-established consensus on how this might, or should, be done. Instead, a variety of criteria are proposed depending, it seems, on the epistemological orientation of the individual concerned. An eminently sensible compromise is Maddi's (1976) suggestion that one should use both rational and empirical criteria in theory evaluation. A *rational*, or conceptual, analysis of a theory involves what Rychlak (1968) refers to as a coherence approach to "truth," one that is concerned with the extent to which propositions are both internally consistent and compatible with available knowledge. In other words, a rational analysis would seek to determine whether a theory is *plausible* in light of, for instance, other conceptualizations in a field of study (Levy, 1970). An *empirical* analysis, on the other hand, may involve two quite different criteria: *validity* and *utility* (Levy, 1970). As is well known, validation involves an attempt to determine the extent to which a proposition corresponds with the facts, the latter being derived from the observable consequences of some empirical manipulation. The utility of a theory has to do with its value to a user. One is interested in how useful the theory is in dealing with, for instance, practical problems in applied settings. In what follows, therefore, I shall discuss each criterion in turn. The *plausibility* of my typology is assessed in light of the decisions made by other typologists; its empirical *validity* is estimated by reference to the small amount of empirical data relevant to the model; and, its *utility* is explored in dealing with problems selected from clinical, vocational, and environmental psychology.

Plausibility

The present typology differs from all existing models, notably in its attempt to incorporate the three personality domains of cognition, affection, and conation. One way of assessing the plausibility of this approach would be to compare and contrast the present model with other, more prominent, personality typologies. In particular, one would be interested in the way in which their constituent dimensions are formulated; how these have been used to delimit types, and the decisions made by theorists about the orthogonality of dimensions. The obvious choice with which to begin the discussion is Jung's well-known typology, after which I turn to those of Coan, Eysenck, McCrae and Costa, and Royce.

Jung. Jung's typology is derived from three dimensions: a basic attitude (extraversion–introversion) and two functional (sensation–intuition, thinking–feeling) dimensions (Jung, 1923). In Chapter 4, I explained that Jung's extraversion–introversion is a direction-of-interest concept, one that contrasts an external with an internal orientation to life. Thus, the extravert is said to subordinate inner life to external necessity with attention being directed at "objective" happenings. The extravert responds to external demands, rather than to inner promptings. Introverts, however, are depicted by Jung as being quite the opposite, concerned primarily with their own subjective, rather than objective, reality. This direction-of-interest conception of extraversion–introversion has proven to be the most durable of Jung's dimensions, although, as mentioned in Chapter 4, it has been subjected to conceptual distortion. My objective-subjective dimension differs from Jung's conception in a number of important ways. While I use Murray's distillation of the Jungian dimension (intraception–extraception) as an important part of objectivity-subjectivity, I also include the elements of power–nurturance and emotional detachment–empathy, all of which are implied in Jung's writing but not dealt with in any systematic way. It is the "functional" dimensions that have given cause for concern, however (Storr, 1973).

The two functional dimensions represent attempts to account for individual differences in perception and judgment, with unsatisfactory results it seems. Thus, the perceptual dimension contrasts *sensation* (perception by means of the senses, preference for realism, concern for objective factual detail, acute observation) with *intuition* (perception by means of insight, preference for patterns and wholes, imagination over facts). Similarly, the judgment dimension contrasts *thinking* (analytic, logical, objective judgments, a concern with value-free "truth") with *feeling* (value judgments predominate, sensitivity to explanations in value terms) (McCaulley, 1981). Unfortunately, the separation of irrational (perception) from rational (judgment) functions seems odd in light of modern views on information processing. As I have argued in Chapter 2, one would expect, for instance, that someone who is analytic in perceptual style would also be analytic in memory and thought. In other words, there appears to be little ground for assuming with Jung that individual differences in perception and thought lie on *orthogonal* dimensions. A more reasonable formulation, therefore, would be to contrast sensation/thinking (akin to an analytical style) with intuition/feeling (holistic style). Such a reorganization seems to "work" reasonably well for sensation/thinking, since both functions emphasize an analytic concern for detail and logical thought, yet they do not refer to a "pure" cognitive style since both include conative factors. Thus, *sensing* is said to involve a preference for hard realistic facts, whereas *thinking* is associated with

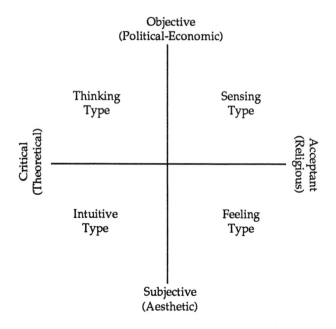

Figure 15. Relations between Jung's functions and the Spranger–Allport values. (Modified from Conley, 1985b.)

objectivity and tough-mindedness. Similarly, while *intuition* clearly is couched in terms of holistic perception, *feeling* is virtually a pure description of subjectivity. In other words, Jung fails to separate his three dimensions, confounding his "functions" with extraversion–introversion— the basic attitudes to life. The outcome of this can be seen in attempts by others to use Jung's typology in both conceptual and empirical research. To illustrate this point, it might be useful to look at a few recent studies in detail.

Conley (1985b) has tried to integrate Jung's formulation with the Spranger–Allport system of values (Fig. 15). The two value dimensions contrast *political/economic* (interest in power and tangible assets, unfeeling) with *aesthetic* (interest in subjective experience, harmony) values, and *critical/theoretical* (empirical, objective observer of "truth") with *religious* (seeker of mystical unity) values. The two-dimensional model so produced bears passing resemblance to mine, especially in its conception of objectivity–subjectivity. However, the critical–acceptant distinction is less clearly related to analytical and holistic orientations, although the latter are implied in Conley's dimension. When one turns to the relationship between this model of personal styles and Jung's typology, Conley has

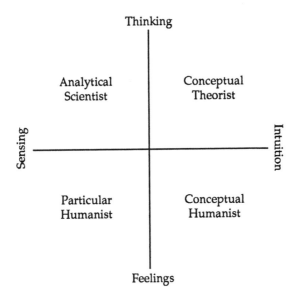

Thinking

Analytical
Scientist

Conceptual
Theorist

Sensing

Intuition

Particular
Humanist

Conceptual
Humanist

Feelings

Figure 16. Intellectual types in relation to Jung's functions. (From Mitroff & Kilmann, 1978.)

some difficulty in allocating Jung's functions to an appropriate quadrant. For example, *sensing* is placed in the political/economic–religious quadrant which, by definition, is said to involve power-seeking and a search for mystical unity, a paradoxical combination that is largely unrelated to Jung's "sensation." In a like manner, *intuition* is lodged in a quadrant defined in terms of objective empiricism and subjective experience, another dubious combination that reflects only some aspects of Jung's "intuition." Conceptual difficulties of this kind could be, of course, due to one or both models. Whether or not Jung's functions are confounded in some way requires us to look at some additional examples.

As part of his research on natural and social scientists, Mitroff employed Jung's functions in developing a taxonomy of scientific types (Fig. 16, Table 5; *cf.* Mitroff, 1974; Mitroff & Kilmann, 1978). His taxonomy is interesting because it combines, in a conceptually coherent manner, the style and content that one would expect to find in my four main types. For example, the analytical scientist (reductionist) is depicted as being concerned with empirical precision in a clearly demarcated discipline (analytic), the perception of himself/herself as an expert in

TABLE 5. INTELLECTUAL (SCIENTIFIC) TYPES

	Analytical Scientist (Reductionist)	Conceptual Theorist (Schematist)	Conceptual Humanist (Romantic)	Particular Humanist (Gnostic)
Nature of Science	Occupies a privileged and preferred position: clearly separable from other fields and clear lines of demarcation between disciplines; value-free, disinterested, apolitical	Occupies a privileged and preferred position; not clearly separable from other fields, all disciplines depend on one another; value-free and apolitical	Does *not* occupy a privileged and preferred position; not clearly separable from other fields and all disciplines depend on one another; science is *not* value-free, it is political	Does *not* occupy a privileged and preferred position; may be subordinate to poetry, art, literature, music, and mysticism as older "superior" ways of knowing; science is political
Nature of Scientific Knowledge	Impersonal, value-free, disinterested; precise, reliable, accurate, valid, reductionistic and realistic, unambiguous; apolitical	Impersonal, value-free, disinterested; imaginative, holistic, ambiguous, uncertain; apolitical	Personal, value-based; imaginative, holistic, uncertain and multiple causation; political and concerned with humanity	Personal, value-based; acausal, non-rational; partisan, political; sometimes action-oriented
Basis of Truth	Consensus, agreement, reliability, external validity, rigor, controlled nature of inquiry	Conflict between antithetical imaginative theories; comprehensive, integrative theory building	Conflict between objective and subjective knowledge; between the knower and the known	Intense personal knowledge and experience
Aims of Science	Precise, unambiguous theoretical and empirical knowledge	To construct the broadest possible conceptual schemes	To promote human development on the widest possible scale	To help people know themselves and to achieve self-determination
Role of Scientists	Disinterested, unbiased, impersonal, sceptical experts and specialists	Disinterested, unbiased, impersonal, imaginative, speculative generalists	Personally involved, admitting of biases, imaginative, speculative generalists	Personally involved, biased, imaginative, poetical interpreters of the particular

Modified from Mitroff and Kilmann (1978).

control of nature (power), maintaining a value-free, disinterested, apolitical posture (emotional detachment), and a concern for external reliability and validity (extraception). What makes Mitroff's work even more interesting is that he has been able to incorporate the results of his earlier empirical work into this conceptual taxonomy without violating either. In the course of this previous research, Mitroff (1974) identified three broad types of scientist among those who studied geological specimens brought back from the Moon by the Apollo astronauts.

> Type I scientists are distinguished by their extreme willingness to speculate far afield from known data, or even ignore data when the situation demanded it, in order to construct highly imaginative conceptual theories. [They] are conceptual theorists of the first rank [who] enjoy finding and creating patterns in disparate data drawn from the most widely scattered scientific fields. Type III scientists represent the other end of the continuum. Here, speculation is disdained and avoided at almost any cost. Type III scientists value precision and fine experimental work above all else. Type IIIs believe in "sticking close to the data".... The Type II represents something in between—capable both of doing good experimental work and of speculating modestly on it.... At times, Type II scientists might even rise to bold speculation; however, they are more akin to Problem Solvers than to Problem Recognizers or Integrators. (Mitroff & Kilmann, 1978, p. 21)

Mitroff is entirely consistent in suggesting that Type I scientists represent his conceptual theorist (thinking–intuition) type (my objective–holistic type), while Type IIIs show the characteristics of the analytical scientist (thinking–sensing) and my objective–analytic type. In turn, Type IIs occupy some intermediate position between the two extremes, showing both analytic and holistic functioning in the objective domain.

Of interest here is how Mitroff could have developed a typology that is entirely consistent with my own, using Jung's functions. It is possible, I believe, because of the confounding of dimensions in Jung's scheme. As mentioned above, the *thinking* function contains elements of tough-minded objectivity, while *feeling* involves sensitivity to one's inner, emotional reactions to events. What Mitroff has done, therefore, is to define the thinking–feeling dimension in such a way as to emphasize its extraversion–introversion aspects, while, at the same time, treating sensation–intuition as an analytic–holistic dimension. The net result is a typology that closely resembles my own. I believe, however, that the formulation of dimensions in my typology eliminates the conceptual confounding that one sees in Jung's model by clearly distinguishing between cognitive and conative dimensions.

Of further interest is a study conducted by Loomis and Saltz (1984) on artistic styles. Four clusters of artistic styles or types emerged from their analysis of subjects' ratings of eight well-known artists. It appeared to

Loomis and Saltz that the clusters could be accounted for in terms of two dimensions (Fig. 17).

> The *figurative vs. nonfigurative* dimension differentiates between representational and abstract art while the *narrative vs. descriptive* dimension distinguishes between art that is fanciful and idiosyncratically arranged and art that is descriptive and arranged in line with collective norms.... Spontaneous [narrative] art refers to products of fantasy and imagination which are not encumbered with the constraints of time and space. Rational [descriptive] art, on the other hand, refers to subject matter arranged in accordance with [the] expected [and] predictable.... Analyzing the figurative vs. nonfigurative distinction, one notes immediately that figurative artists paint recognizable elements. People, animals, trees, and soup cans all appear on the canvas as they appear in the physical world. Nonfigurative artists, however, do not paint recognizable elements. They are concerned with color, with abstract forms, or with the process of painting. In terms of Jung's theory it appears that figurative artists are oriented toward the outer world while nonfigurative artists are oriented toward the inner world. This difference in orientation can be interpreted as representing the difference between extraversion and introversion. (Loomis & Saltz, 1984, p. 29)

Or, in my terms, the difference can be referred to as the objective–subjective dimension. Loomis and Saltz go on to say that

> looking at the work of artists who are labeled spontaneous ... one is struck by the unexpected quality of their arrangements. Chagall paints a chicken floating over a small town ... and the others,... display a similar disregard for logical constraints. This contrasts with the work of the four artists who are labeled as rational. In their art there is a systematic, orderly quality. People and furniture are on the ground, not up in the air ... and, in the nonfigurative art of Mondrian, rectangles of color are prescribed and defined. (Loomis & Saltz, 1984, p. 29)

Here I part company with Loomis and Saltz, however, when they attempt to interpret the difference between spontaneous and rational styles in terms of a contrast between Jung's irrational and rational functions. For reasons already mentioned, I believe this to be an unworkable distinction and suggest, instead, that the styles in question might be more adequately characterized as analytic (rational) and holistic (spontaneous). Thus, the artistic styles revealed by Loomis and Saltz are encouragingly consistent with my four main types and might be more clearly understood using my typology rather than the Jungian dimensions.

In sum, Jung proposes three orthogonal dimensions, a generic extraversion–introversion dimension that resembles my objectivity–subjectivity distinction, and two function dimensions that are problematic. It seems that the three dimensions are not conceptually distinct, as we have

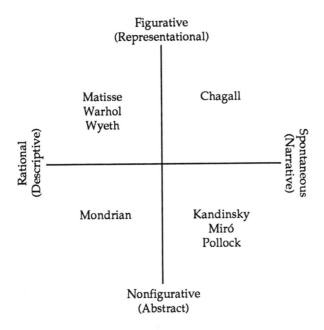

Figure 17. Artistic types. (From Loomis & Saltz, 1984.)

witnessed in the studies discussed above. Additional research with the Myers-Briggs Type Indicator (MBTI) appears to confirm this suspicion, although this method of assessment is itself suspect. McCrae and Costa (1989a), for instance, find that the MBTI does not measure qualitatively distinct types corresponding to Jung's conceptions, leading them to the conclusion that Jung's theory is either incorrect or is inadequately operationalized by the MBTI. Despite qualms about this test, some interesting findings emerge from its use in exploring the relationship between Jung's functions and measures of objectivity–subjectivity derived from other research traditions. Thus, a clear link is found between objectivity and sensation/thinking and between subjectivity and intuition/feeling (Caine *et al.*, 1981; Coan, 1979; Forisha, 1983). What this implies, of course, is a conceptual overlap between Jung's attitude and functional dimensions, one that is clarified, I believe, in my own model.

One final point needs to be made before leaving Jung's typology, namely the absence of an emotionality dimension. As McCrae and Costa note, the MBTI is conspicuously lacking in a neuroticism factor, an omission that reflects the fact that "emotional instability versus adjustment did not enter into Jung's definitions of types" (McCrae &

Costa, 1989a, p. 36). It is not clear why this is so, given the prominent role afforded to emotionality in the models to which we now turn.

Coan. Using factor analytical methods, Coan has studied the structure of epistemological values (Coan, 1968, 1979) and the characteristics of the optimal personality (Coan, 1974). What is interesting, for our purposes, is that Coan has identified generic dimensions that appear to be similar, if not identical, to those incorporated into my typology.

1. *Epistemological values.* A content analysis of major psychological theories (Coan, 1968) and the further analysis of the self-reported epistemological orientations of psychologists (Coan, 1979) led Coan to recognize several first-order factors, among the most notable of which are *objectivism–subjectivism* and *elementarism–holism* (Fig. 18). Objectivism refers to a preference for studying overt behaviour rather than strictly experiential or psychological subject matter. Where "internal" processes are studied, they are reduced to mechanical metaphors and treated from the perspective of an external, scientific observer. Subjectivism, on the other hand, is concerned with internal experience as the subject-matter of psychology and takes the perspective of a self-reflective observer.

The set of values being contrasted by this factorial dimension is similar to the extraceptive–intraceptive conception of Murray (1938) and others that I have included in my version of the objective–subjective dimension. Similarly, Coan's *elementarism* (a preference for dealing with elementary or specific variables and relationships) and *holism* (a preference for dealing with complex global patterns and relationships) have much in common with my analytic–holistic dimension. However, Coan couches this latter dimension in terms of epistemological values, whereas I prefer to treat it as a cognitive style distinction.

Since Coan's factors are oblique, he feels comfortable in combining these first-order factors into what is referred to as a grand polarity between *restrictive* and *fluid* orientations. His descriptions of these higher-order poles (Coan, 1979, p. 153) are remarkably similar to my OA (restrictive) and SH (fluid) types. The assumption is that, at their most generic level, epistemological values can be described most effectively as a grand polarity akin to the tough–tender dichotomy of James's (1907) and Kimble's (1984) scientist–humanist distinction and that this polarity combines the *objective–subjective* and *elementarism–holism* dimensions. The implications for my model will be discussed shortly.

2. *The optimal personality.* Based on a factor analysis of a battery of personality and ability tests aimed at "illuminating the realm of variables that enter into various concepts of the optimal personality" (Coan, 1974, p. 36), Coan isolated two important factors: (*i*) *distress proneness* (*i.e.,* an emotionality dimension similar to Eysenck's N and Cattell's Anxiety), and

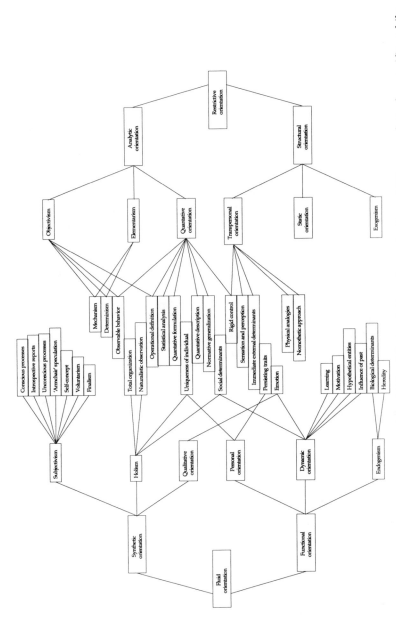

Figure 18. A bipolar hierarchy of theoretical variables. The variables shown in the middle are relatively specific, while those on the left and right sides represent more general and mutually opposing trends. (From Coan, 1974.)

(*ii*) *objective* versus *personal orientation, i.e.,* a confident impersonal attitude (oriented to control, manipulation, and mastery) versus a more humanistic attitude (oriented toward relationships and a greater sensitivity to the inner realm). A factor of somewhat lesser importance turned out to be *analytic versus global*, differing intellectual attitudes that contrast a search for analytic understanding with that of an appreciation of unanalysed totalities. The appearance of a *distress* (N) factor in this analysis, and not in the study of epistemological values, is understandable in light of the data base for each study. The intellectual exercise of theory-building would tend to emphasize the cognitive and conative elements of human functioning, as I have explained earlier. Similarly, the *objective–personal* orientation factor emphasizes mastery and control, not extraception, as one sees in the equivalent factor in the values analysis. I interpret this as support for including both components (mastery and extraception) in a more comprehensive conception of this factor, as I have done in my model. Finally, Coan combines his first-order factors into the two higher-order categories of *restrictive–fluid* (objective, analytical, impersonal versus subjective, global, personal) and *general discomfort* (distress). This is equivalent to collapsing my cognitive and conative dimensions into one, while retaining an independent emotionality dimension.

In sum, Coan's identification of three generic dimensions which are conceptually similar to mine affords some support for my choice of traits, although his use of these differs from my own preferences. Like Coan, Conway (1989) and others, see some virtue in subsuming the analytic–holistic dimension under a broad objective–subjective umbrella. Indeed, there is some empirical support for such a procedure, for measures of objectivity–subjectivity and analytical–holistic styles show moderately low correlations (Caine *et al.*, 1981). My reason for not following this path, however, is that, by doing so, one is unable to represent *objective–holistic* and *subjective–analytic* types in one's model. Use of the "grand polarity" commits such individuals to personological oblivion.

Eysenck, and McCrae and Costa. Starting from widely differing standpoints, Eysenck, and McCrae and Costa have produced virtually identical models of personality (*cf.* Eysenck & Eysenck, 1985; McCrae & Costa, 1984, 1985, 1987, 1989a,b). In Eysenck's case, his early work with traumatized servicemen immediately after World War II was followed by more extensive research with a variety of clinical populations and, increasingly, a massive experimental research effort. McCrae and Costa, on the other hand, base their model on factor analytic studies of personality descriptions in ordinary language. In both cases, the authors have converged on a three-dimensional model of personality comprising: *Neuroticism* (negative emotionality), *Extraversion* (positive emotionality), and a third dimension referred to by Eysenck as *Psychoticism* and by McCrae and Costa as *Openness to Experience*. Although Eysenck believes Psychoticism and Openness to be opposite poles of the same dimension, McCrae and Costa demur, arguing that the link remains to be demonstrated (Eysenck & Eysenck, 1985, p. 139).

One of the main difficulties in resolving this conceptual difference lies in the confused interpretation of the factor from which McCrae and Costa derive their concept of Openness. As mentioned in Chapter 1, the fifth of the Robust Traits was originally interpreted as a "culture" factor, reflecting an interest in, and expression of, sophisticated intellectual and artistic tastes. Subsequently, its core meaning came to be intellectual and artistic interests, the nonintellective, motivational attitudes that characterize intellectual achievement. In their conception of Openness, however, McCrae (1987), and McCrae and Costa (1984, 1987) appear to use a narrower conception of this "Intellect" factor, discounting the elements of sophistication and perseverance, while emphasizing those features related to creativity. It is for this reason that Digman (1989) regards Openness as subordinate to the more superordinate Intellect factor. *Openness to Experience*, therefore, connotes a sensitivity to such aspects of inner experience as fantasy, aesthetics, feelings, ideas, and values. As such, it is similar to the notion of intraception, a major component of my conception of subjectivity. Not surprisingly, therefore, Openness correlates significantly with (among other things) measures of divergent thinking (McCrae, 1987), creativity in many professions, and subjective epistemological values (Conway, 1989). Missing from Openness, however, is reference to power–love and emotional detachment–empathy, elements that are important, I believe, in defining subjectivity. I conclude, therefore, that Openness refers to the intraceptive aspect of my dimension. In a similar vein, Eysenck's Psychoticism refers to one element of my objective pole (the hostile, tough-minded aspect) but has little to say about the more benign mastery that complements the picture of objectivity. Finally, neither model includes a cognitive dimension. Although Eysenck has long recognized the role of intelligence in personality, most of his attention has been focused on the model of temperament discussed here.

In sum, both models support my interest in objectivity–subjectivity and emotionality but differ from my typology in their inclusion of orthogonal dimensions of positive and negative emotionality. My reasons for combining these into a simple *affect intensity* dimension have been discussed at length in Chapter 3, and merely reflect a preference for an alternative conception of affective space.

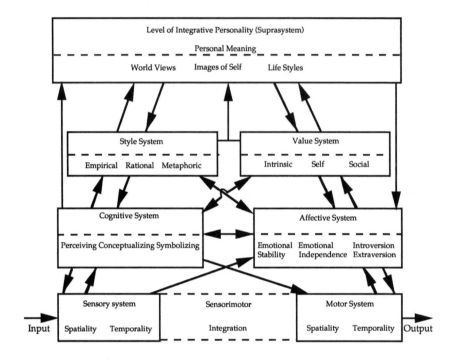

Figure 19. Royce's systems theory of personality. (From Powell & Royce, 1978.)

Royce. After a lifetime studying epistemological values and the factorial structure of personality, Royce has produced a comprehensive and decidedly complex personality theory (Fig. 19; Royce & Powell, 1983).[2] Like mine, it is best seen as a speculative essay which, although drawing on a great deal of empirical data, is essentially a personal statement. The model is composed of personality "systems" (sensory, motor, cognitive, affective, style, value) which interact at different levels in the personality hierarchy to produce individual differences in world view, self-image, and lifestyle. The very complexity of Royce's scheme makes it virtually impossible to describe in a few pages. What I shall do, therefore, is focus on that aspect of most relevance to my own theory: the nature and origins of his *stylistic types.*

---

[2] By referring to this work as Royce's theory, I do not wish to detract from the contributions made by Royce's various collaborators, reference to whom can be found in Royce and Powell (1983).

Unlike my tendency to recognize polarities, Royce favours triads. In fact, his theory appears to be an elaboration and justification of his early work on epistemological values in which he recognized three basic "styles." *Empiricism* involves a view of reality, largely determined by a commitment to external experience which is tested by the reliability and validity of observations. The major underlying cognitive processes involve active perception and the seeking of sensory experience. *Rationalism* involves a commitment to rationality in which the validity of a particular view of "reality" is assessed in terms of logical consistency. The major underlying cognitive processes are clear thinking and the rational analysis and synthesis of ideas. *Metaphorism* is a commitment to metaphorical expression in which the validity of ideas is tested by the universality of particular insights and awareness. Of importance are those conscious and unconscious processes involved in developing symbols (metaphors).

At first glance, there would seem to be a rough correspondence between Royce's stylistic types and my prototypes. Thus, the empirical type shows some of the characteristics of the objective–analytic individual; the rational type is similar to my objective–holistic prototype, and there is a resemblance between the metaphoric style and the subjective–holistic person. Royce does not recognize any style or type that shows subjective–analytic qualities. To help in exploring these relationships further, I have summarized the cognitive, affective, and conative characteristics of Royce's types in Table 6. Turning first to the cognitive components of each style, the empirical and metaphorical styles are reminiscent of my contrast between analytic and holistic thinking. Thus, the literal, concrete, detailed, precise, compartmentalized cognition of empirical types is essentially how I describe analytical processing. Likewise, the more imaginative, divergent, and integrative orientation of the metaphorical style is central to the notion of holism. Somewhat more difficult to understand, however, is the mixture of abstract, integrative ability and analytic, field-independent style proposed for the rational type. This is not what one would find in the objective–holistic individual but, rather, would be more indicative of a versatile type.

Royce's treatment of the affective system differs considerably from mine. Rather that recognizing an orthogonal affective dimension, Royce proposes that each stylistic type is characterized by a specific emotional state. The empirical type is said to be socially introverted, inhibited, and prone to high impulse control. While this may be the case in some instances, the logic of my own model suggests that some objective–analytic types can exhibit signs of social extraversion. Many empirical scientists, for instance, are socially uninhibited and gregarious. The proposed relationship between rationality and emotional independence

TABLE 6. ROYCE'S PERSONALITY TYPES

	Empirical	Rational	Metaphoric
Cognitive System	*Perceptual ability.* The spatiovisual ability, flexibility and speed of closure that facilitate the manipulation of the directly perceptible qualities of things. *Extensive scanning style.* An intensive and extensive attention to tasks; to the incidental aspects of the field; sharp precise memories, compartmentalization; concrete thinking; intolerance of ambiguity.	*Conceptual ability.* The verbal reasoning and comprehension skills that facilitate the development of a repertoire of concepts together with the ability to generate abstract, integrative concepts. *Field independent style.* An analytic rather than global way of perceiving, an ability to overcome the influence of embedding contexts.	*Symbolizing ability.* An imaginative fluency that allows the representation of a number of objects or ideas in a single form, as seen in artistic and literary production. *Divergent style?* Low compartmentalization and a capacity for conceptual integration.
Affective System	*Introversion.* General and social inhibition; high impulse control; low surgency and a preoccupation with veridicalness and exactness.	*Emotional independence.* Lack of sociability; autonomy; little interest in people; an intellectual and impersonal approach to problems.	*Emotional instability.* An exuberant playful, expansive, impetuous, nervous demeanour; a physiognomic style in which percepts are suffused with emotional qualities.
Conative (value) System	*Self.* Emphasis on being oneself, maintaining independence and behaviour according to one's own standards. Strong emphasis on affective reactions and inner as well as outer events. The external world is important only insofar as it provides stimulation for creativity.	*Intrinsic.* Emphasis on mastering intellectual and physical challenges. Elegant mental solutions prized. Value placed on not being changed affectively by environment. One must prevent emotional reactions from colouring the external world as it really appears to the objective observer.	*Social.* A concern with movements toward and away from other people. Being helpful and being praised or comforted by others is most desirable. Relations to others are important in terms of one's own affective reactions.

From Royce and Powell (1983).

is consistent with the notion of objectivity and emotional detachment, but in my own model I have treated emotional independence as an aspect of conation, not as an affective style. More confusing, however, is the suggestion of a link between metaphorism and emotional instability (neuroticism). Royce depicts the latter as a matter of playful exuberance, an emotional state which is said to typify creative individuals (Simonton, 1988) but one that is hardly consistent with the conception of neuroticism as general distress.

Finally, the value (conative) components of Royce's descriptions of types show a similar range of consistencies and inconsistencies with my own prototypes. Thus, the empiricist's emphasis on autonomy and being oneself is consistent with my understanding of an objective-analytic orientation, but the concern for affective reactions and inner reality is not. Such a mixture of qualities appears to confuse objective and subjective value systems, something one would not expect to observe amongst objective individuals. The need to achieve mastery over the external environment and to maintain emotional control as defining features of the rational type is quite consistent with the notion of an objective-holistic individual. Similarly, the concern for helpful social relationships and the affective quality of life, said to characterize the metaphoric style, fits comfortably with the view that the latter is similar to the subjective-holistic type.

In sum, the similarity between Royce's model and my own is more apparent than real. At first glance, there does seem to be some similarity between the two sets of types, but closer inspection reveals a number of differences. I suspect that what is happening here is that we start with different personal conceptions of personality prototypes and, accordingly, build different pictures. The net result is that Royce appears to combine qualities that, according to my picture, should not go together. A conceptual analysis of the kind undertaken here, therefore, cannot determine which picture is "correct," in any absolute sense, but is useful in ascertaining the internal consistency of a model.

General summary. The purpose of this review has been to estimate the plausibility of my personality typology in light of the models offered by more eminent theorists. In particular, I was interested in which dimensions have been used, how they are conceptualized, and whether they are treated as orthogonal characteristics. Considerable support for the use of cognitive, affective, and conative dimensions is apparent. While those models seeking to summarize epistemological behaviour emphasize the cognitive and conative domains and models of adjustment or temperament emphasize emotionality, taken together, they confirm my choice of personality domains. Strongest support for the conceptualization of each dimension is available for the objective–subjective and emotionality traits, while the analytic-holistic distinction is prominent in Coan's analyses and implicit in those of Jung and Royce. The inclination to combine the cognitive and conative dimensions into a grand polarity is evident in Coan's work, but this is interpreted as a matter of preference rather than some fundamental inconsistency with my model. Finally, none of the questions raised in this section attend to the way in which the various dimensions interact with one another within each type. I shall deal with this issue in the sections that follow.

Validity

Of interest here is the extent to which empirical research identifies patterns of relationships between the generic dimensions that are consistent with my typological formulations. Unfortunately, given the recent development of the model, there has been little time for it to be subjected to extensive empirical evaluation, with the result that the available empirical evidence is both scanty and circumstantial. However, what is available is interesting and suggestive. Most of the relevant research has focused on the *analytic–holistic* and *objective–subjective* dimensions, there being relatively little interest in their interaction with *emotionality*. Within this limited research, only two components of the *analytic–holistic* dimensions are afforded sustained attention, namely field dependence–independence and convergence–divergence. However, this is no particular problem, for I believe that either of these two styles can be used to operationalize the broader stylistic dimension. For instance, you may remember that field-independent and -dependent individuals were characterized in Chapter 2 as differing in perceptual styles, specifically in their ability to analyse and restructure perceptual fields. The more field independent the individual, the more likely he or she is to restructure percepts to match a given task. In contrast, the field-dependent person is more likely to accept the field as given. Similar differences in the predilection for analysis is also evident amongst convergers and divergers, who were said to differ in their styles of encoding and recall. Convergers are inclined to restrict encoding to the denotative aspects of stimuli, linking concepts into tight logical networks. Divergers, however, make more use of connotative and contextual cues, thereby developing looser, possibly less "logical," conceptual networks. What is interesting about these perceptual and memory styles is that they share cognitive correlates. Thus, for instance, Hudson's "divergers" share with Witkin's "field-dependent" individuals a common tendency to see the world in preconceived patterns (B. Frank, 1983). Similarly, field-independent and -dependent subjects show differences in memory tasks that are akin to those found amongst convergers and divergers (Bennink, 1982). At the same time, convergent and field-independent individuals are clearly more skilled at logical problem-solving than their divergent, field-dependent contemporaries (Henneman & Rouse, 1984; Myer & Hensley, 1984; Roberge & Flexer, 1983). What all this suggests is that regardless of the way in which one operationalizes the analytic–holistic dimension, whether it be the Witkin or the Hudson conception, one is likely to pick up the same pattern of correlations with other cognitive and noncognitive variables. Thus, the correlations between field dependence–independence, convergence–divergence, and variables that reflect my *objective–subjective* dimension reveal a consistent pattern. In what follows, therefore, I shall make use of the excellent reviews provided by Witkin & Goodenough (1977, 1981), Witkin *et al.* (1979), and Hudson (1968, 1970, 1972), sketching their findings in broad terms.

Witkin has incorporated the concept of field dependence–independence, together with its personality correlates into the broader conception of "psychological differentiation." In addition to individual differences in perceptual style, therefore, the latter refers to differences in social behaviour, impulse control, and defence mechanisms, as well as to forms of cerebral lateralization. In this scheme, the more psychologically differentiated (field-independent) individual is said to show a greater sense of separate self, more definite boundaries between self and others, and a greater segregation of internal psychological functions. In contrast, the less differentiated (field-dependent) individual shows greater integration and connectedness both internally and externally with the outside world. Clearly, Witkin is referring to a broad psychological difference resembling the agency–communion distinction of Angyal and Bakan (Chapter 4, pp. 113-114). Hudson, likewise, has explored the broader correlates of convergence–divergence but has not developed an overarching conception within which to integrate his findings. One should bear in mind, however, that in using the terms "convergence–divergence" he is referring to something more complex than simply a cognitive style.

Both Witkin and Hudson have demonstrated a consistent relationship between field independence/convergence and a concern for *power* (authoritarianism/manipulativeness), *autonomy* (distancing oneself from others), and *ambition* (achievement striving). This is a robust finding that has been assessed through a variety of means, including questionnaires, autobiographical sketches, and projective tests. In contrast, field-dependent/divergent individuals appear to be more cooperative and accommodating, showing little concern for power but seeking personal closeness and attachment instead. It is interesting that similar patterns of relationships have been found in various studies of creativity in arts and

science. For instance, Helson was able to identify several stylistic orientations amongst mathematicians and writers of literary fantasy that
resembled what Neumann (in Helson, 1973a) has called *matriarchal* and
patriarchal consciousnesses (Helson & Crutchfield, 1970; Helson, 1973a,b).
The former closely resembles the field-dependent/divergent style, while
the latter is clearly a matter of field independence/convergence. Of
interest to us here is the nonassertive, more inner-directed nature of the
matriarchal type, in contrast to the more assertive, mastery-orientation of
the patriarchal consciousness.

When one turns to *emotional detachment–empathy*, the picture of the field
independent/converger that emerges is of an emotionally overcontrolled,
highly constrained individual who carefully channels the expression of
impulses and emotions. Especially important is the separation of emotion
and thought, the attempt to exclude intrusive and wayward emotions
from influencing the production and expression of ideas. Simonton (1988),
for instance, in his empirical studies of creative artists and scientists, was
moved to recognize *classical* types within each group who appear to seek
order, perfection, precision, and high control in their work, in contrast to
romantic types who evince a profusion of rich, expressive, novel ideas in
a relatively uncontrolled manner. The classical–romantic distinction is
clearly similar to my objective–subjective contrast and it is interesting that
Simonton also recognizes the relationship between this and what is
evidently a convergent–divergent difference.

In the interpersonal domain, the field independent/converger shows
relatively little expression of strong emotion and tends actively to dislike
conflict and hostility. One accommodation to the latter is a preference for
conflict-free, impersonal work situations where the potential for emotional turmoil is reduced (Holton, 1978; Albert & Runco, 1987). When exposed to situations that require more emotional involvement in interpersonal matters, the field independent/converger may become resistant and
uncooperative (Gruenfeld & Thung-Rung, 1984). All of this is not to say
that field independent/convergers do not feel strong emotions. For
instance, Hudson found that when convergers do allow themselves the
liberty of such emotional expression, often it is accompanied by extremely
violent and ghoulish images. Presumably the reason for this is that,
having learned to control their emotional expression, they may be
unpractised in expressing strong emotions in a socially skillful manner.
In contrast, field dependent/divergers are less emotionally constrained,
seeming to enjoy both the experience and expression of a variety of emotions. Hence, they seek the interpersonal closeness that may engender
such emotion and are clearly more involved with others. Thus, they
attend to others' faces more closely and spontaneously include human

figures in their drawings more frequently than do field independent/convergers.

With regard to cognitive empathy, field independent/convergers are clearly *extraceptive*. Perhaps as a result of their inclination to wall themselves off from others, to rely on their own judgment, they give the appearance of being impervious—unwilling to accommodate themselves to the views of other people. Indeed, Hudson found that convergers are simply not sensitive to others' "subjectivity." In contrast, field dependent/divergers seek out and make more use of information from those around them, especially in ambiguous situations. Similarly, they attend to social nuances and the more intangible aspects of social intercourse, using this fund of information to develop greater interpersonal skills than one sees in the more field independent-individual. It follows that field dependent/divergers might be labelled *intraceptive*. In a similar vein, both Helson and Katz have identified a link between intraception and, matriarchal and divergent thinking, respectively (Helson & Crutchfield, 1970; Helson, 1973a,b; Katz, 1984).

Finally, both Witkin and Hudson concur on the nature of the defence mechanisms associated with each cognitive style. Field independent/convergers make use of specialized, articulated defences such as emotional isolation, intellectualization, and projection. This is consistent with the tendency found in people with this style to compartmentalize and to separate their experiences. Thus, separating feeling from thought and dampening the former, while leaving thoughts amenable to manipulation, is precisely what one would expect to find in objective–analytic types. On the other hand, field dependent/divergers use relatively unspecialized defences that block out unpleasant events in their entirety, sweeping away whole chunks of experience until it is possible to deal with them in a more effective manner. Therefore, one sees use of denial and repression by holistic types. Some indirect support for these differences comes from studies of dreaming in artists and scientists (Albert & Runco, 1987). The comparison between what might be more accurately labelled as "romantic artists" and "classical scientists" reveals more vivid and frequent dreams amongst the former. Albert and Runco suggest that this may be due to the greater openness of artists to primary process thinking. Scientists, on the other hand, appear to distance themselves from immediate experience, even when dreaming, using "externally derived rational systems" to control imagery (Albert & Runco, 1987, p. 84). In other words, they are prone to the use of intellectualization. Albert and Runco explain these differences in terms of the density of barriers between emotion/impulse and cognition. Their explanation is similar to that proposed by Block and Block (1979) in their research on *ego control*. The latter refers to the degree of "permeability" of the ego, *i.e.*, the capacity of the ego to contain impulses, feelings, and desires. The personality correlates of over-controlled individuals, who are said to show excessive boundary impermeability, appear to be consistent with the field-independent/convergent style, whereas the under-controller (one who exhibits excessive boundary permeability) is clearly more field-dependent/divergent.

All of these connections between the *analytic–holistic* cognitive style dimension (field dependence–independence, convergence–divergence) and various components of the *objective–subjective* dimension (power, emotional detachment, extraception–intraception) are consistent with the way in which my typology is formulated. However, Witkin and Hudson have focused their attention on only two of the types in my model, the OA and SH quadrants. Thus, the pattern of correlations relating field independence/convergence to power, emotional detachment, and extraception form the basis of what I have called the OA or *reductionist* type, while the association between field dependence/divergence and nurturance, emotional empathy, and intraception make up my SH or *romantic* type. There is no particular significance in the fact that neither Witkin nor Hudson have identified the remaining two types (OH, SA). Their theoretical assumptions would not allow them to predict the occurrence of these types, so they are neither found nor discussed. Similarly, neither author incorporated a temperament or emotionality dimension into their deliberations—an omission that requires us to look elsewhere for pertinent information on the interaction of this latter dimension with other aspects of personality. Unfortunately, there is little of direct relevance. For instance, the massive body of literature on the effect of anxiety on cognition examines cognitive performance under different levels of state and trait anxiety (Eysenck & Eysenck, 1985; Persson & Sjoberg, 1978), Typically, a curvilinear relationship is found in which performance first increases and then declines with increasing stress. In addition, some research finds a narrowing of attention and category width in response to anxiety. However interesting this research might be, it does not tell us about the effect of emotionality on the adoption of different cognitive styles (analytic–holistic) and value positions (objective–subjective).

A recent study by Larsen *et al.* (1987), however, offers some clues about the nature of these relationships. The authors concluded that individuals high in affect intensity engaged in the cognitive operations of *personalization* (responded in personal/emotional terms), *empathy* (showed an interest in the thoughts and feelings of others), *globalization* (emphasized global associations of test stimuli), *elaboration* (were inclined to fantasy), and *generalization* (went beyond the immediate context) to a greater extent than those who scored low on the affect intensity dimension. In other words, high affect intensity is related to a tendency toward subjective behaviour (personalization, empathy) and holistic thinking (globalization, elaboration, generalization). These findings are in direct contrast to the more traditional literature (Persson & Sjoberg, 1978) in which anxiety is observed to result in the narrowing of categories and more analytical perception. What would seem to be an empirical paradox can be clarified by reference to Block (1982), who makes use of Piaget's notions of *assimilation* (the integration of external elements into evolving or completed structures) and *accommodation* (any modification of conceptual structure by the elements it assimilates) in discussing the matter. Personal equilibrium, or well-being, is achieved by some judicious balance between the two processes, one that maintains stability (assimilation) while allowing change (accommodation). According to Block, assimilation is the first line of adaptation to life's demands, an attempt to construe events in terms of available conceptual structures. If this fails, then we may switch to accommodative procedures, which may entail prolonged anxiety as reconstruction of events occurs. If anxiety becomes excessive, we may revert to assimilation, perseverating with inappropriate ways of seeing the world. What Block calls excessive assimilation (the overenthusiastic application of schemas) would seem to resemble certain aspects of global/holistic thinking, whereas excessive accommodation is akin to analytic thinking with its ever-changing perceptual–cognitive activity. Of interest here is Block's hypothesis that the readiness to alternate between assimilation and accommodation is an important individual difference variable, one that is influenced by the level of anxiety experienced by the individual. In his view, high anxiety will result in the shift to more holistic (assimilative) behaviour, a proposition that is consistent with Larsen *et al.* (1987), above.

My interpretation of these matters, however, leads to a different hypothesis from that of Block. I propose that high levels of emotionality lead, not to a switch from accommodation to assimilation but rather to the individual becoming fixated on one or the other. That is, very high levels of anxiety (or affect intensity) will push individuals to extreme behaviours on the *analytic–holistic* and *objective–subjective* dimensions. High levels of emotionality, therefore, act to lock individuals into patterns of cognitive and conative behaviour that may be maladaptive. Ironically, very low levels of emotionality may result in precisely the same consequences for the simple reason that the individuals may not be moved to change or may not be bothered to do so.

In sum, while there is a modicum of support for my typology, particularly with regard to the interaction of the cognitive and conative dimensions, the role of emotionality awaits further research.

Utility

The utility of a theory has to do with its usefulness in helping to understand and to solve problems, especially those of a practical nature. In what follows, the extent to which the present model is useful in dealing with problems selected from clinical, vocational, and environmental psychology is examined.

(*a*) *Clinical psychology.* The problem of interest here is that of personality classification, more particularly the difficulties involved in classifying personality disorders. As noted in Chapter 1, opinion in psychology has shifted from the use of classical categories to conceptualizations based on personality dimensions and/or prototypes. In contrast, the profession of psychiatry retains a strong interest in diagnostic categories based on classical assumptions; however, the situation is changing. The continuing interchange between the two disciplines is facilitating research on the possible dimensional and prototypical nature of psychiatric classification which, in turn, is influencing conceptions of diagnostic categories. In what follows, I shall review some of this research, indicating in so doing, how my own model might help in understanding the nature of, and relationships between, personality disorders. To begin with, it would be useful to clarify some of the assumptions involved in the psychiatric approach to classification found in DSM–III and DSM–III–R.[3]

DSM–III, Axis II is composed of sets of diagnostic criteria organized into diagnostic categories that seek to distinguish between the various personality disorders. In developing the latest version, the selection of both criteria and categories, rather than being guided by some coherent theoretical position was, instead, "developed intentionally and explicitly to be *atheoretical*" (Millon, 1986b). According to Millon, the reason for this was to avoid potential disputes between different theoretical schools and, thereby, to enhance the acceptance of the new manual. However, the negotiations which culminated in DSM–III were highly political in nature, with various factions seeking to have their particular interests included in the final version (Bayer & Spitzer, 1985; Rothblum *et al.*, 1986). Thus, DSM–III is atheoretical only in the sense that no single school of thought is dominant, although Blashfield (1984) suggests that Millon's (1981) personality system played a significant role in current conceptions of Axis II.

Axis II, however, is beset by a number of problems. The DSM–III version was based on the assumption of classical categories: mutually

---

[3] The third edition of the *Diagnostic and Statistical Manual of Mental Disorders* (DSM–III) and its recent revision (DSM–III–R) describe the American Psychiatric Association's widely used classification of mental disorders.

exclusive categories defined by sets of necessary and sufficient criteria (Livesley, 1985). Unfortunately, personality disorders are inherently too variable to fit easily into such rigid categories, the result being unreliable classification and endless borderline instances (Livesley, 1985). Although an effort was made to overcome these problems in the revised version of DSM–III (DSM–III–R) by modifying assumptions about the nature of diagnostic categories, opinions differ over the outcome. Some observers suggest that there is greater evidence of the use of polythetic categories (a set in which no single feature is essential to group membership and in which all instances are of equal importance) but that DSM–III–R remains a mixture of classical (monothetic) and polythetic categories (Livesley, 1985; Widiger *et al.*, 1988). Thus, the latest revisions attempt to introduce the notion of prototypicality but fall short of this goal (Frances & Widiger, 1986; Morey, 1988b). More sceptical are Romney and Bynner (1989) who see little movement in DSM–III–R away from classical assumptions. Thus, the unreliability and overlap between categories of personality disorder continues to be seen as a major problem (Benjamin, 1986; Blashfield & Breen, 1989; Kass *et al.*, 1985; Kiesler, 1986; Morey, 1988a,b; Romney & Bynner, 1989). For instance, in a typical study, Morey (1988b) had clinicians rate their patients on a checklist of 166 diagnostic criteria describing eleven personality disorders common to DSM–III and DSM–III–R. Morey found that, when the DSM–III criteria were used, only four personality disorders (narcissistic, histrionic, paranoid, and schizoid) had an overlap of at least fifty percent with another disorder. However, when the DSM–III–R criteria were used, eight of the eleven disorders showed this degree of overlap. Thus, the most recent version of DSM–III appears to result in more, rather than less, diagnostic confusion. Given these difficulties, the question is what might be done to improve the quality of personality disorder classification.

Two broad approaches can be, and are being, used: category research (attempts to refine prevailing categories) and dimensional research (attempts to understand the dimensional structure of DSM–III and/or provide a new dimensional model from which to derive new sets of diagnostic categories).

1. *Category research*. A variety of multivariate strategies, such as cluster analysis, are being used to identify the empirical relationships between diagnostic symptoms. One such attempt to determine the internal structure of the DSM–III–R disorders is shown in Fig. 20 (Morey, 1988a).

The separation of Axis–II into two large clusters that appear to reflect differences in interpersonal power is interesting in light of the prominent role afforded to objectivity–subjectivity in my own model. However, of immediate concern to us here is the credence one can attribute to such analyses. Morey himself suggests that it is debatable whether such an

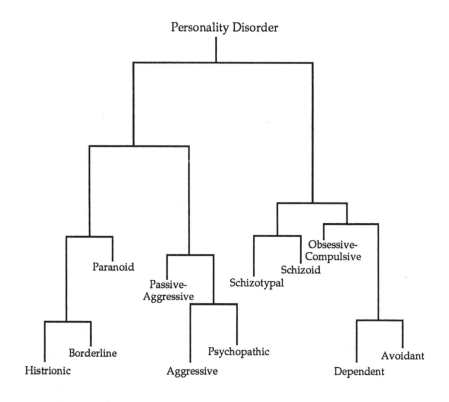

Figure 20. A cluster analysis of DSM–III–R personality disorders. (From Morey, 1988a.)

empirical approach to classification leads to taxonomic coherence. Blashfield (1984) makes the same point in noting that different cluster analytic techniques can generate decidedly different solutions to the same data set. Since no single technique has gained ascendency, one is faced with competing and disparate interpretations. In discussing the more extreme forms of naive empiricism (the idea that one can generate taxonomies on a purely empirical basis) as misguided, both Blashfield and Morey argue for the essential role of a coherent theoretical position from which to derive interpretations of empirical data and personality taxonomies. Needless to say, this augurs well for my own model.

A second line of research on diagnostic categories has sought to determine whether clinicians have some well-formed prototypical conception of the various personality disorders and the extent to which they use DSM criteria in delimiting these prototypes. Typical studies have clinicians sort lists of diagnostic criteria according to their conception of the typical exemplar of a personality disorder, rather than that of an average patient. One such study concluded that clinicians do seem to have "reliable concepts of all categories of personality disorder and that these concepts possess an internal structure based on judged prototypical qualities" (Livesley, 1986, p. 732). In contrast, Blashfield simply asked clinicians to allocate diagnostic criteria to disorder categories without the admonition to focus on prototypical exemplars (Blashfield & Breen, 1989; Blashfield & Haymaker, 1988). Perhaps this is why he found that the majority of subjects failed to sort 30 percent of the criteria into the correct DSM–III–R category, there being considerable overlap in their diagnoses.

While prototype analysis may help to clarify prevailing categories, for instance, by suggesting weightings for specific criteria (Widiger *et al.*, 1988) or providing some guidelines for selecting behavioural indices for criteria, one is still left with an *ad hoc* set of thirteen categories for which there appears to be limited theoretical or empirical support. Prototypical analysis, therefore, might be more productive within the context of a dimensional approach, to which we now turn.

2. *Dimensional research.* Factor analysis and multidimensional scaling have been used to investigate the dimensional structure of disorder categories (Blashfield *et al.*, 1985; Hyler & Lyons, 1988; Kass *et al.*, 1985; Morey *et al.*, 1985; Widiger *et al.*, 1987). While factorial solutions vary in their identification of from two to four underlying dimensions, there is considerable agreement about their interpretation. For instance, the three dimensional structure proposed by Widiger *et al.* (1987) includes: *social involvement* (schizoid/paranoid versus dependent/avoidant/borderline/ histrionic), *assertiveness* (narcissistic/histrionic versus schizoid/avoidant/ dependent/passive-aggressive), and *anxious ruminations* versus *behavioural acting out* (schizotypal/compulsive/paranoid/avoidant versus antiso-cial/passive-aggressive/schizoid/borderline). Widiger *et al.* (1987) claim considerable consistency between their solution and other models. Thus, *social involvement* is similar to that found by Blashfield *et al.* (1985). It also resembles the affiliation dimension of the Interpersonal Circumplex (see Chapter 4) and Millon's self–other dimension (which will be discussed shortly). *Assertiveness* is consistent with the circumplex dimension of power/dominance and Millon's activity–passivity. Similarly, *anxious rumination–behavioural acting out* closely resembles Blashfield's acting out and (according to Widiger *et al.*, 1987) Jung's introversion–extraversion.

On the face of it, the three dimensions identified by Widiger and others bear passing resemblance to the three components of my objective–subjective dimension: *power* (assertiveness), *emotional detachment* (social involvement), and *extraception* (anxious rumination–acting out). The fit is not exact, of course, but it does imply that the DSM–III categories are based primarily on a conative dimension. No purely cognitive or affective dimensions are evident. This is something of a puzzle because several disorders are defined in cognitive and affective terms. For instance, the compulsive category emphasizes cognitive problems, while those labelled as histrionic struggle with labile emotions. Therefore, to catch the full flavour of clinical descriptions, classification needs to cover the cognitive, affective, and conative domains. The extent to which established dimensional models do so is something to which we now turn.

A pair of dimensional models are discussed frequently as a potential basis for reformulating the DSM disorders: Millon's three-dimensional theory and the Interpersonal Circumplex. Millon's (1986b,c) model comprises: *self–other* (the orientation for reinforcement toward self or other), *pleasure–pain* (the tendency to be attracted toward pleasure or to avoid pain), and *active–passive* (the tendency either to initiate or to react to events). By combining the self–other and the pleasure–pain dimensions, Millon produces five categories: *dependent* (other-directed), *independent* (self-oriented), *ambivalent* (self-other ambivalence), *detached* (diminished capacity to experience pleasure/pain), and *discordant* (the blending of pleasure/pain). When crossed with the active–passive dimension, ten basic personality types are produced, each with its associated personality disorder:

passive-detached (schizoid)	active-detached (avoidant)
passive-dependent (dependent)	active-dependent (histrionic)
passive-independent (narcissistic)	active-independent (antisocial)
passive-ambivalent (compulsive)	active-discordant (aggressive)
passive-discordant (masochistic)	active-ambivalent
	(passive-aggressive)

Widiger *et al.* point out, however, that Millon's system remains programmatic for, like mine, "there has not yet been an empiric study of the extent to which this dimensional structure provides an adequate model for the DSM–III personality disorders" (Widiger *et al.*, 1987, p. 557). Further, none of Millon's dimensions bear any conceptual relationship to mine. *Self–other* is related neither to Jung's nor to my interpretation of introversion–extraversion. My objective–subjective distinction refers to an inner–outer difference, between psychological and behavioural interests, not to whether one is oriented toward oneself or toward others, although the latter may be a consequence of objectivity and subjectivity. Likewise, *pleasure–pain* appears to be a biological element in Eysenck's social extraversion, while *active–passive* is related to temperamental factors such as impulsivity. In neither case do these latter dimensions bear on my cognitive and affective dimensions. I would conclude, therefore, that Millon's

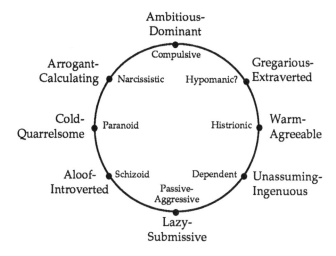

Figure 21. Relationships between the interpersonal circumplex and the DSM–III personality disorders. Wiggins (1982) interpersonal traits lie outside the perimeter, while the corresponding Axis II diagnoses are inside. (From Romney & Bynner, 1989.)

scheme lacks the comprehensiveness required to do justice to the variability of personality disorders.

Wiggins (1982) has used his version of the Interpersonal Circumplex (IPC) as a basis for speculation about the relationships between personality traits and disorders (Fig. 21). In this scheme, disorders are thought to be exaggerated or extreme forms of each dimensional pole, with a new disorder *hypomanic* (extreme gregariousness) being identified to complete the the picture. Wiggins cautions us, however, that

> since categories of psychiatric diagnosis are thought to be fuzzy sets organized around prototypes derived from clinical experience, there is no reason to expect a one-to-one correspondence between such categories and the octants of a more formal interpersonal system. Instead, it is more reasonable to expect that there will be a characteristic profile of the interpersonal variables associated with each diagnostic category. (Wiggins, 1982, p. 213)

While this presents no particular problem in developing a classification scheme, there are other more serious difficulties. Kiesler notes that the IPC focuses solely on interpersonal traits so that "there is no proper place for respondents to rely on inferences about subjects' motives, feeling states, cognitions, or other covert events" (Kiesler, 1986, p. 579). Although this may be an advantage in restricting the possibility of erroneous inferences, it does limit one to only a fraction of the phenomena that go to make up disorders. One virtue of the IPC, however, is that it does lend itself to the development of prototypical classifications.

In a recent study, Romney and Bynner (1989) were able to provide only partial support for Wiggins's hypotheses on the relationship between interpersonal traits and personality disorders. All the relationships proposed by Wiggins, with the exception of those for the compulsive and passive-aggressive, were confirmed. Interestingly, they found that the compulsive disorder did not fit onto the circumplex probably because "a disorder with a strong cognitive component such as compulsive personality disorder is unlikely to have an unambiguous location in the *interpersonal* space defined by Affiliation and Dominance" (Romney & Bynner, 1989, p. 534). This is consistent with Frances and Widiger, who argue: "The compulsive personality, for example, involves such cognitive features as indecisiveness ... and the schizoid and schizotypal disorders are differentiated largely by cognitive impairments in the latter disorder" (Frances & Widiger, 1986, p. 390). The absence of a cognitive dimension from circumplexes leads them to conclude: "To the extent that personality disorders involve more than interpersonal disorders, the circumplex will be an inadequate model" (Frances & Widiger, 1986, p. 390).

In sum, there is growing interest in the possibility of conceptualizing personality disorders as prototypes and in the prospect that this process could be facilitated by understanding the dimensional structure of disorders. Attempts to do so have had mixed results. Both cluster and factor analyses have identified groupings that appear to revolve around a power dimension, which is, in essence, an interpersonal trait. Similarly, formal dimensional models like those of Millon and Wiggins emphasize interpersonal qualities. However, personality disorders are best seen as involving more than just interpersonal difficulties, as is apparent in trying to classify the compulsive disorder. Thus, since an interpersonal focus is something of a limitation, there is a need for a broader theoretical basis. For instance, the overlap between the avoidant and dependent disorders (Blashfield & Breen, 1989) could be reduced by the addition of a cognitive dimension, and the histrionic/narcissistic confusion might be remedied by use of an affective dimension. All of this is, of course, another way of saying that I believe my model may have something to offer to the classification of disorders.

3. *The present model.* To begin with, I adopt a conception of disorder that is common to all intrapsychic conflict models, the view that an imbalance between conflicting psychological forces or processes is maladaptive. To put it another way, extremely inflexible behaviour in

which the individual persists with a particular style, or pursues a particular goal where this is clearly inappropriate, is characteristic of a personality disorder. In terms of my model, therefore, the persistence of behaviour at one extreme of a dimension, despite changing circumstances, is seen as problematic. Kiesler is of a like mind when he comments: "The abnormal person, rather than possessing the flexibility of the normal individual to use the broad range of interpersonal behaviors warranted by different social situations, is locked into a rigid and extreme use of a limited class of interpersonal actions" (Kiesler, 1986, p. 572). The kinds of disorder associated with the extreme poles of each of my dimensions are described in what follows.

Disorders of *cognitive style* are clearly described in Shapiro's (1965) classical description of neurotic styles, which is organized around the analytic–holistic distinction. Thus, his "obsessive–compulsive" shows a disordered form of analytical thinking in which the person's attentional style is intense, sharply focused, and restricted, with a tendency to ignore the incidental, peripheral aspects of stimuli and events. The net result is that, while this obsessive preoccupation with detail may result in the development of factual knowledge in a restricted area, the broader picture is lost. In contrast, the "hysterical" (histrionic) style is holistic. Attention is easily caught by transient events (making the hysterical person susceptible to the immediately obvious) and is easily distracted by the opinions of others. An incapacity for persistent concentration and the tendency to fuse memories means that the hysteric is left with impressions of events which, although vivid, are commonly lacking in factual detail. Thus, thinking is global and diffuse, with a tendency to rely on guesses and hunches rather than upon careful evaluation of the facts. Similar viewpoints on the narrowly focused attentional style of "obsessives" have been offered by Pollak (1979) and Claridge (1985). The more diffuse style of "hysterics" is described in Pollak (1981).

As with cognitive style, disorders of *emotional style* are exhibited as an involuntary excess, *i.e.*, extremes of instability (dysphoria, euphoria) and stability (flat affect, unreactivity). The disruptive effects of emotional instability are discussed by Horowitz *et al.*, who describe the case of Ellen, a borderline personality.

> Her most disturbing out-of-control experiences [were] entry into a chaotically jumbled state, in which she felt out of control. Ideas and feelings were experienced as jumbles of intensely vivid but disconnected sequences of imagery.... She could tolerate manageable states of irritable anger, but these could rapidly escalate to furious rage, in which Ellen was flooded by profound anger. In addition ... there was a third relatively uncontrolled state, that of flooded despairing sadness. This state contained an element of panic, with a piercing and unbearable quality that the patient described as

"like vomiting" her grief.... Ellen oscillated confusingly between self-pity, anger, compliance, and anxious and disparaging laughter. (Horowitz *et al.*, 1984, p. 271)

At the other extreme of emotional stability, Rachman's research on bomb-disposal experts in Northern Ireland (Rachman, 1984; Rachman *et al.*, 1983) suggests "the existence of a small group of people who are unusually competent and calm, and who may be particularly well suited for carrying out hazardous tasks" (Rachman *et al.*, 1983, p. 163). In particular, soldiers who had been decorated for gallantry in bomb disposal showed significantly lower physiological responsiveness to stressful situations than even other experts in the same line of business. However, the fact that these men survived in their chosen field suggests that they were not so emotionally unreactive as to become careless. Clinically significant levels of emotional unreactivity, as in the *schizoid* personality, are, presumably, more severe.

Disorders of *conative content* are illustrated, and their vicissitudes are examined, in an interesting discussion of objectivity–subjectivity by Smail (1984). In his view, we live in an "objectified" culture, one in which the essence of human relationships is manipulation, exploitation, deception, and competition. In conversation, we bristle with mutual suspicion and hostility, carefully avoiding intimacy by being judgmental and defensive. The purpose of "objectification" is to avoid the painful realities that our personal sensitivity might impose upon us. Objectification starts early when, as children, we learn to dissemble, to attend to appearances, to conform to parental standards, and, most important of all, to practice impression management. It is those who become both skilled at impression management and comfortable in the roles they adopt that are commonly seen as psychologically "healthy." If it is to be carried off with success, such a state of bliss requires a denial of personal insight and a pervasive emotional anasthaesia. On the other hand, there are those who are unable to escape their subjectivity, even though they may wish to do so. They appear to be afflicted by an intuitive sensitivity that makes their interaction with the "objective" world of impression management a painful experience. Yet, some persist in their efforts to explore their own experiences and to establish intimate contact with others. An unfortunate but familiar pattern is of the sensitive child born into an insensitive family, ending up with a sense of personal failure and worthlessness. They are to be found standing in corners "aching with a sense of their own futility ... searching despairingly and vainly for words that will introduce them to others as worthy of attention" (Smail, 1984, p. 47). Most people, therefore, give up "subjectivity" as a bad job, the very rarity of those who can function successfully in this mode being a sad reflection on the nature of our society. In this context, then, disorders of conative

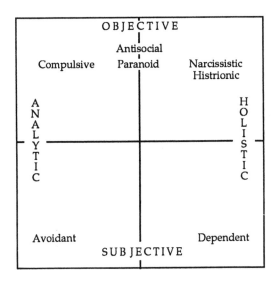

Figure 22. Personality types and disorders. (From A. Miller, 1988.)

content would be seen as extreme forms of objectivity and subjectivity. The extremely objective person, in Smail's sense, would be one whose life is a matter of impression management and the manipulation of both self and others (antisocial, narcissistic). The personal world of intuitive insight, emotional sensitivity and intimacy, caring, compassion, and so on, must be avoided at all costs as a potential source of troublesome ideas and feelings. In contrast, the extremely subjective person is likely to experience the objective world as one which makes it difficult to live as a "subject" and to establish some "genuine" contact with others. As a result, the intuitively sensitive may, according to Smail, lead lives of psychological pain and loneliness and experience the feeling of being a fundamental failure as a human being (avoidant).

When one turns to the descriptions of personality disorders in DSM–III (Millon, 1981), it is possible to identify extreme behaviours of the kind noted above on all three dimensions in many of the classical disorders (Table 7). In turn, this allows one to speculate about the dimensional basis of each disorder as well as their relationship with one another (Fig. 22). My bases for these speculations are as follows:

(i) *The objective–analytic type* combines an objective preoccupation with power, interpersonal control, and emotional detachment with an analytical concern for factual detail and logical precision. When taken to an extreme, these characteristics express themselves in overcontrol and a narrow focus on trivial detail, precisely the kind of behaviour that

TABLE 7. CHARACTERISTICS OF DSM-III DISORDERS IN RELATION TO
THE DIMENSIONS OF PERSONAL STYLES

	Objective/Subjective	Analytic/Holistic	Emotional Stability/Instability
Compulsive	*objective:* preoccupied with self-control; avoids introspection and attains little self-insight; seeks emotional detachment; little ability to express warmth and tenderness; rigidly structures environment; overly concerned with rules, procedures and formalities.	*analytic:* exhibits a narrow, small-minded outlook; a preoccupation with trivial detail and objective "facts," all of which preclude the possibility of developing a broader perspective.	*unstable:* sits atop a powder-keg of inner turmoil, his/her greatest task being to control the intense feelings that lurk below a cloak of respectability; commonly prone to anxiety disorders.
Antisocial	*objective:* power-oriented, tough, unsentimental; obtains gratification by humiliating and dominating others; callous, insensitive and vindictive; absence of self-insight; contemptuous of intimacy, compassion, emotional warmth.	*analytic and holistic:* most exhibit clarity and logic in their thinking (implying analytic capacity) but rarely exhibit foresight; the success of some variants implies a versatile cognitive style.	*unstable:* frequent signs of emotional distress and dysphoria; an irrascible temper that flares easily into fury and vindictiveness.
Paranoid	*objective:* inordinate fear of losing independence and power to shape events in accord with grandiose sense of self; mistrusts others, seeks to avoid entrapment by becoming hard, obdurate, vigilant; lacks self-insight, compassion, warmth.	*analytic and holistic:* lives in a world of fantasy and delusion composed of fixed beliefs, and unrealistic perceptions (holistic); hypervigilant, intense and narrow search for confirmation of expectations (analytic).	*unstable:* finds it difficult to relax; appears tense, edgy, irritable, disputatious, factious, abrasive; prone to extremes of mood and general anxiety disorders.

	Objective/Subjective	Analytic/Holistic	Emotional Stability/Instability
Narcissistic	*objective:* shows interpersonal exploitativeness, uses others to indulge self; emotional detachment, low empathy, lack of regard for others; avoids introspection and lacks self-insight.	*holistic:* preoccupied with pretentious, unrealistic fantasies; takes liberties with the "facts" in refashioning "reality" to his/her own liking. Imaginative, cognitively expansive.	*stable:* affect is generally relaxed; a pervasive sense of well-being; a buoyancy of mood; does not characteristically develop anxiety disorders.
Histrionic	*objective:* avoids introspection; experiences a barren intrapsychic world, an inner emptiness; compensates by actively seeking attention, reassurance; manipulative, seductive; intensely extraceptive.	*holistic:* prone to flights of (romantic) fantasy; thought processes scattered; little interest in careful analysis; pays fleeting attention to detail; inability to think in a concentrated, logical fashion.	*unstable:* lively, dramatic and exhibitionistic; highly labile emotions, overly reactive, easily excitable, capricious and given to angry outburst or tantrums; intensely expressive.
Dependent	*subjective:* overly strong needs for affection and nurturance; noncompetitive, avoids autonomy; subordinates own needs to those of others; emotionally warm, tender, considerate; friendly, obliging, generous, obsequious.	*holistic:* tends to be naive, unperceptive, uncritical; inclined to see only the pleasant side of troubling events; minimally introspective, a pollyanna perspective on life.	*stable:* a pacific temperament; docile, friendly, but with a tendency to maudlin sentimentality
Avoidant	*subjective:* desires affection and acceptance but socially anxious; empathetic; intensely sensitive to rejection, humiliation; uncertain about the sincerity of others; inclined to retreat to the introspective world of thoughts and feelings.	*analytic:* sensitive, acutely perceptive observer; hyperalert to feelings and intentions of others; vigilant scanning for signs of rejection; tends to be excessively introspective and self-conscious.	*unstable:* experiences recurrent anxiety and mood disharmonies, affective dysphoria, easily distressed by rejection; upset by lack of social ease; prone to anxiety disorders.

Note: based on descriptions from *Disorders of Personality: DSM–III Axis II* by T. Millon (1981). New York, Wiley; from A. Miller (1988).

typifies the compulsive personality disorder (Table 7). Compulsive behaviour is also associated with high levels of anxiety and other emotional difficulties, which suggests that this disorder can be identified more precisely as an emotionally unstable variant of the objective–analytical style (Fig. 22). There does not appear to be a DSM–III equivalent of the emotionally stable variant, although Millon (1981, p. 288) suggests the possibility of a schizoid–compulsive combination that would fit into this stylistic category.

(*ii*) *The objective–holistic type* shows the same impersonal, manipulative orientation that one sees in the objective–analytic style. However, power/control is not always achieved by the direct manipulation of events; it is often achieved through more symbolic manipulation. Thus, the holistic aspect of this style shows itself in the development of belief systems and fantasies that are imposed on "objective" reality. Therefore, the objective–holistic style is imaginative but impersonal. More extreme forms of this style would start to exhibit a callous indifference to others, together with a drift into delusional fantasy composed of beliefs that are not checked against "reality." The DSM–III disorder that is most consistent with this style is the narcissistic type (Table 7), which is also described as being emotionally relaxed, suggesting that it can be interpreted as the emotionally stable variant of the objective–holistic style (Fig. 22). The emotionally unstable variant, which combines fear and hostility with narcissism, can be identified with the histrionic disorder, while even more aggressive variants are best interpreted as the narcissistic–antisocial (aggressive) mixed personality disorder (Millon, 1981, p. 172). The antisocial and paranoid disorders are clearly objective, unstable styles, but their location on the analytic-holistic dimension is more uncertain (Table 7). There appear to be a number of antisocial disorders, most of which exhibit clarity and logic in thinking, together with a record of success in manipulating others. This suggests the presence of a versatile cognitive style, one that does not limit the person's flexibility in pursuing his or her nefarious ends. Similarly, the paranoid's combination of hypervigilance with delusional fantasy suggests the presence of a mixed cognitive style. I have, therefore, placed both disorders in a central (versatile) position on the cognitive style dimension (Fig. 22).

(*iii*) *The subjective–analytic type* shows a primary interest in subjective experience and some lack of interest in the practical, objective world. The analytic component leads to a tendency to analyse personal experience, a psychologically minded search for self-insight and empathetic understanding of others. Thus, there is an inclination to withdraw into a reflective, narrowly preoccupied world of introspective thought at the expense of engagement with the broader reality. Extreme forms of this style involve an excessive concern for psychological involvement, intimacy, and affection, coupled with distress at difficulty in achieving these ends. Overindulgence in analytic, introspective thought would tend to result in obsessive rumination about the minutiae of personal experience. The avoidant personality disorder appears to fall into this category (Table 7) as the emotionally unstable variant of the subjective–analytic style (Fig. 22). No emotionally stable variant is described in DSM–III, although a schizotypal-avoidant combination is mentioned by Millon (1981).

(*iv*) *The subjective–holistic type* might be most conveniently typified as being "experiential." That is, there is a primary interest in personal-emotional experiences but little interest in introspective analysis. Thus, the subjective–holist lives in a world of personal episodes, events, and unanalysed personal experiences. There is little or no interest in factual detail or in the intricacies of the practical world. Like the subjective–analytic approach to life, the subjective–holistic style is one in which the individual seeks to behave as a "subject," by establishing some degree of intimacy with others. The holistic element shows itself, however, in an imaginative, rather global, orientation that in extreme cases drifts into fantasy and delusion. The DSM–III disorder that appears to exhibit this style, *i.e.*, the dependent personality, is clearly subjective, holistic, and emotionally stable (Fig. 22, Table 7).

The difficulty I have had in fitting the remaining DSM–III disorders into the style model would appear to raise doubts about the validity of either the model or the DSM–III classification system, or both. I am not sure which of these alternatives is the case. However, in support of my model, I am inclined to take the view of Millon (1981, p. 332) who, in speaking about the borderline disorder, suggests that it might be viewed more appropriately as a level of disorder rather than as a diagnostic category. This approach could well be extended to include the passive–aggressive, schizoid and schizotypal disorders.

For instance, a primary defining feature of the schizoid and schizotypal disorders appears to be an excessive emotional stability or unreactive indifference. Their indifference to both the objective and the subjective worlds (as well as their characterization as socially introverted but not intraceptive or introspective) makes it difficult to place them meaningfully on the objective–subjective dimension. Similarly, the apparent perceptual insensitivity and defective perceptual scanning of the schizoid (which implies an holistic form of thought) may simply reflect their indifference to the world around them, an indifference that may also exhibit itself in the poverty of their attempts at holistic thought. There is the same difficulty in placing the schizotypal disorder on the analytic–holistic dimension. The tendency to thought disorder and word salad implies a gross form of analytic thinking, but, at the same time, schizotypals are also described as developing recurrent illusions, magical and telepathic thinking, daydreams, fantasies, and metaphorical thinking—all characteristic of a more holistic tendency. What might be happening here is that the schizoid and schizotypal categories may be heterogeneous, a disparate array of individuals who share a common emotional indifference. It is possible, therefore, that these disorders reflect extreme behaviour on the emotional stability–instability dimension and, as such, could be subsumed under other category labels as the emotionally stable (unreactive, indifferent) variants. For instance, Millon (1981) recognizes schizotypal–avoidant and schizoid–dependent mixed types.

At the other extreme of emotional instability, one finds the borderline and passive–aggressive disorders, both of which exhibit emotional lability and difficulty in emotional control. Once again, the problem of their classification might be most sensibly resolved by viewing them as levels of disorder rather than as diagnostic categories. Such a strategy would result in their being subsumed under the four main types (in my model) as unstable variants. Along these lines, Millon recognizes borderline–dependent and borderline–compulsive mixed personalities, as well as noting that borderline characteristics are occasionally displayed in combination with narcissistic and avoidant personalities (Millon, 1981, p. 356).

In sum, my attempt to use the model in interpreting the DSM–III personality disorders (as described by Millon, 1981) results in a classification that appears to have some face validity. Thus, the pattern of disorders that results is consistent with the findings of the multivariate analyses discussed earlier. For instance, the close relationships between the histrionic and narcissistic (as well as avoidant and dependent) disorders is maintained, as is the contrast between the larger clusters of antisocial/paranoid/narcissistic/histrionic and dependent/avoidant. It differs from other studies in locating the compulsive disorder at the objective pole. Widiger *et al.* (1987), for instance, would prefer to locate it midway between objectivity and subjectivity. However, the present analysis does allow one to distinguish between previously confounded diagnostic categories such as avoidant/dependent, as well as to identify ways in which some disorders need to be reconceptualized.

(*b*) *Vocational psychology.* The issue of interest here is the nature and development of professional competence. This is problematic in the sense that there is little consensus on what "professional competence" might be and even less agreement on how it might be fostered through education, etc. Such a degree of uncertainty is unfortunate, given the central role of professionals in society, as well as the status and privileges they enjoy

(Friedson, 1984). Professionals lay claim to this status on grounds of special expertise and ethical responsibility (Baum, 1987), but whether the majority of professionals actually exhibit such competencies is a much debated question (Lynton & Elman, 1987; Schon, 1987). At the heart of the controversy is the problem of defining professional competence. Once defined, it may then be possible to resolve some of the disputes over the need for educational reform. I believe that my model speaks to both issues.

It is relatively easy to agree on a general definition of professional competence, such as *the ability to perform effectively in a particular job or role* (Grant, 1979), but it is much more difficult to be specific. Attempts to do so commonly involve some form of job analysis in which the various knowledge and skills needed for effective performance are assessed. While job analysis is particularly useful in dealing with those occupations where performance skills can be easily observed (*e.g.*, auto-mechanic), problems arise in the professional domain where the crucial tasks are mental and, therefore, covert (Schoon, 1985). In addition, traditional job analysis tends to result in lists of phenotypic skills rather than identifying genotypic competencies. The latter, if identifiable, are preferable, for they may generalize across jobs and are, therefore, more useful in informing educational policy. To complicate matters further, many professions are engaged in internecine warfare over their role in society. In professional psychology, for instance, differences of opinion over the most appropriate balance between "basic" science and "professional" knowledge and skills have resulted in differing models of competence (Stern, 1984). Persistent dispute is fueled by a minority view that the role of psychology in modern society (and hence job definitions within the profession) has become that of a co-conspirator in an outmoded and autocratic system of health care (Rothblum *et al.*, 1986). The fact that many professions cannot agree on their role in society does not exactly facilitate either job analysis or the definition of competence. A common response to all this is for professions to avoid the question of effective job performance and turn inwards toward what one might call an incestuous definition of competence, one that focuses on the assumed "core" of a discipline. Proficiency with the technical knowledge and skills that are thought to define the discipline becomes the acid test of competence. Needless to say, arguments over the nature of this "core" abound, and attempts to accommodate differing persuasions result in increasingly bloated curricula.

Some observers, however, see much of this debate as parochial, one that misses the obvious point that professional education and the notions of competence that underlie it are fundamentally flawed (Pacey, 1983;

Schon, 1987; Wenk, 1988). Professional educators, they say, have tended to make the wrong choice when faced with a basic professional dilemma:

> In the varied topography of professional practice, there is a high, hard ground overlooking a swamp. On the high ground, manageable problems lend themselves to solution through the application of research-based theory and technique. In the swampy lowland, messy, confusing problems defy technical solution. The irony of this situation is that the problems of the high ground tend to be relatively unimportant to individuals of society at large ... while in the swamp lie the problems of greatest human concern. The practitioner must choose. Shall he remain on the high ground where he can solve relatively unimportant problems according to prevailing standards of rigor, or shall he descend to the swamp of important problems and nonrigorous inquiry? (Schon, 1987, p. 3)

It appears that many professions have taken to the high ground, asserting a narrow preoccupation with what Schon calls *technical rationality* in their definition of competence. Technical rationality is an offspring of positivist philosophy which asserts that only empirically demonstrable phenomena can form the basis of "knowledge." Extreme positivists, therefore, maintain that anything that cannot be "operationalized" and empirically tested is of no value in developing an understanding of a problem. In practice, this posture results in a preoccupation with *empirical* "fact" (as opposed to intuitive insight), a detached *objectivity* (rather than subjective involvement), a preference for *reductive* analysis (in contrast to holistic synthesis), and *quantitative* rather than qualitative analyses (Linstone *et al.*, 1984; A. Miller, 1985). There is no doubt that the precision and effort to attain objective detachment that one sees in the best forms of positivist thinking make it an ideal vehicle for dealing with certain kinds of well-structured, circumscribed problems. However, when one turns to real-world *messes*, a strict adherence to technical rationality becomes a liability. This message has been propounded by philosophers of science (Berman, 1984; Capra, 1982; Drengson, 1983), as well as by some members of the professional community itself (Dalton, 1986; Linstone *et al.*, 1984; Pacey, 1983; Rivage-Seul, 1987; Robottom, 1987; Udwadia, 1986; Vanderburg, 1989).

The rejection of technical rationality as either the sole, or the most important component of, professional practice has resulted in three main proposals for a broader conception of professional competence:

1. Intellectual training has to be extended beyond a preoccupation with reductive–analytical (positivist) thinking to include practice in holistic–intuitive modes of problem-solving. In other words, a concerted effort is needed to develop and to refine *professional judgment* (Schon, 1987; Sewell, 1974).

2. Professional work is more than detached, intellectual problem-solving. It takes place within a social context and has sociopolitical consequences. At the same time, effective professional action requires an ability to manoeuver through the tangled web of social and bureaucratic obstacles. Therefore, some form of "social" competencies are an important aspect of professional life (Dorcey, 1986; Petulla, 1987).

3. Professionals can no longer pretend to be disinterested experts who wash their hands of social responsibility, for there are clear ethical implications surrounding their actions. Ethical awareness is, therefore, an important component of professional life, one that requires some understanding of one's personal motives and values (Morrill, 1980; Rivage-Seul, 1987; Yeazell, 1986).

In other words, all of these authors are talking about the need for three levels or kinds of competence: *technical* (that which expands our ability to control the world around us); *practical* (the knowledge required to get things done in a given social context); and, *personal* (the ability to free ourselves from those psychosocial pressures that inhibit our capacity to understand ourselves and others). The fact that a tripartite model of professional competence is emerging from the current round of debate is both intriguing and unsettling in light of Holliday and Chandler's (1986) conclusion that similar competencies have been recognized over the centuries as the core constituents of "wisdom." It appears, therefore, that recent analyses have rediscovered ancient truths.

Recent research on "practical" and "personal" competencies has generated lists of qualities that appear to be important in professional practice (Boyatzis, 1982; Stark et al., 1986). However, the problem is that much of this work is atheoretical. Consequently, there is no way of knowing whether these capabilities can be fostered through education or how one might go about this task. If, on the other hand, research were to be embedded in a personality model, individual differences in competence could be specified more clearly and the potential for change estimated. It is in this regard that my model might be useful. For instance, it provides a dimensional basis that helps one understand the nature of, and relationships between, the three sets of competencies noted above. Thus, there is reason to recognize two kinds of *technical* competence: the detailed, analytical knowledge of the objective world (objective–analytic), and a tacit understanding of the way in which physical systems work (objective–holistic). Similarly, two kinds of *personal* competence are plausible: an introspective understanding of the inner world of self and others (subjective–analytic), complemented by a tacit sense of appropriate and effective interpersonal behaviour (subjective–holistic). *Practical/social* competence, on the other hand, is more difficult to place within the model. Presumably, it requires a combination of interpersonal skills, coupled with an objective understanding of social and organizational structures. If this is the case, then its major defining elements would be drawn from the OH and SH quadrants.

A more interesting implication of the model, however, is that the most versatile professional is one who has developed competencies in all four quadrants of the present model, the question being whether formal education can encourage such versatility. One obvious problem, in this regard, is that many students enter higher education with distinct, and rather narrow, preferences for particular cognitive styles and epistemological values (Witkin *et al.*, 1977). Requiring them to become more versatile implies that they would have to adopt styles and values that may be uncongenial to them. For instance, it is difficult to persuade an analytical person to become more holistic, and vice versa (see Chapter 2), because preferred styles serve a psychodynamic function. That is, they are ways of reassuring individuals that they have some control over their lives. Thus, a person's choice of style is emotionally tinged. Any attempt to persuade or to force a person to change his or her style will be met with a strong emotional reaction. People cling to their styles like limpets and can become quite distraught if there is any intimation that they should change. One sees this in the rather brittle quality of professional relationships when experts are thrown together in interdisciplinary groups. Barmark and Wallen (1979), for instance, in a study of a Swedish ecology project, found that the empirical (objective–analytic) and systems (objective–holistic) biologists were unable to cooperate effectively with one another because they were either unwilling or incapable of adjusting their incompatible intellectual styles. To make matters worse, scientists of different stylistic persuasions have a tendency to view one another with amused contempt (Mitroff & Kilmann, 1978). It follows that any attempt to have students change their preferred style may well be greeted with varying degrees of hostility and resistance. The most vociferous response is likely to come from the extremely specialized individuals, those with the strongest emotional and intellectual commitment to a particular style. This has interesting implications for curriculum design because it suggests that the use of electives or interdisciplinary programmes as a "broadening" device will be ineffective with such stylistic specialists. Perhaps they should be left to hone the one tool with which they seem happy. What I conclude from all this is consistent with the aphorism: "To those that hath shall be given." The students who are likely to become versatile are those who show a predisposition to such flexible behaviour. In psychological terms, they would occupy the middle range of the analytic–holistic and objective–subjective dimensions and, have less emotional attachment to any particular style. Such people do exist and, interestingly enough, gravitate toward such disciplines as biology, geography, and psychology (Hudson, 1968).

While shifts on the analytic–holistic dimension are possible under the right circumstances, changes toward more objective or subjective behaviour are more difficult to achieve. At stake are a person's most basic values and their most deeply rooted conceptions of themselves as persons. The strength of the emotions that are released by attempts to have "objective" students function in a more "subjective" way is well illustrated by my own experiences in a small agricultural college in Northern Ireland. What I was required to teach seemed to me to be relatively innocuous, simply a smattering of psychological concepts that I hoped would be of use to prospective professionals heading for managerial positions. Nothing had prepared me for their response. A small minority seemed relatively interested in such ideas; a larger proportion were apathetic; and a substantial minority reacted with such vicious anger that I was at a loss to explain their behaviour. As they sat in class, glaring out balefully from behind sullen masks, it slowly occurred to me that what I considered to be relatively innocuous was to them profoundly disturbing. In effect, I was forcing them to indulge in introspective thought, to talk about feelings and emotions, inner thoughts, attitudes, and biases, all of which they found inexplicably threatening. Some of them could hardly contain their anger, to the point that around the campus they took to throwing things at me, either verbal abuse or anything physical on which they could lay their hands. In later years, I experienced the same, albeit less physical, reaction when teaching forestry students, among whom a similar minority reacted with barely suppressed fury when I began to discuss the "inner" world. To say the very least, such a reaction tends to cramp one's teaching style, with unfortunate consequences for such matters as moral and ethical education. If students are to understand the moral and ethical dimensions of their work, they need to be comfortable in discussing their own moral values. A prerequisite for this is a capacity for introspective thought and self-analysis. If some students reject the latter out of hand, their moral development will be hindered. Perhaps this may help to explain the findings of a survey I conducted some years ago (A. Miller, 1984) which found that a sample of students in forest resource management were either morally egocentric (Kohlberg's preconventional level) or morally conventional (Kohlberg's conventional level). Only one student out of a sample of ninety-two showed signs of the higher-order morality involved in Kohlberg's postconventional reasoning.

It is not clear how familiar professional faculty are with these issues for, rather than encouraging versatility, traditional professional education may well stifle it. Indeed, mainstream departments in science and engineering appear to assume that objective–analytic skills are the *sine qua non* of excellence and those students who are deficient in such skills must endure judicious doses of technical rationality. The problem is that, in the process, most departments neglect the other three types of intellectual skill, a fact that is attracting scathing criticism of professional education. For instance, Wenk (1988) assures us that current engineering programs in the United States are obsolete. At best they train technicians capable only of occupying modest roles in large organizations but unable to cope with the complexity of real-world problems. In fact, modern engineers are not really engineers at all (Sample, 1988). At the root of this debacle is a preoccupation with a narrow science/mathematics knowledge base and a lack of attention to more holistic skills in synthesis and design (Cady *et al.*, 1988; Felder, 1987). A similar refrain can be heard from Australia, where Bawden and Valentine (1984) believe that post-secondary education in agriculture has failed to grapple with the problems posed by reductionist science. In their view, students are not being prepared to handle the complexities of modern agriculture. When one turns to forestry education in Canada, Thirgood (1988) characterizes the system as excessively preoccupied with a narrow technical domain, at the expense of liberal education. The situation seems to be no better in the sciences where Fischbach and Sell (1986) find chemistry being taught in a purely analytical fashion through the use of well-formed problems with clear solutions, quite unlike the world in which chemists actually find themselves. Meanwhile, according to Huszagh and Infante (1989), biology is dominated by mediocrities interested only in amassing vast quantities of information, while being hostile to more speculative, holistic theory—the very activity needed to integrate data and produce new ideas. Even when one turns to environmental science, where one would expect to find more innovative pedagogy, the typical curriculum (at least in England) remains technocentric, emphasizing a mechanistic and reductionist world view (O'Sullivan, 1986). It would seem, therefore, that mainstream curricula in the applied and pure sciences are preoccupied with objective–analytic activity, spend much less time in developing objective–holistic skills, and virtually ignore the need for competence in the subjective–analytic and holistic areas.

In sum, the present model provides a useful basis for understanding the nature of, and relationships between, several generic competencies. It specifies the higher-order goal of professional versatility and allows one to estimate the difficulties involved in developing a broader repertoire of competencies. When the model is used to assess the results of current programmes in professional schools, it appears that many are one-sided, emphasizing a narrow set of competencies at the expense of others that are essential in the development of professional versatility. I conclude, therefore, that the model has some utility in this domain.

(c) *Environmental psychology*. In this section, I shall attempt to demonstrate the utility of the present model in understanding the psychological nature of environmental conflicts.

It does not require much exposure to environmental disputes before one begins to recognize clearly defined factions which seem to adopt mutually antagonistic postures almost regardless of the particular issue at hand. Indeed, much of the conflict between factions is less concerned with ecological substance than it is about personal styles. In other words, what one sees in environmental and many other disputes is a clash between mutually incompatible personality types. Unfortunately, there has been limited interest in pursuing this kind of personological analysis; the result is that little or no research is available for discussion. Apart from occasional studies such as Efron (1984) on the influence of intellectual style on estimates of the risk associated with exposure to carcinogens, and Petak (1980) on the relationship between epistemological values and environmental planning, the only substantive work is that of Cotgrove (1982), a sociologist who sought to understand the postures of influential groups in society (environmentalists, industrialists, public officials) in terms of their world views and intellectual styles. I am indebted to his work not only for clarifying my understanding of the relationship between personality and environment, but also for stimulating me to study the matter more empirically than is my custom. Recently, for instance, I undertook to analyse the writings and public pronouncements of the various factions involved in a local environmental dispute: the spruce budworm epidemic in New Brunswick. What I found were clear indications of the presence of the four main personality types (A. Miller, 1984/5). Since this is the only piece of work that relates my model to an environmental dispute, it might be worth looking at it in some detail.

The spruce budworm is an endemic pest that has reached epidemic levels of infestation in the spruce-fir forests of eastern Canada, particularly in New Brunswick. The insect became a significant pest only when the provincial forest industries became dependent on the production of pulp and paper for their commercial viability. Since 1952, in an attempt to protect valuable softwood species, the provincial government has undertaken, a chemical spray programme which covers an area of up to three million hectares annually. The spray programme is implemented each year in the face of growing resistance from environmental groups who demand that the use of chemical pesticides be stopped on the grounds of threats to public health and to the environment. Thus, the "spruce budworm problem," like so many environmental issues, is an often acrimonious argument involving scientists, bureaucrats, industrialists, producers, environmental groups, and a perplexed public. The questions of interest in this regard are how the four personality types perceive the budworm problem, and how this perception influences the kinds of solution that are generated. What one would anticipate is that each type would tend to see a different "problem," or to focus on different aspects of it. Not only would this limit the kinds of solutions produced, but it also means that there is little common ground upon which to establish dialogue with other types. In what follows, an attempt is made to depict the behaviour of each type.

1. *Reductionist (analytical scientist).* This is the style of thinking that predominates among government and industrial scientists, as well as among those bureaucrats whose training is scientific. In essence, it reflects the reductive–analytical training at the core of traditional scientific and technical education. Such individuals see themselves as impartial, objective, technical persons involved in obtaining the kind of scientific information that will allow the refinement and improvement of the basically sound pest management strategies already in place. Typically, they contrast themselves with what they see as the overemotional, irrational, and largely uninformed environmentalists who appear bent on disrupting the ongoing scientific process, a process that is best left to technical experts. For example, the former Minister of Natural Resources notes in a presentation to the Canadian Pest Management Society:

> The real danger we face in our forest industry today is not the budworm itself, the real danger lies ... in that adverse public influence ... which [is] based on inaccurate information, on hearsay, on gossip, on innuendo and on fear. If ... a negative public influence is permitted to grow and to prevail, then the budworm battle will be lost, not through failure of the spray programme ... but rather through our own failure to maintain public confidence in the difficult decisions which must be made if we are to save our softwood forests and the lifestyle in N[ew] B[runswick]. which is so dependent upon them. (Bird, 1979, p. 2)

The "separation" aspect of this type is seen in attempts to limit the "problem" by asserting the primacy of its technical and engineering aspects. This does not mean that reductionists are unaware of the political and social elements, but rather that they do not see the latter as part of the "real problem" and, thus, not really within their professional jurisdiction. Hence, the words of admonishment from Bird, pointing out that scientists need to expand their conception of their responsibility and to reassure the public: "To build public confidence and to maintain a positive public influence concerning the budworm protection programme ... to communicate with our citizens effectively about the problems and the solutions" (Bird, 1979, p. 3). The implication is that the reductionist's view of the problem is correct, that the solutions they have developed are the best available, and that scientists should take an active role in convincing the public that this is so. This belief that the technical experts should "educate" the public for their own good (together with the view that members of the public are something of a nuisance) is a theme often advanced by resource managers.

It follows from the above that the perception of the "spruce budworm problem" by reductionists is very narrow. This limited view is founded on the belief that the basic aim of the pest control programme should be to minimize damage to the host species, thereby protecting the economic viability of the pulp industries. Thus the problem is defined as a budworm epidemic, a single insect species that has exceeded tolerable levels and needs to be brought back under control. The terms used in describing policy reflect these basic assumptions. One sees, for example, concentration on the insect in "pest control," on biocidal strategies in "spray programmes," and on protecting the host in "crop protection programmes." Since broader ecological and sociopolitical factors are not part of the problem definition and are not reflected in the available terminology, they cannot be incorporated into problem solutions. As Baskerville notes: "the historical crop protection programme has been treated as a simple, straightforward procedure and this has aided in the formation of a rather unrealistic view of the problem on the part of many professionals" (Baskerville, 1976, p. 1).

Given the reductionist perception of the problem as largely technical and a matter of insect control, it follows that the solutions that have been developed are primarily technical and biocidal. The solution to the budworm problem is to kill the insect in sufficient numbers so as to minimize damage to the host species. This is seen as being highly successful, barring a few unfortunate side effects, while alternative strategies are said not to be available:

> There are some simple, yet profound truths.... The budworm protection programme has been a tremendous success. It has preserved our forest environment and our forest economy. Another truth is that there are no options presently available to deal with the budworm, except the existing spray programme. Of the entire fifteen optional areas of research and development mentioned by Dr. Baskerville in his 1976 report, none except the spraying of insecticides has been advanced to even reasonable levels of effectiveness. The main truth is that, although the spray programme is not very desirable ... it is the only option available to us at this time, and may remain so for years to come. (Bird, 1979, p. 5)

It would be interesting at this point to consider how the reductionists deal with criticism and evidence that is contrary to their beliefs. Perkins (1982) argues that the chemical control paradigm has fallen out of favour among research entomologists in agriculture, although this demise has not yet been reflected in farming practice. Presumably, among scientists, there has been a shift toward more ecologically based strategies such as integrated pest management. In order to make this shift, it would be necessary for those involved to reconsider the way in which they perceive the problem, broadening it to incorporate other aspects of the environment. A similar change appears to be occurring in New Brunswick with regard to the spruce budworm problem, although there remains an entrenched body of professionals who, rather than reformulating the problem, simply reaffirm their commitment to established perceptions, advocating more intensive efforts along the same lines:

> Our funding of research, testing and monitoring activities must continue to increase. Only by the most cautious selection of the best chemical formulations we can find, by careful development of the best application technique, and by intensive control and monitoring of the results of our efforts, can we successfully combat the budworm. (Bird, 1979, p. 7)

However, critics of the analytical scientist's way of perceiving and dealing with the "problem" will not be placated. They argue that the analytical approach is not impartial and objective, as scientists claim, but rather shows an unfortunate tendency to reductionist views and technological determinism, a partiality toward the needs of the major forest industries, a passion for secrecy, a strong wish to maintain managerial control in the hands of technical experts, and an unwillingness to incorporate public views into the decision-making process. Perhaps most damning of all is the criticism that the reductionist approach leads the analytical scientists to deal only with the symptoms of the problem (the budworm plague) rather than the roots of the problem (inadequate forest policy).

2. *Schematist.* Schematists share with the analytical scientist a faith in objectivity, scientific method, empirical data, and rational procedures, but differ over the question of reductionism. Rather than the narrow perspective of the analytical scientist, the schematist seeks to develop a more comprehensive picture of the problem at hand, one that takes into account its many, interconnected parts. Systems modellers are a good example of what might be called "objective holism." They appear to believe that it is possible, given time and effort, to depict the complex relationships in ecosystems in mathematical terms, their goal being to develop the techniques for doing so. In addition, there is no implication of the anti-establishment rhetoric that one usually associates with the romantic

style. Systems theorists seem to be comfortable working within the established order.

The spruce budworm problem has been the focus of intensive modelling efforts involving scientists at all levels from provincial to international (Holling, 1978). The MFRC–UBC model that has emerged is, perhaps, the most comprehensive insect-forest simulation in existence (Cuff & Baskerville, 1983). Underlying this model is a perception of the budworm problem that differs in significant ways from that of the analytical scientist. The shift in perception is typified by use of the term "budworm–forest" problem. This subtle change in title reflects a more comprehensive view in which the problem is seen, not primarily as an insect infestation, but as a question of forest–insect dynamics and ecosystem resilience. Expansion of the problem definition, in this way, opens up the possibility of more varied "solutions," of which the biocidal strategy is but one. According to the schematist perspective, a solution to the "budworm–forest" problem would involve the development of a more resilient ecosystem (in contrast to the brittleness of current monocultures) through the development of adaptive management strategies (Holling, 1978). The latter would require the use of ecological models in policy formation together with a more varied repertoire of pest control procedures; in other words, the development of appropriate forms of integrated pest management. Thus, "solutions" are seen as long-term and comprehensive and involve restructuring of the forest base.

Unfortunately, adoption of this holistic perspective has been slow, and progress towards holistic goals limited. Those involved in budworm modelling in New Brunswick are finding that their models are not being used, at least to the extent that they would wish. Indeed, this seems to be a widespread phenomenon, with ecological modellers finding that their efforts are not informing policy formation to any significant degree (Clarke, 1983). In response to this problem, holists could make some attempt to question their assumptions and reconceptualize "the problem." As with analytical scientists, however, many appear to redouble their efforts along the same lines, seeking more and better data, and even more comprehensive models. The question, however, is whether this is a sensible strategy for, as Van Melsen (1980) notes, the ideal of an holistic science, with its implication of total knowledge, may be unattainable.

Critics would argue that the big, ecosystem models are too complex and esoteric to be of much use, since their builders are often the only people who can understand them (Clarke, 1983; Mar, 1974). Furthermore, large models may give the appearance of soundness, but on closer inspection reveal empirical gaps filled by guesswork and assumption. When one adds to this the fact that many models have never been checked against empirical observation, then questions of validity become significant (Cuff & Baskerville, 1983). The more vociferous critics of quantitative modelling argue that the activity is an exercise in speculation that shows signs of delusions of grandeur, taking positivist and rational thought to its logical and absurd extreme (Hoos, 1974). The most damning criticism of budworm and other similar attempts at modelling is that it totally omits the psychosocial domain. This appears to result from a number of factors, not the least of which are the predominantly biophysical training of modellers together with the difficulty in incorporating qualitative psychosocial variables into quantitative models. Since psychosocial variables are not part of the definition of the "budworm–forest" problem, they cannot become part of the solution. Schematists, therefore, are limited to primarily biophysical solutions, unless they are willing and able to expand their problem definition.

3. *Romantic.* Of all the intellectual types discussed here, romantics are the most varied and the most difficult to typify. There are, however, some common characteristics underlying this way of thinking. Most romantics do not reject objectivity, but are suspicious of a total reliance on it. Rather, they would seek a greater respectability for the subjective aspects of thought, such as intuitions, feelings, and values, as well as a more central role for laypeople in environmental decisions. It follows that romantics tend to take an integrative view, one that can include both subjective and objective data, as well as technical and psychosocial factors. However, the more extreme examples of this type of thinking may depend on their "sense" of the problem at hand, basing this and possible solutions on an ideological commitment to, for example, the oneness of Humankind and Nature. Thus, there may be a certain impatience with analytical detail and, hence, an unfamiliarity with the complexities of technical data.

Romantics are to be found scattered throughout the scientific community but are more concentrated and perhaps more evident in environmental interest groups. Many of the latter would see themselves as protecting human rights against the growing totalitarianism of science, technology, and big business—a trend they see as being both politically dangerous and dehumanizing in scale. A particular target for their anger is the technical expert, someone, they argue, who simply fuels technological depredations while professing objectivity and impartiality. Thus, in formulating the "problem," environmentalists and other romantics have three main aims: (*i*) to point out the subjective bias in the work of technical experts, (*ii*) to obtain participation in the environmental decision-making process, thereby breaking the monopoly of the technical expert, and (*iii*) to resist "bigness" in environmental management in the form of centralization of power and industrial concentration. In contrast to these trends, they seek to encourage decentralization, small-scale industry, and a form of resource pluralism (Cotgrove, 1982).

Given these aims, it follows that romantics emphasize the psychosocial, "human" aspects of environmental problems. Thus, the budworm problem is seen by the romantic as a "budworm–forest–people" issue, with the "people" aspect being composed of, not only the general public, but also technical and bureaucratic personnel. The latter, therefore, are seen as part of the problem as well as, potentially, part of the solution. Although the problem is expanded to its broadest perspective by some romantics, there is also a tendency to pay less attention to its technical aspects. This difference in orientation means that solutions to the budworm dilemma are sought in somewhat different directions from that of the analytical scientist and holist. For example, the question becomes not how to kill the moth (analytical scientist) or how to develop a more resilient ecosystem by technical means (holist), but, rather, how to develop a man–forest interaction that will guarantee the development of a healthy society and forest resource. For many romantics, this does not simply mean full employment in current forest industries and continued dependence on business monopolies, monocultures, and the whims of world markets, but implies a radical restructuring of the forest and its dependent forest industries in pursuit of decentralization of power and individual self-sufficiency. Consequently, a romantic solution to the "budworm–forest–people" problem has political overtones. It requires, for implementation, the development of a political decision-making structure that encourages genuine public participation in environmental policy-making and a continuing dialogue over such matters as pest-control strategies. An interesting example of this view has been provided by a New Brunswick environmental group:

> The primary goal of forestry management should be to maximize the productive use of the forest—and by "productive" I mean that the forest sustains both economic and recreational activities to the maximum extent possible without harming or eroding the forest as a resource. Unfortunately, the spray program has been used for over thirty years as a substitute for proper forest management.... Like the World War I general who has no *new* ideas, the only thing industry and government officials can come up with is more spray. The Canadian Forestry Service says that the budworm situation in the New Brunswick forest parallels the situation in 1974 and that insufficient control in 1975 caused deterioration in the health of the forest. Yet in 1975, 6.8 million acres were sprayed—much of it twice—with three or four different chemicals, and in 1976, 10 million acres were sprayed with five different chemicals. What in heaven's name is "sufficient"? When, after three decades, the budworm is spreading and the forest is in worse shape, it is shockingly clear that the spray program has failed as an effective management tool.... In New Brunswick we need a mixed forest and we need

a wider variety of economic activities to go with that mixed forest. This means rethinking our ideas about how to use the forest. It means getting fresh ideas about how to resuscitate the forest economy. For all of the jobs that forestry supposedly provides, there is enormous unemployment in New Brunswick. Can't we figure out better ways to use the forest to sustain high employment and a healthier economy? Must we continue to depend so heavily on pulp and paper, which, in New Brunswick, means dependence on softwoods and on sprays? (Schuyler, 1982, pp. 1–3).

Thus, while romantics reject a total reliance on chemical control, they appear to go beyond advocacy of integrated pest management, adding a political dimension to their request (or demand) for a reformulation of forest policy. This is a very different perception of the spruce budworm problem from those described so far for it offers the option of seeing the budworm issue as a non-problem. In other words, there is a "spruce budworm problem" only as long as the province of New Brunswick places such emphasis on the pulp and paper industry.

Critics of the romantic position argue that such views are technically and economically naive. Everyone, including the technical experts, would like to have a mixed forest, with a different species composition and age structure, together with a more diversified industrial base, but the technical difficulties are immense. Even if some of the latter could be solved, one is still left with developing new markets, training people in new skills, relocating skilled workers, and investing in new industrial plants. On top of this, there are the political problems involved in achieving public consensus and persuading the electorate to bear the cost of a massive restructuring. In the meanwhile, the more immediate problem of protecting softwoods still remains. Thus, the romantic perspective is seen by critics as excessively idealistic.

4. *Gnostic.* Although the role of gnostics in the budworm case is indirect and intangible, it is nevertheless important, for it provides a philosophical background to the debate. For the gnostic, the origins of environmental problems lie within the individual psyche, caused by Humankind's wrong relations with Nature which, in turn, derive from unexamined conflicts within us. As a consequence, we have developed a distorted view of ourselves and our place in nature, one that displays the kind of arrogance that lends itself to the destruction we see around us (Van Melsen, 1980). Thus, the budworm problem may be seen as a budworm–forest–people problem, but, in actuality, it is really a symptom of a deeper malaise, that of our warped consciousness. Solutions to the "problem," therefore, are necessarily personal and introspective, a matter of coming to grips with our distorted values and irrational desires. Once this healing process begins, then the environmental consequences of this unhealthy mentality can be dealt with (Roszak, 1973). This "mystical"

view (if that is the right way to describe it) is now a well-established component of a growing criticism of positivist science and its consequences (Jones, 1983; Nandy, 1983). As such, it appears to offer the fundamental truth that our "environmental problems" are in large part a function of our excessive demands on a fragile ecosystem and that we need to undertake a fundamental reappraisal of our values.

To its critics, however, the remoteness of this perspective from the practicalities of the "real" world makes it appear naive, even criminally negligent. For example, in New Brunswick, the gnostic view is associated with the minority position of non-intervention in the forest, *i.e.*, the chemical spray programme should be stopped and nature allowed to take its course. The immediate consequence of this would be massive softwood destruction followed by additional problems such as increased fire hazard and large-scale unemployment. Evidently, to the gnostic, these risks are worth taking in pursuit of the more important, long-term goal of a healthy man–environment relationship. However, even this goal may be unrealistic for, as critics have pointed out, calls for the development of a healthy psyche (with its implications of moderation and frugality) have echoed down the centuries, particularly in religious thought. One might question the extent to which the majority listen to these admonitions:

> Despite [evidence] that people have begun to rediscover the moral ideal of self-imposed restraint, the obstacles to a wholesale move in that direction remain very imposing. It may well turn out that human appetite will not be, cannot be, moderated. On a planet teeming with four or eight or twelve billion people, examples of restraint may remain what they are now: a series of minor, isolated gestures, unthinkable to the starving, unacceptable to the aspiring, unappealing to the affluent. (Worster, 1983, p. 174)

In sum, I have attempted to demonstrate the way in which the four main personality types perceive an environmental problem. In each case, the "problem" is seen differently, with the consequence that radically different solutions are proposed. Apparently, the proponents of each style tend to believe that they see to the heart of the matter and, therefore, know best how to deal with the problem. However, it is clear to the observer that each type has only a partial understanding of the spruce budworm problem, and that none has a monopoly on the whole "truth." To get closer to the latter, some integration of all four perspectives is needed, in the hope that the weaknesses of each will be compensated for by the strengths of others. Thus, the narrowly technical perspective of the reductionists could be supplemented by the broader views of the schematists and the socio-political sophistication of the romantics. On the other hand, the flights of fancy indulged in by the latter could be brought under control following scrutiny by the reductionists. The implication of all this is that an integrated perspective can be achieved only through constructive dialogue between the various personality types or by the development of versatile individuals who can sustain such a dialogue within their own heads. Thus, the present typology provides a useful framework within which to organize and interpret the behaviours of environmental disputants. While the analysis summarized above is clearly an oversimplification of events, it does, however, establish a coherent basis for further research.

CONCLUSIONS

In seeking to resurrect the "personality typology" as a credible conceptual tool, I have drawn attention to the recent rehabilitation of nomothetic traits, as well as noting the evidence in support of a small group of generic dimensions that appear repeatedly in factorial studies. In addition, I have outlined one of the ways in which three of these dimensions can be used to define a new typology. While evidence in support of the latter is scanty, if one is willing to extend one's purview beyond "validating" evidence to include other forms of corroboration, then a reasonable case can be made for the plausibility and utility of the present model. I present the model, therefore, as a set of hypotheses that have heuristic value in both research and practice.

References

Adler, A. (1964). *Problems of neurosis.* New York: Harper.

Albert, R. & Runco, M. (1987). The possible different personality dispositions of scientists and nonscientists. In D. Jackson & J. Rushton (Eds.), *Scientific excellence: Origins and assessment.* Newbury Park, California: Sage.

Alexander, P. (1984). Training analogical reasoning skills in the gifted. *Roeper Review, 6,* 191–193.

Allport, G. (1961). *Pattern and growth in personality.* New York: Holt, Rinehart & Winston.

Anderson, J. (1980). *Cognitive psychology: And its implications.* San Francisco: Freeman.

Arkes, H. & Freedman, M. (1984). A demonstration of the costs and benefits of expertise in recognition memory. *Memory & Cognition, 12,* 84–89.

Ashworth, C., Blackburn, I. & McPherson, F. (1982). The performance of depressed and manic patients on some repertory grid measures: A cross-sectional study. *British Journal of Medical Psychology, 55,* 247–255.

Ashworth, C., Blackburn, I. & McPherson, F. (1985). The performance of depressed and manic patients on some repertory grid measures: A longitudinal study. *British Journal of Medical Psychology, 58,* 337–342.

Averill, J. (1974). An analysis of psychophysiological symbolism and its influence on theories of emotion. *Journal for the Theory of Social Behaviour, 4,* 147–190.

Averill, J. (1982). *Anger and aggression: An essay on emotion.* New York: Springer-Verlag.

Babladelis, G. (1984). *The study of personality.* New York: Holt, Rinehart & Winston.

Bannister, D. & Fransella, F. (1966). A grid test of schizophrenic thought disorder. *British Journal of Social and Clinical Psychology, 5,* 95–102.

Bargh, J. (1984). Automatic and conscious processing of social information. In R. Wyer & T. Srull (Eds.), *Handbook of social cognition, Volume 3.* Hillsdale, N.J.: Erlbaum.

Barmark, J. & Wallen, G. (1979). The interaction of cognitive and social factors in steering a large scale interdisciplinary project. Paper presented at the First International Conference on Interdisciplinary Research Groups, Schloss Reisenberg, Germany (April, 1979).

Baron, J. (1985). What kinds of intelligence components are fundamental? In S. Chapman, J. Segal & R. Glaser (Eds.), *Thinking and learning skills, Volume 2.* Hillsdale, N.J.: Erlbaum.

Baron, J., Badgio, P. & Gaskins, I. (1986). Cognitive style and its improvement: A normative approach. In R. Sternberg (Ed.), *Advances in the psychology of human intelligence, Volume 3.* Hillsdale, N.J.: Erlbaum.

Baskerville, G. (1976). Report of the task force for evaluation of budworm control alternatives. Cabinet Committee on Economic Development, Province of New Brunswick, Canada.

Bastick, T. (1982). *Intuition: How we think and act.* Chichester: Wiley.

Bates, J. (1987). Temperament in infancy. In J. Osofsky (Ed.), *Handbook of infant development.* New York: Wiley.

Batson, C., Bolen, M., Cross, J. & Neuringer-Benefiel, H. (1986). Where is the Altruism in the Altruistic Personality? *Journal of Personality and Social Psychology,* 50, 212–220.

Batson, C., Fultz, J. & Schoenrade, P. (1987). Distress and empathy: Two qualitatively distinct vicarious emotions with different motivational consequences. *Journal of Personality,* 55, 19–39.

Baum, H. (1987). *The invisible bureaucracy: The unconscious in organizational problem-solving.* New York: Oxford University Press.

Bawden, R. & Valentine, I. (1984). Learning to be a capable systems agriculturalist. *Journal of Programmed Learning & Educational Technology,* 21, 273–287.

Bayer, R. & Spitzer, R. (1985). Neurosis, psychodynamics, and DSM–IIII: A history of the controversy. *Archives of General Psychiatry,* 42, 187–196.

Becker, E. (1973). *The denial of death.* New York: Free Press.

Bem, D. (1983). Toward a response style theory of persons in situations. In M. Page (Ed.), *Nebraska symposium on motivation,* 1982. Lincoln, Nebraska: University of Nebraska Press.

Benjamin, L. (1986). Adding social and intrapsychic descriptors to Axis I of DSM–III. In T. Millon & G. Klerman (Eds.), *Contemporary directions in psychopathology: Toward the DSM–IV.* New York: Guilford.

Benjamin, L. (1987). Use of the SASB dimensional model to develop treatment plans for personality disorders. I: Narcissism. *Journal of Personality Disorders,* 1, 43–70.

Bennink, C. (1982). Individual differences in cognitive style, working memory and semantic integration. *Journal of Research in Personality,* 16, 267–280.

Benson, D. & Zaidel, E. (1985). *The dual brain.* New York: Guilford.

Berg, E., Lunetta, V. & Tamir, P. (1981–82). Index of distinctness—a measure of the intensity of cognitive processes. *Journal of Educational Research,* 75, 197–203.

Berman, M. (1984). *The reenchantment of the world.* New York: Bantam.

Bieri, J., Atkins, A., Briar, S., Leaman, R., Miller, H. & Tripodi, T. (1966). *Clinical and social judgment.* New York: Wiley.

Bird, J. (1979). New Brunswick's spruce budworm programme: Public influence and effects on decision making. An address to the Canadian Pest Management Society, Fredericton, New Brunswick.

Birtchnell, J. (1984). Dependence and its relationship to depression. *British Journal of Medical Psychology,* 57, 215–225.

Blaney, P. (1986). Affect and memory: A review. *Psychological Bulletin, 99,* 229–246.

Blashfield, R. (1984). *The classification of psychopathology: Neo-Kraepelian and quantitative approaches.* New York: Plenum.

Blashfield, R. & Breen, M. (1989). Face validity of the DSM–III–R personality disorders. *American Journal of Psychiatry,* 146, 1575–1579.

Blashfield, R. & Haymaker, D. (1988). A prototype analysis of the diagnostic criteria for DSM–III–R personality disorders. *Journal of Personality Disorders,* 2, 272–280.

Blashfield, R., Sprock, J., Pinkston, K. & Hodgin, J. (1985). Exemplar prototypes of personality disorder diagnoses. *Comprehensive Psychiatry,* 26, 11–21.

Block, J. (1982). Assimilation, accommodation, and the dynamics of personality development. *Child Development,* 53, 281–295.

Block, J. & Block, J. H. (1979). The role of ego-control and ego-resiliency in the organization of behavior. In W. Collins (Ed.), *Minnesota symposium on child development, Volume 13.* Hillsdale, N.J.: Erlbaum.

Block, J., Buss, D., Block, J. H. & Gjerde, P. (1981). The cognitive style of breadth of categorization: Longitudinal consistency of personality correlates. *Journal of Personality and Social Psychology,* 40, 770–779.

Block, J. & Ozer, D. (1982). Two types of psychologists: Remarks on the Mendelsohn, Weiss, and Feimer contribution. *Journal of Personality and Social Psychology,* 42, 1171–1181.

Bower, G. (1981). Mood and memory. *American Psychologist,* 36, 129–148.

Boyatzis, R. (1982). *The competent manager.* New York: Wiley.

Brand, C. (1984). Personality dimensions: An overview of modern trait psychology. In J. Nicholson & H. Beloff (Eds.), *Psychology Survey 5.* Leicester: British Psychological Society.

Branden, B. (1986). *The passion of Ayn Rand.* New York: Doubleday.

Brandt, L. (1982). *Psychologists caught: A psycho-logic of psychology.* Toronto: University of Toronto Press.

Breger, L. (1974). *From instinct to identity.* Englewood Cliffs, N.J.: Prentice-Hall.

Briggs, S. (1987). Rachel Carson: Her vision and her legacy. In G. Marco, R. Hollingworth & W. Durham (Eds.), *Silent spring revisited.* Washington, D.C.: American Chemical Society.

Brody, N. (1986). Conscious and unconscious processes in the psychology of motivation. In D. Brown & J. Veroff (Eds.), *Frontiers of motivational psychology.* Berlin: Springer-Verlag.

Brooks, P. (1972). *The house of life: Rachel Carson at work.* Boston: Houghton Mifflin.

Broughton, R. (1990). The prototype concept in personality assessment. *Canadian Psychology,* 31, 26–37.

Brumby, M. (1982). Consistent differences in cognitive styles shown for qualitative biological problem-solving. *British Journal of Educational Psychology,* 52, 244–257.

Bruner, J. (1984). Narrative and paradigmatic modes of thought. Invited address, American Psychological Association Conference, Toronto, Canada.

Bruner, J. (1986). Thought and emotion: Can Humpty Dumpty be put together again. In D. Bearison & H. Zimiles (Eds.), *Thought and emotion: Developmental perspectives*. Hillsdale, N.J.: Erlbaum.

Buck, R. (1984). *The communication of emotion*. New York: Guilford.

Buck, R. (1985). Prime theory: An integrated view of motivation and emotion. *Psychological Review*, 92, 389–413.

Burnham, J. (1968). Historical background for the study of personality. In E. Borgatta & W. Lambert (Eds.), *Handbook of personality theory and research*. Chicago: Rand-McNally.

Buss, Allan R. & Poley, W. (1976). *Individual differences: Traits and factors*. New York: Gardner.

Buss, Arnold H. (1989). Personality as traits. *American Psychologist*, 44, 1378–1388.

Buss, Arnold H. & Finn, S. (1987). Classification of personality traits. *Journal of Personality and Social Psychology*, 52, 432–444.

Buss, Arnold H. & Plomin, R. (1984). *Temperament: Early developing personality traits*. Hillsdale, N.J.: Erlbaum.

Buss, D. & Craik, K. (1984). Acts, dispositions, and personality. *Progress in Experimental Personality Research*, 13, 241–301.

Cady, K., Phoenix, S. & Rhodin, T. (1988, December). Restructuring graduate engineering education: The M.Eng. program at Cornell. *Engineering Education*, 157–163.

Caine, T., Wijesinghe, O. & Winter, D. (1981). *Personal styles in neurosis: Implications for small group psychotherapy and behaviour therapy*. London: Routledge & Kegan Paul.

Campbell, J. & Reynolds, J. (1984). A comparison of the Guilford and Eysenck factors of personality. *Journal of Research in Personality*, 18, 305–320.

Campos, J. & Barrett, K. (1984). Toward a new understanding of emotions and their development, In C. Izard, J. Kagan & R. Zajonc (Eds.), *Emotions, cognition and behavior*. Cambridge, Mass.: Cambridge University Press.

Cantor, N. & Mischel, W. (1977). Traits as prototypes: Effects on recognition memory. *Journal Personality and Social Psychology*, 35, 38–48.

Cantor, N. & Mischel, W. (1979). Prototypes in person perception. *Advances in Experimental Social Psychology*, 12, 3–52.

Caplan, P. (1984). The myth of women's masochism. *American Psychologist*, 39, 117–123.

Caplan, P. (1987). The name game: Psychiatry, misogyny, and taxonomy. *Women and Therapy: A Feminist Quarterly*, 6, 187–202.

Capra, F. (1982). *The turning point: Science, society and the rising culture*. Toronto: Bantam.

Carlson, R. (1984). What's social about social psychology? Where's the person in personality research? *Journal of Personality and Social Psychology*, 47, 1304–1309.

Carlson, R. (1985). Masculine/feminine: A personological perspective. *Journal of Personality*, 53, 384–399.

Carson. R. (1989). Personality. *Annual Review of Psychology*, 40, 227–248.

Cattell, R. (1970). The integration of functional and psychometric requirements in a quantitative and computerized diagnostic system. In A. Mahrer (Ed.), *New approaches to personality classification*. New York: Columbia University Press.

Cattell, R. & Kline, P. (1977). *The scientific analysis of personality and motivation.* London: Academic Press.

Chi, M., Glaser, R. & Rees, E. (1982). Expertise in problem solving. In R. Sternberg (Ed.), *Advances in the psychology of human intelligence, Volume 1.* Hillsdale, N.J.: Erlbaum.

Chwalisz, K., Diener, E. & Gallagher, D. (1988). Autonomic arousal feedback and emotional experience: Evidence from the spinal cord injured. *Journal of Personality and Social Psychology,* 54, 820–828.

Cialdini, R., Schaller, M., Houlihan, D., Arps, K. & Fultz, J. (1987). Empathy-based helping: Is it selflessly or selfishly motivated? *Journal of Personality and Social Psychology,* 52, 749–758.

Claridge, G. (1985). *Origins of mental illness.* Oxford: Blackwell.

Claridge, G. (1986). Eysenck's contribution to the psychology of personality. In S. Modgil & C. Modgil (Eds.), *Hans Eysenck: Consensus and controversy.* Philadelphia: Palmer.

Clark, L. & Watson, D. (1988). Mood and the mundane: Relations between daily life events and self-reported mood. *Journal of Personality and Social Psychology.* 54, 296–308.

Clarke, W. (1983). Sustainable development of the biosphere: A strategic exploration of interactions among energy, agriculture and the world environment. Unpublished document, Institute for Energy Analysis, Oak Ridge, Tennessee, U.S.A.

Coan, R. (1968). Dimensions of psychological theory. *American Psychologist,* 23, 715–722.

Coan, R. (1974). *The optimal personality: An empirical and theoretical analysis.* New York: Columbia University Press.

Coan, R. (1979). *Psychologists: Personal and theoretical pathways.* New York: Irvington Publishers.

Cofer, N. & Appley , M. (1984). Motivation and personality. In N. Endler & J. Hunt (Eds.), *Personality and the behavioral disorders, Volume 1,* New York: Wiley.

Cohn, C. (1987). Sex and death in the rational world of defense intellectuals. *Signs,* 12, 687–718.

Conley, J. (1985a). Longitudinal stability of personality traits: A multitrait–multi-method–multioccasion analysis. *Journal of Personality and Social Psychology,* 49, 1266–1282.

Conley, J. (1985b). A personality theory of adulthood and aging. In R. Hogan & W. Jones (Eds.), *Perspectives in personality, Volume 1.* Greenwich, Connecticut: JAI Press.

Conway, J. (1989). Epistemic values and psychologists: A world of individual differences. Unpublished manuscript, University of Saskatchewan.

Cooper, L. (1982). Strategies for visual comparison and representation: Individual differences. In R. Sternberg (Ed.), *Advances in the psychology of human intelligence, Volume 1.* Hillsdale, N.J.: Erlbaum.

Cooper, L. & Mumaw, R. (1985). Spatial aptitude. In R. Dillon (Ed.), *Individual differences in cognition, Volume 2.* Orlando: Academic.

Costa, P. & McCrae, R. (1988). Personality and adulthood: A six-year longitudinal study of self-reports and spouse ratings on the NEO Personality Inventory. *Journal of Personality and Social Psychology,* 54, 853–863.

Cotgrove, S. (1982). *Catastrophe or cornucopia*. Chichester: Wiley.

Cotton, J. (1981). A review of research on Schacter's theory of emotion and mis-attribution of arousal. *European Journal of Social Psychology*, 11, 365–397.

Cuff, W. & Baskerville, G. (1983). Ecological modelling and management of spruce budworm infested fir—spruce forests of New Brunswick, Canada. In W. Lauenroth, G. Skogerboe & M. Flug (Eds.), *Analysis of ecological systems: State-of-the-art in ecological modelling*. New York: Elsevier.

Dalton, L. (1986). Why the rational paradigm persists—the resistance of professional education and practice to alternative forms of planning. *Journal of Planning Education & Research*, 5, 147–153.

Daly, E., Lancee, W. & Polivy, J. (1983). A conical model for the taxonomy of emotional experience. *Journal of Personality and Social Psychology*, 45, 443–457.

Davies, D., Jones, D. & Taylor, A. (1984). Selective and sustained-attention tasks: Individual and group differences. In R. Parasuraman & D. Davies (Eds.), *Varieties of Attention*. Orlando: Academic.

Davis, C. & Cowles, M. (1988). A laboratory study of temperament and arousal: A test of Gale's hypothesis. *Journal of Research in Personality*, 22, 101–116.

Davis, M. (1983). The effects of dispositional empathy on emotional reactions and helping: A multidimensional approach. *Journal of Personality*, 51, 167–184.

Davis, M., Hull, J., Young, R. & Warren, G. (1987). Emotional reactions to dramatic film stimuli: The influence of cognitive and emotional empathy. *Journal of Personality and Social Psychology*, 52, 126–133.

Davis, R. (1986). Testing Kohn's self-reliance hypothesis among high school adolescents. *Adolescence*, 21, 443–447.

Deci, E. & Ryan, R. (1985a). *Intrinsic motivation and self-determination in human behavior*. New York: Plenum.

Deci, E. & Ryan, R. (1985b). The general causality orientations scale: Self-determination in personality. *Journal of Research in Personality*, 19, 109–134.

Delis, D. & Ober, B. (1986). Cognitive neuropsychology. In T. Knapp & L. Robertson (Eds.), *Approaches to cognition*. Hillsdale, N.J.: Erlbaum.

Derryberry, D. & Rothbart, M. (1984). Emotion, attention, and temperament. In C. Izard, J. Kagan & R. Zajonc (Eds.), *Emotions, cognition and behavior*. Cambridge, Mass.: Cambridge University Press.

Diener, E., Larsen, R., Levine, S. & Emmons, R. (1985). Intensity and frequency: Dimensions underlying positive and negative affect. *Journal of Personality and Social Psychology*, 48, 1253–1265.

Digman, J. (1989). Five robust trait dimensions: Development, stability, and utility. *Journal of Personality*, 57, 195–214.

Digman, J. & Inouye, J. (1986). Further specification of the five robust factors of personality. *Journal of Personality and Social Psychology*, 50, 116–123.

Dorcey, A. (1986). *Bargaining in the governance of Pacific coastal resources: Research and reform*. Vancouver, B.C.: Westwater Research Center, University of British Columbia.

Drengson, A. (1983). *Shifting paradigms: From technocrat to planetary person*. Victoria, B.C.: Lightstar Publishing Co.

Dweck, C. & Leggett, E. (1988). A social-cognitive approach to motivation and personality. *Psychological Review*, 95, 256–273.

Efron, E. (1984). *The apocalyptics: Cancer and the big lie.* New York: Simon & Schuster.

Eisenberg, N. & Strayer, J. (1987). Critical issues in the study of empathy. In N. Eisenberg & J. Strayer (Eds.), *Empathy and its development.* Cambridge: Cambridge University Press.

Ekman, P. (1984). Expression and the nature of emotion. In K. Scherer & P. Ekman (Eds.), *Approaches to emotion.* Hillsdale, N.J.: Erlbaum.

Entwistle, N. (1981). *Styles of learning and teaching.* Chichester: Wiley.

Epstein, S. (1979). The stability of behavior: I. On predicting most of the people much of the time. *Journal of Personality and Social Psychology, 37,* 1097–1126.

Epstein, S. (1983). A research paradigm for the study of personality and emotions. In M. Page (Ed.), *1982 Nebraska Symposium on motivation.* Lincoln, Nebraska: University of Nebraska Press.

Epstein, S. (1984). Controversial issues in emotion theory. In P. Shaver (Ed.), *Review of Personality and Social Psychology, Volume 5,* Beverley Hills: Sage.

Epstein, S. & O'Brien, E. (1985). The person–situation debate in historical and current perspective. *Psychological Bulletin, 98,* 513–537.

Eysenck, H. (1967). *The biological bases of personality.* Springfield, Illinois: Thomas.

Eysenck, H. (1985). *Decline and fall of the Freudian empire.* Harmondsworth, Middlesex: Penguin.

Eysenck, H. & Eysenck, M. (1985). *Personality and individual differences.* New York: Plenum.

Eysenck, H., Wakefield, J. & Friedman, A. (1983). Diagnosis and clinical assessment: The DSM–III. *Annual Review of Psychology, 34,* 167–193.

Fahrenberg, J. (1987). Concepts of activation and arousal in the theory of emotionality (neuroticism): A multivariate conceptualization. In J. Strelau & H. Eysenck (Eds.), *Personality dimensions and arousal.* New York: Plenum.

Fahrenberg, J., Foerster, F., Schneider, H., Muller, W. & Myrtek, M. (1986). Predictability of individual differences in activation processes in a field setting based on laboratory measures. *Psychophysiology, 23,* 323–333.

Farley, F. (1985). Psychobiology and cognition: An individual differences model. In J. Strelau, J. Farley & A. Gale (Eds.), *The biological bases of personality and behavior, Volume 1.* Washington: Hemisphere.

Farley, F. (1986). The Big T in personality. *Psychology Today, 20,* 43–52.

Fehr, B. & Russell, J. (1984). Concept of emotion viewed from a prototype perspective. *Journal of Experimental Psychology: General, 113,* 464–486.

Felder, R. (1987). On creating creative engineers. *Engineering Education,* 222–227.

Feshbach, S. (1984). The "personality" of personality theory and research. *Personality and Social Psychology Bulletin, 10,* 446–456.

Fischbach, F. & Sell, N. (1986). A structured approach to teaching applied problem solving through technology assessment. *Journal of Chemical Education, 63,* 522–525.

Fiske, S., Kinder, D. & Larter, W. (1983). The novice and the expert: Knowledge-based strategies in political cognition. *Journal of Experimental Social Psychology, 19,* 381–400.

Fiske, S. & Pavelchak, M. (1986). Category-based versus piecemeal-based affective responses. In R. Sorrentino & E. Higgins (Eds.), *Handbook of motivation and cognition*. New York: Guilford.

Fiske, S. & Taylor, S. (1984). *Social cognition*. New York: Random House.

Fletcher, B. (1981). Wholistic and analytic stimulus processing: The development of selective perceptual strategies. *Quarterly Journal of Experimental Psychology*, 33A, 167–176.

Fletcher, G., Danilovics, P., Fernandez, G., Peterson, D. & Reeder, G. (1986). Attributional complexity: An individual difference measure. *Journal of Personality and Social Psychology*, 51, 875–884.

Floyd, A. (1976). *Cognitive styles*. Milton Keynes: Open University.

Folkman, S. (1984). Personal control and stress and coping processes: A theoretical analysis. *Journal of Personality and Social Psychology*, 46, 839–852.

Folkman, S. & Lazarus, R. (1985). If it changes it must be a process: A study of emotion and coping during three stages of a college examination. *Journal of Personality and Social Psychology*, 48, 150–170.

Ford, M. & Lowery, C. (1986). Gender differences in moral reasoning: A comparison of the Justice and Care orientations. *Journal of Personality and Social Psychology*, 50, 777–783.

Ford, N. (1981). Recent approaches to the study and teaching of 'effective learning' in higher education. *Review of Educational Research*, 51, 345–377.

Forisha, B. (1983). Relationship between creativity and mental imagery: A question of cognitive styles? In A. Sheikh (Ed.), *Imagery: Current theory, research and application*. New York: Wiley.

Fowler, W. (1977). Sequence and styles in cognitive development. In F. Weizmann & I. Uzgiris (Eds.), *The structuring of experience*. New York: Plenum.

Frances, A. & Widiger, T. (1986). Methodological issues in personality disorder diagnosis. In T. Millon & G. Klerman (Eds.), *Contemporary directions in Psychopathology: Toward the DSM–IV*. New York: Guilford.

Frank, B . (1983). Flexibility of information processing and the memory of field-independent and field-dependent learners. *Journal of Research in Personality*, 17, 89–96.

Frank, J. (1987). The drive for power and the nuclear arms race. *American Psychologist*, 42, 337–344.

Fransella, F. (1981). *Personality: Theory, measurement and research*. London: Methuen.

Franz, C. & White, K. (1985). Individuation and attachment in personality development: Extending Erickson's theory. In A. Stewart & M. Lykes (Eds.), *Gender and personality*. Durham: Duke University Press.

Friedman, H. & Booth-Kewley, S. (1987). The "disease-prone personality": A meta-analytic view of the construct. *American Psychologist*, 42, 539–555.

Friedson, E. (1984). Are professions necessary? In T. Haskell (Ed.), *The authority of experts*. Bloomington, Indiana: Indiana University Press.

Fromm, E. (1973). *The anatomy of human destructiveness*. Greenwich: Fawcett.

Funder, D. (1983). The "consistency" controversy and the accuracy of personality judgments. *Journal of Personality*, 51, 346–359.

Funder, D. & Harris, M. (1986). On the several facets of personality assessment: The case of social acuity. *Journal of Personality*, 54, 528–550.

Gale, A. (1986). Extraversion–introversion and spontaneous rhythms of the brain: Retrospect and prospect. In J. Strelau, F. Farley & A. Gale (Eds.), *The biological bases of personality and behavior, Volume 2*. Washington: Hemisphere.

Gangestad, S. & Snyder, M. (1985). On the nature of self-monitoring. *Review of Personality and Social Psychology*, 6, 65–85.

Garber, B. & Miller, M. (1986). Of beasties and butterflies: Evidence for the stability and domain specificity of individual differences in categorization. *Journal of Personality*, 54, 645–658.

Gardner, R., Holzman, P., Klein, G., Linton, H. & Spence, D. (1959). Cognitive control: A study of individual consistencies in cognitive behavior. *Psychological Issues*, 1, Monograph 4.

Gartner, C. (1983). *Rachel Carson*. New York: Frederick Ungar.

Gathercole, S. & Broadbent, D. (1984). Combining attributes in specified and categorized target search: Further evidence for strategic differences. *Memory & Cognition*, 12, 329–337.

Gifford, R. & O'Connor, B. (1987). The interpersonal circumplex as a behavior map. *Journal of Personality and Social Psychology*, 52, 1019–1029.

Gilligan, C. (1982). *In a different voice*. Cambridge: Harvard University Press.

Gitomer, D. & Pellegrino, J. (1985). Developmental and individual differences in long-term memory retrieval. In R. Dillon (Ed.), *Individual differences in cognition, Volume 2*. Orlando: Academic.

Glass, A. & Holyoak, K. (1986). *Cognition*. New York: Random House.

Glass, A., Holyoak, K. & Santa, J. (1979). *Cognition*. Reading, Mass.: Addison-Wesley.

Goldsmith, H., Buss, A.H., Plomin, R., Rothbart, M., Thomas, A., Chess, S., Hinde, R. & McCall, R. (1987). Roundtable: What is temperament? Four approaches. *Child Development*, 1987, 58, 505–529.

Goleman, D. (1985). *Vital lies, simple truths: The psychology of self-deception*. New York: Simon & Schuster.

Goodenough, D., Oltman, P. & Cox, P. (1987). The nature of individual differences in field dependence. *Journal of Research in Personality*, 21, 81–99.

Grant, G. (1979). Implications of competence-based education. In G. Grant *et al.* (Eds.). *On competence: A critical analysis of competence-based reforms in higher education*. San Francisco: Jossey-Bass.

Gray, J. (1971). *The psychology of fear and stress*. New York: McGraw–Hill.

Gray, J., Owen, S., Davis, N. & Tsaltas, E. (1983). Psychological and physiological relations between anxiety and impulsivity. In M. Zuckerman (Ed.), *Biological bases of sensation seeking, impulsivity and anxiety*. Hillsdale, N.J.: Erlbaum.

Greenberg, L. & Safran, J. (1987). *Emotion in Psychotherapy*. New York: Guilford.

Gruenfeld, L. & Thung-Rung Lin (1984). Social behavior of field independents and dependents in an organic group. *Human Relations*, 37, 721–741.

Guilford, J. (1967). *The nature of human intelligence*. New York: McGraw–Hill.

Guilford, J. (1975). Factors and factors of personality. *Psychological Bulletin*, 82, 802–814.

Haaken, J. (1988). Field dependence research: A historical analysis of a psychological construct. *Signs: Journal of Women in Culture and Society*, 13, 311–330.

Hampson, S., John, O. & Goldberg, L. (1986). Category breadth and hierarchical structure in personality: Studies of asymmetries in judgments of trait implications. *Journal of Personality and Social Psychology, 51,* 37–54.

Harvey, O., Hunt, D. & Schroder, H. (1961). *Conceptual systems and personality organization.* New York: Wiley.

Helson, R. (1973a). The heroic, the comic, and the tender: Patterns of literary fantasy and their authors. *Journal of Personality, 41,* 163–184.

Helson, R. (1973b). Heroic and tender modes in women authors of fantasy. *Journal of Personality, 41,* 493–512.

Helson, R. & Crutchfield, R. (1970). Creative types in mathematics. *Journal of Personality, 38,* 177–197.

Henneman, R. & Rouse, W. (1984). Measures of human problem solving performance in fault diagnosis tasks. *IEEE Transactions on Systems, Man, and Cybernetics, 14,* 99–112.

Hermans, H. (1988). On the integration of nomothetic and idiographic research methods in the study of personal meaning. *Journal of Personality, 56,* 785–809.

Hesteren, F., Sawatsky, D. & Zingle, H. (1982). Conceptual complexity and the helping relationship. *Canadian Counsellor, 17,* 4–13.

Hicks, L. (1984). Conceptual and empirical analysis of some assumptions of an explicitly typological theory. *Journal of Personality and Social Psychology, 46,* 1118–1131.

Higgins, R. (1982). *The seventh enemy.* London: Hodder and Stoughton.

Hilgard, E. (1980). The trilogy of mind: Cognition, affection and conation. *Journal History of the Behavioral Sciences, 16,* 107–117.

Hill, C. (1987). Affiliation motivation: People who need people ... but in different ways. *Journal of Personality and Social Psychology, 52,* 1008–1018.

Hirschberg, N. (1978). A correct treatment of traits. In H. London (Ed.), *Personality: A new look at metatheories.* New York: Hemisphere Publishing Corporation.

Hoffman, M. (1986). Affect, cognition, and motivation. In R. Sorrentino & E. Higgins (Eds.), *Handbook of motivation and cognition.* New York: Guilford.

Hoffman, R. (1980). Metaphor in science. In R. Honeck & R. Hoffman (Eds.), *Cognition and figurative language.* Hillsdale, N.J.: Erlbaum.

Hogan, R. (1983). A socioanalytic theory of personality. In M. Page (Ed.), *1982 Nebraska symposium on motivation.* Lincoln, Nebraska: University of Nebraska Press.

Holliday, S. & Chandler, M. (1986). *Wisdom: Explorations in adult competence.* Basel: Karger.

Holling, C. (1978). *Adaptive environmental assessment and management.* New York: Plenum.

Holloway, E. & Wampold, B. (1986). Relation between conceptual level and counseling-related tasks: A meta-analysis. *Journal of Counseling Psychology, 33,* 310–319.

Holton, G. (1978). *The scientific imagination: Case studies.* Cambridge: Cambridge University Press.

Holyoak, K. (1984). Analogical thinking and human intelligence. In R. Sternberg (Ed.), *Advances in the psychology of human intelligence, Volume 2.* Hillsdale, N.J.: Erlbaum.

Hooker, K., Blumenthal, J. & Siegler, I. (1987). Relationships between motivation and hostility among Type A and Type B middle-aged men. *Journal of Research in Personality*, 21, 103–113.

Hoos, I. (1974). Criteria for "good" futures research. *Technological Forecasting and Social Change*, 6, 113–132.

Horney, K. (1950). *Neurosis and human growth*. New York: Norton.

Horowitz, M., Marmar, C., Krupnick, J., Wilner, N., Kaltreider, N. & Wallenstein, R. (1984). *Personality styles and brief psychotherapy*. New York: Basic Books.

Houts, A., Cook, T. & Shadish, W. (1986). The person–situation debate: A critical multiplist perspective. *Journal of Personality*, 54, 52–105.

Howard, D. (1983). *Cognitive psychology*. New York: MacMillan.

Howard, G. & Conway, C. (1986). Can there be an empirical science of volitional action? *American Psychologist*, 41, 1241–1251.

Hudson, L. (1968). *Contrary imaginations*. Harmondsworth: Penguin.

Hudson, L. (1970). *Frames of mind*. Harmondsworth: Penguin.

Hudson, L. (1972). *The cult of the fact*. New York: Harper & Row.

Hunt, D., Butler, L., Noy, J. & Rosser, M. (1978). *Assessing conceptual level by the paragraph completion method*. Toronto: Ontario Institute for Studies in Education.

Hunt, M. (1982). *The universe within*. New York: Simon & Schuster.

Huszagh, V. & Infante, J. (1989). The hypothetical way of progress. *Nature*, 338, 109.

Hyler, S. & Lyons, M. (1988). Factor analysis of the DSM–III personality disorder clusters: A replication. *Comprehensive Psychiatry*, 29, 304–308.

Isen, A. (1984). Toward understanding the role of affect in cognition. In R. Wyer & T. Srull (Eds.), *Handbook of Social Cognition, Volume 3*. Hillsdale, N.J.: Erlbaum.

Isen, A., Daubman, K. & Gorgoglione, J. (1987). The influence of positive affect on cognitive organization: Implications for education. In R. Snow & M. Farr (Eds.), *Aptitude, learning and instruction, Volume 3: Conative and affective process analysis*. Hillsdale, N.J.: Erlbaum.

Izard, C. (1982). Comments on emotion and cognition: Can there be a working relationship? In M. Clark & S. Fiske (Eds.), *Affect and cognition*. Hillsdale, N.J.: Erlbaum.

Izard, C. (1984). Emotion–cognition relationships in human development. In C. Izard, J. Kagan & R. Zajonc (Eds.), *Emotion, cognition and behavior*. Cambridge, Mass.: Cambridge University Press.

Izard, C., Kagan, J. & Zajonc, R. (1984). Introduction. In C. Izard, J. Kagan, & R. Zajonc (Eds.), *Emotion, cognition and behavior*. Cambridge, Mass.: Cambridge University Press.

Izard, C. & Malatesta, C. (1987). Perspectives on emotional development. I: Differential emotions theory of early emotional development. In J. Osofsky (Ed.), *Handbook of infant development*. New York: Wiley.

Jacoby, L. & Brooks, L. (1984). Nonanalytic cognition: Memory, perception, and concept learning. In G. Bower (Ed.), *The psychology of learning and motivation, Volume 18*. Orlando: Academic.

James, W. (1907). *Pragmatism*. New York: Longmans, Green & Co.

Jaquish, G. (1983). Intra-individual variability in divergent thinking in response to audio, visual, and tactile stimuli. *British Journal of Psychology,* 74, 467–472.

John, O., Angleitner, A. & Ostendorf, F. (1988). The lexical approach to personality: A historical review of trait taxonomic research. *European Journal of Personality,* 2, 171–203.

Jones, A. (1983). Beyond industrial society: Towards balance and harmony. *The Ecologist,* 13, 141–147.

Jung, C. (1923). *Psychological types.* Princeton: Princeton University Press.

Kagan, J. & Kogan, N. (1970). Individual variation in cognitive processes. In P. Mussen (Ed.), *Carmichael's Manual of Child Psychology, Volume 1.* New York: Wiley.

Kagan, J., Reznick, J. & Snidman, N. (1987). The physiology and psychology of behavioral inhibition in children. *Child Development,* 58, 1459–1473.

Kaplan, A. (1986). The "self-in-relation": Implications for depression in women. *Psychotherapy,* 23, 234–242.

Kass, F., Skodol, A., Charles, E., Spitzer, R. & Williams, J. (1985). Scaled ratings of DSM–III personality disorders. *American Journal of Psychiatry,* 142, 627–630.

Katz, A. (1983). What does it mean to be a high imager? In J. Yuille (Ed.), *Imagery, Memory and Cognition.* Hillsdale, N.J.: Erlbaum.

Katz, A. (1984). Creative styles: Relating tests of creativity to the work patterns of scientists. *Personality and Individual Differences,* 5, 281–292.

Keller, E. (1985). *Reflections on gender and science.* New Haven: Yale University

Kelly, G. (1955). *The psychology of personal constructs* (2 volumes). New York: Norton.

Kenrick, D. (1986). How strong is the case against contemporary social and personality psychology? A response to Carlson. *Journal of Personality and Social Psychology,* 50, 839–844.

Kenrick, D. & Dantchik, A. (1983). Interactionism, idiographics, and the social psychological invasion of personality. *Journal of Personality,* 51, 286–307.

Kendrick, D. & Funder, D. (1988). Profiting from controversy: Lessons from the person–situation debate. *American Psychologist,* 43, 23–34.

Kiesler, D. (1986). The 1982 interpersonal circle: An analysis of DSM–III personality disorders. In T. Millon & G. Klerman (Eds.), *Contemporary directions in psychopathology: Toward the DSM–IV.* New York: Guilford.

Kihlstrom, J. (1984). Conscious, subconscious, unconscious: A cognitive perspective. In K. Bowers & D. Meichenbaum (Eds.), *The unconscious reconsidered.* New York: Wiley.

Kimble, G. (1984). Psychology's two cultures. *American Psychologist,* 39, 833–839.

Kogan, N. (1971). Educational implications of cognitive styles. In G. Lesser (Ed.), *Psychology and educational practice.* Glenview, Illinois: Scott, Foresman.

Kogan, N. (1976). *Cognitive styles in infancy and early childhood.* Hillsdale, N.J.: Erlbaum.

Kogan, N. (1982). Cognitive styles in older adults. In T. Field, A. Huston, H. Quay, L. Troll & G. Finley (Eds.), *Review of human development.* New York: Wiley.

Kogan, N. (1983). Stylistic variation in childhood and adolescence: Creativity, metaphor, and cognitive styles. In P. Mussen (Ed.), *Handbook of child psychology, Volume 3: Cognitive development*. New York: Wiley.

Kohlberg, L. (1969). Stage and sequence: The cognitive-developmental approach to socialization. In D. Goslin (Ed.), *Handbook of socialization theory and research*. Skokie, Ill.: Rand-McNally.

Kuhl, J. (1986). Motivation and information processing: A new look at decision making, dynamic change, and action control. In R. Sorrentino & E. Higgins (Eds.), *Handbook of motivation and cognition: Foundations of social behavior*. New York: Guilford.

Lacey, J. (1967). Somatic response patterning and stress: Some revisions of activation theory. In M. Appley & R. Trumbull (Eds.), *Psychological stress*. New York: Appleton-Century-Crofts.

Lamiell, J. (1987). *The psychology of personality. An epistemological inquiry*. New York: Columbia University Press.

Landfield, A. (1971). Personal construct systems in psychotherapy. Chicago: Rand-McNally.

Lang, P. (1984). Cognition in emotion: Concept and action. In C. Izard, J. Kagan & R. Zajonc (Eds.), *Emotion, cognition and behavior*. Cambridge, Mass.: Cambridge University Press.

Larsen, R. & Diener, E. (1985). A multitrait–multimethod examination of affect structure: Hedonic level and emotional intensity. *Personality and Individual Differences*, 6, 631–636.

Larsen, R., & Diener, E. (1987). Affect intensity as an individual difference characteristic: A review. *Journal of Research in Personality*, 21, 1–39.

Larsen, R., Diener, E. & Cropanzano, R. (1987). Cognitive operations associated with individual differences in affect intensity. *Journal of Personality and Social Psychology*, 53, 767–774.

Larsen, R., Diener, E. & Emmons, R. (1986). Affect intensity and reactions to daily life events. *Journal of Personality and Social Psychology*, 51, 803–814.

Laughlin, P. (1973). Selection strategies in concept attainment. In R. Solso (Ed.), *Contemporary issues in cognitive psychology*. Washington, D.C.: Winston.

Lazarus, R. (1971). *Personality*. Englewood Cliffs, N.J.: Prentice-Hall.

Lazarus, R. (1984). On the primacy of cognition. *American Psychologist*, 39, 124–129.

Lazarus, R., Coyne, J. & Folkman, S. (1984). Cognition, emotion and motivation: The doctoring of Humpty Dumpty. In K. Scherer & P. Ekman (Eds.), *Approaches to emotion*. Hillsdale, N.J.: Erlbaum.

Lerner, J. & Lerner, R. (1983). Temperament and adaptation across life: Theoretical and empirical issues. In P. Baltes & O. Brim (Eds.), *Life-span development and behavior, Volume 5*. New York: Academic.

Lesgold, A. (1984). Acquiring expertise. In J. Anderson & S. Kosslyn (Eds.), *Tutorials in learning and memory*. San Francisco: Freeman.

Leventhal, H. (1982). The integration of emotion and cognition: A view from the perceptual-motor theory of emotion. In M. Clark & S. Fiske (Eds.), *Affect and cognition*. Hillsdale, N.J.: Erlbaum.

Leventhal, H. & Tomarken, A. (1986). Emotion: Today's problems. *Annual Review of Psychology*, 37, 565–610.

Levey, A. & Martin, I. (1981). Personality and conditioning. In H. Eysenck (Ed.), *A model for personality*. New York: Springer.

Levi-Montalcini, R. (1988). *In praise of imperfection: My life and work*. New York: Basic Books.

Levinson, D., Sharaf, M. & Gilbert, D. (1966). Intraception: The evolution of a concept. In G. DiRenzo (Ed.), *Concepts, theory, and explanation in the behavioral sciences*. New York: Random House.

Levy, L. (1970). *Conceptions of personality: Theories and research*. New York: Random House.

Lifton, P. (1985). Individual differences in moral development: The relation of sex, gender and personality to morality. In A. Stewart & M. Lykes (Eds.), *Gender and personality*, Durham: Duke University Press.

Linstone, H., Meltsner, A., Adelson, M., Clary, B., Cook, P., Hawke, S., Miller, R., Mysior, A., Pearson, J., Shuman, J., Umbdenstock, L., Wagner, D. & Will, S. (1984). *Multiple perspectives in decision making*. New York: Elsevier.

Livesley, W. (1985). The classification of personality disorder: 1. The choice of category concept. *Canadian Journal of Psychiatry*, 30, 353–358.

Livesley, W. (1986). Trait and behavioral prototypes of personality disorder. *American Journal of Psychiatry*, 143, 728–732.

Loevinger, J. (1976). *Ego development: Conceptions and theories*. San Francisco: Jossey-Bass.

Loomis, M. & Saltz, E. (1984). Cognitive styles as predictors of artistic styles. *Journal of Personality*, 52, 22–35.

Lykes, M. (1985). Gender and individualistic vs. collectivist notions about the self. In A. Stewart & M. Lykes (Eds.), *Gender and Personality*. Durham: Duke University Press.

Lynton, E. & Elman, S. (1987). *New priorities for the university: Meeting society's needs for applied knowledge and competent individuals*. San Francisco: Jossey-Bass.

Maddi, S. (1976). *Personality theories: A comparative analysis*. Homewood, Illinois: Dorsey Press.

Maddi, S. (1984). Personology for the 1980s. In R. Zucker, J. Arnoff, & A. Rabin (Eds.), *Personality and the prediction of behavior*. New York: Academic.

Mahoney, M. (1976). *Scientist as subject: The psychological imperative*. Cambridge, Mass.: Ballinger.

Mandler, G. (1975). *Mind and emotion*. New York: Wiley.

Mandler, G. (1985). *Cognitive psychology*. Hillsdale, N.J.: Erlbaum.

Mangan, G. (1982). *The biology of human conduct: East–West models of temperament and personality*. Oxford: Pergamon.

Mar, B. (1974). Problems encountered in multidisciplinary resources and environmental simulation models development. *Journal of Environmental Management*, 2, 83–100.

Martindale, C. (1981). *Cognition and consciousness*. Homewood, Illinois: Dorsey.

Mason, A. & Blankenship, V. (1987). Power and affiliation motivation, stress, and abuse in intimate relationships. *Journal of Personality and Social Psychology*, 52, 203–210.

Matlin, M. (1983). *Cognition*. New York: Holt, Rinehart & Winston.

McAdams, D. (1982). Intimacy motivation. In A. Stewart (Ed.), *Motivation and society*. San Francisco: Jossey-Bass.

McAdams, D. (1984). Love, power and images of the self. In C. Malatesta & C. Izard (Eds.), *Emotion in adult development*. Beverley Hills: Sage.

McAdams, D. (1985). The "Imago": A key narrative component of identity. In P. Shaver (Ed.), *Review of personality and social psychology, Volume 6*. Beverley Hills: Sage.

McCaulley, M. (1981). Jung's theory of psychological types and the Myers-Briggs Type indicator. In P. McReynolds (Ed.), *Advances in psychological assessment*. San Francisco: Jossey Bass.

McClelland, D. (1975). *Power: The inner experience*. New York: Irvington.

McCrae, R. (1987). Creativity, divergent thinking, and openness to experience. *Journal of Personality and Social Psychology, 52*, 1258–1265.

McCrae, R. & Costa, P. (1984). *Emerging lives, enduring dispositions: Personality in adulthood*. Boston: Little Brown.

McCrae, R. & Costa, P. (1985). Updating Norman's "adequate taxonomy": Intelligence and personality dimensions in natural language and in questionnaires. *Journal of Personality and Social Psychology, 49*, 710–721.

McCrae, R. & Costa, P. (1987). Validation of the five-factor model of personality across instruments and observers. *Journal of Personality and Social Psychology, 52*, 81–90.

McCrae, R., & Costa, P. (1989a). Reinterpreting the Myers-Briggs Type Indicator from the perspective of the five-factor model of personality. *Journal of Personality, 57*, 17–40.

McCrae, R., & Costa, P. (1989b). The structure of interpersonal traits: Wiggins' circumplex and the five-factor model. *Journal of Personality and Social Psychology, 56*, 586–595.

McKenna, F. (1984). Measures of field dependence: Cognitive style or cognitive ability? *Journal of Personality and Social Psychology, 47*, 593–603.

McReynolds, P. (1989). Special review. *Personality and Individual Differences, 10*, 133.

Mehrabian, A. & Epstein, N. (1972). A measure of emotional empathy. *Journal of Personality, 40*, 525–543.

Mendelsohn, G., Weiss, D. & Feimer, N. (1982). Conceptual and empirical analysis of the typological implications of patterns of socialization and femininity. *Journal of Personality and Social Psychology, 42*, 1157–1170.

Mershon, B. & Gorsuch, R. (1988). Number of factors in the personality sphere: Does increase in factors increase predictability of real-life criteria. *Journal of Personality and Social Psychology, 55*, 675–680.

Messick, S. (1976). Personality consistencies in cognition and creativity. In S. Messick (Ed.), *Individuality in learning*. San Francisco: Jossey-Bass.

Messick, S. (1984). The nature of cognitive styles: Problems and promise in educational practice. *Educational Psychologist, 19*, 59–74.

Messick, S. (1987). Structural relationships across cognition, personality and style. In R. Snow & M. Farr (Eds.), *Aptitude, learning and instruction, Volume 3. Conative and affective process analyses*. Hillsdale, N.J.: Erlbaum.

Meyer, G. & Shack, J. (1989). Structural convergence of mood and personality: Evidence for old and new directions. *Journal of Personality and Social Psychology*, 57, 691–706.

Millar, D. (1980). A repertory grid study of obsessionality: Distinctive cognitive structure or distinctive cognitive content? *British Journal of Medical Psychology*, 53, 59–66.

Miller, A. (1978). Conceptual Systems Theory: A critical review. *Genetic Psychology Monographs*, 97, 77–126.

Miller, A. (1981). Conceptual matching models and interactional research in education. *Review of Educational Research*, 51, 33–84.

Miller, A. (1984). Professional competence in environmental management. *International Journal of Environmental Studies*, 22, 91–101.

Miller, A. (1984/5). Psychosocial origins of conflict over pest control strategies. *Agriculture, Ecosystems and Environment*, 12, 235–251.

Miller, A. (1985). Technological thinking: Its impact on environmental management. *Environmental Management*, 9, 179–190.

Miller, A. (1987). Cognitive styles: An integrated model. *Educational Psychology*, 7, 251–268.

Miller, A. (1988). Toward a typology of personality styles. *Canadian Psychology*, 29, 263–283.

Miller, A. & Wilson, P. (1979). Cognitive differentiation and integration: A conceptual analysis. *Genetic Psychology Monographs*, 99, 3–40.

Miller, J. B. (1986). *Toward a new psychology of women*. Boston: Beacon Press.

Miller, M. & Thayer, J. (1989). On the existence of discrete classes in personality: Is self-monitoring the correct joint to carve? *Journal of Personality and Social Psychology*, 57, 143–155.

Millon, T. (1981). *Disorders of personality: DSM–III, Axis II*. New York: Wiley.

Millon, T. (1986a) On the past and future of DSM–III: Personal recollections and projections. In T. Millon & G. Klerman (Eds.), *Contemporary directions in psychopathology: Toward DSM–IV*. New York: Guilford.

Millon, T. (1986b). A theoretical derivation of pathological personalities. In T. Millon & G. Klerman (Eds.), *Contemporary directions in psychopathology: Toward the DSM–IV*. New York: Guilford.

Millon, T. (1986c). Personality prototypes and their diagnostic criteria. In T. Millon & G. Klerman (Eds.), *Contemporary directions in psychopathology: Toward the DSM–IV*. New York: Guilford.

Mischel, W. (1968). *Personality and assessment*. New York: Wiley.

Missler, R. (1986). Analytic and synthetic cognitive functioning: A critical review of evidence bearing on field dependence. *Journal of Research in Personality*, 20, 1–33.

Mitroff, I. (1974). *The subjective side of science*. Amsterdam: Elsevier.

Mitroff, I. & Kilmann, R. (1978). *Methodological approaches to social science*. San Francisco: Jossey Bass.

Moore, B. (1987). Commentary on Part III. In N. Eisenberg & J. Strayer (Eds.), *Empathy and its development*. Cambridge: Cambridge University Press.

Morais, J. (1982). The two sides of cognition. In J. Mehler, E. Walker & M. Garrett (Eds.), *Perspectives on mental representation*. Hillsdale, N.J.: Erlbaum.

Morey, L. (1988a). The categorical representation of personality disorder: A cluster analysis of DSM–III–R personality features. *Journal of Abnormal Psychology*, 970, 314–321.

Morey, L. (1988b). Personality disorders in DSM–III and DSM–III–R: Convergence, coverage, and internal consistency. *American Journal of Psychiatry*, 145, 573–577.

Morey, L., Waugh, M. & Blashfield, R. (1985). MMPI scales for DSM–III personality disorders: Their derivation and correlates. *Journal of Personality Assessment*, 49, 245–251.

Morrill, R. (1980). *Teaching values in college*. San Francisco: Jossey-Bass.

Moscovitch, M. (1979). Information processing and the cerebral hemispheres. In M. Gazzaniga (Ed.), *Handbook of behavioral neurobiology, Volume 2*. New York: Plenum.

Murray, H. (1938). *Explorations in personality*. New York: Oxford University Press.

Mussen, P., Conger, J., Kagan, J. & Geiwitz, J. (1979). *Psychological development: A life-span approach*. New York: Harper & Row.

Myer, K. & Hensley, J. (1984). Cognitive style, gender, and self-report of principle as predictors of adult performance on Piaget's water level task. *Journal of Genetic Psychology*, 144, 179–183.

Myrtek, M. (1984). *Constitutional psychophysiology*. New York: Academic.

Nandy, A. (1983). The pathology of objectivity. *The Ecologist*, 13, 202–207.

Neimark, E. (1983). There is one classification system with a long developmental history. In E. Scholnick (Ed.), *New trends in conceptual representation*. Hillsdale, N.J.: Erlbaum.

Neimeyer, R., Neimeyer, G. & Landfield, A. (1983). Conceptual differentiation, integration and empathic prediction. *Journal of Personality*, 51, 185–191.

Neiss, R. (1988). Reconceptualizing arousal: Psychobiological states in motor performance. *Psychological Bulletin*, 103, 345–366.

Neisser, U. (1979). The concept of intelligence. *Intelligence*, 3, 217–227.

Nickerson, R., Perkins, D. & Smith, E. (1985). *The teaching of thinking*. Hillsdale, N.J.: Erlbaum.

Noller, P., Law, H. & Comrey, A. (1987). Cattell, Comrey, and Eysenck personality factors compared: More evidence for the five robust factors? *Journal of Personality and Social Psychology*, 53, 775–782.

Norman, W. (1963). Toward an adequate taxonomy of personality attributes: Replicated factor structure in peer nomination personality ratings. *Journal of Abnormal and Social Psychology*, 66, 574–583.

Norris, F., Jones, H. & Norris, H. (1970). Articulation of the conceptual structure in obsessional neurosis. *British Journal of Social and Clinical Psychology*, 9, 264–274.

Norris, F. & Norris, H. (1972). The obsessive-compulsive syndrome as a neurotic device for the reduction of self-uncertainty. *British Journal of Psychiatry*, 121, 277–288.

Orlofsky, J. & Frank M. (1986). Personality structure as viewed through early memories and identity status in college men and women. *Journal of Personality and Social Psychology*, 50, 580–586.

Ormerod, M. & Billing, J. (1982). A six orthogonal factor model of adolescent personality derived from the HSPQ. *Personality and Individual Differences, 3*, 107–118.

Osgood, C., Suci, G. & Tannenbaum, P. (1957). *The measurement of meaning.* Illinois: University of Illinois Press.

O'Sullivan, P. (1986). Environmental science and environmental philosophy—Part I. Environmental science and environmentalism. *International Journal of Environmental Studies, 28,* 97–107.

Pacey, A. (1983). *The culture of technology.* Cambridge, Mass.: MIT Press.

Paivio, A. (1971). *Imagery and verbal processes.* New York: Holt, Rinehart & Winston.

Pask, G. (1976). Styles and strategies of learning. *British Journal of Educational Psychology, 46,* 128–148.

Paulhus, D. & Martin, C. (1987). The structure of personality capabilities. *Journal of Personality and Social Psychology, 52,* 354–365.

Pellegrino, J. & Goldman, S. (1983). Developmental and individual differences in verbal and spatial reasoning. In R. Dillon & R. Schmeck (Eds.), *Individual differences in cognition, Volume 1.* New York: Academic.

Perkins, J. (1982). *Insects, experts, and the insecticide crisis.* New York: Plenum.

Persson, L., & Sjoberg, L. (1978). The influence of emotions on information processing. Goteborg, Sweden: Goteborg Psychological Reports 8(7), University of Goteborg.

Pervin, L. (1983). The stasis and flow of behavior: Toward a theory of goals. In M. Page (Ed.), *Nebraska Symposium on Motivation 1982.* Lincoln, Nebraska: University of Nebraska Press.

Pervin, L. (1985). Personality: Current controversies, issues, and directions. *Annual Review of Psychology, 36,* 83–114.

Petak, W. (1980). Environmental planning and management: The need for an integrative perspective. *Environmental Management, 4,* 287–295.

Peterson, C. (1988). *Personality.* San Diego: Harcourt Brace Jovanovich.

Petulla, J. (1987). *Environmental protection in the United States: Industries agencies, environmentalists.* San Francisco: San Francisco Study Center.

Phares, E. (1988). *Introduction to personality.* 2nd Ed. Glenview, Illinois: Scott, Foresman.

Plath, S. (1982). *The journals of Sylvia Plath.* New York: Dial Press.

Pollak, J. (1979). Obsessive-compulsive personality: A review. *Psychological Bulletin, 86,* 225–241.

Pollak, J. (1981). Hysterical personality: An appraisal in light of empirical research. *Genetic Psychology Monographs, 104,* 71–105.

Pollio, H. & Smith, M. (1980). Metaphoric competence and complex human problem solving. In R. Honeck & R. Hoffman (Eds.), *Cognition and figurative language.* Hillsdale, N.J.: Erlbaum.

Powell, A., & Royce, J. (1978). Paths to being, life style, and individuality. *Psychological Reports, 42,* 987–1005.

Powell, G. (1981). Personality and social behaviour. In H. Eysenck (Ed.), *A model for personality.* New York: Springer.

Prentky, R. (1979). Creativity and psychopathology: A neurocognitive perspective. *Progress in Experimental Personality Research, 9,* 1–39.

Prior, M., Crook, G., Stripp, A., Power, M. & Joseph, M. (1986). The relationship between temperament and personality: An exploratory study. *Personality and Individual Differences, 7,* 875–881.

Rachman, S. (1984). Fear and courage. *Behavior Therapy, 15,* 109–120.

Rachman, S., Hallam, R., Cox, D. & O'Connor, K. (1983). Fear and courage among military bomb disposal operators. *Advances in Behaviour Research and Therapy, 4,* 97–175.

Ray, J. (1981). Authoritarianism, dominance and assertiveness. *Journal of Personality Assessment, 45,* 390–397.

Reisenzein, R. (1983). The Schacter theory of emotion: Two decades later. *Psychological Bulletin, 94,* 239–264.

Revelle, W. (1983). Factors or fictions, and other comments on individuality theory. *Journal of Personality, 51,* 707–714.

Richardson, J. (1983). Student learning in higher education. *Educational Psychology, 3,* 305–331.

Riding, R. & Ashmore, J. (1980). Verbalizer–Imager learning style and children's recall of information presented in pictorial versus written form. *Educational Studies, 6,* 141–145.

Riding, R. & Boardman, D. (1983). The relationship between sex and learning style on graphicacy in 14 year-old children. *Educational Review, 35,* 69–79.

Riding, R. & Calvey, I. (1981). The assessment of verbal imagery learning styles and their effect on the recall of concrete and abstract prose passages by 11 year-old children. *British Journal of Psychology, 72,* 59–64.

Rivage-Seul, M. (1987). Peace education: Imagination and the pedagogy of the oppressed. *Harvard Educational Review, 57,* 152–169.

Roberge, J. & Flexer, B. (1983). Cognitive style, operativity, and mathematical achievement. *Journal for Research in Mathematics Education, 14,* 344–353.

Robertson, L. (1986). From gestalt to neo-gestalt. In T. Knapp & L. Robertson (Eds.), *Approaches to cognition.* Hillsdale, N.J.: Erlbaum.

Robottom, I. (1987). Two paradigms of professional development in environmental education. *The Environmentalist, 4,* 291–298.

Romney, D. & Bynner, J. (1989). Evaluation of a circumplex model of DSM–III personality disorders. *Journal of Research in Personality, 23,* 525–538.

Ronning, R., McCurdy, D. & Ballinger, R. (1984). Individual differences: A third component in problem-solving instruction. *Journal of Research in Science Teaching, 21,* 71–82.

Rosch, E. (1978). Principles of categorization. In E. Rosch & D. Lloyd (Eds.), *Cognition and categorization.* Hillsdale, N.J.: Erlbaum.

Rosch, E. (1983). Prototype classification and logical classification: The two systems. In E. Scholnick (Ed.), *New trends in conceptual representation.* Hillsdale, N.J.: Erlbaum.

Ross, A. (1987). *Personality: The scientific study of complex human behavior.* New York: Holt, Rinehart & Winston.

Ross, M. & Fletcher, G. (1985). Attribution and social perception. In G. Lindzey & E. Aronson (Eds.), *The handbook of social psychology*. 3rd Ed. New York: Random House.

Roszak, T. (1973). *Where the wasteland ends*. New York: Anchor Books.

Rothbart, M. (1986). A developmental model for individual differences in temperament. Unpublished manuscript quoted in Goldsmith *et al.*, 1987.

Rothblum, E., Solomon, L. & Albee, G. (1986). A sociopolitical perspective of DSM–III. In T. Millon & G. Klerman (Eds.), *Contemporary directions in psychopathology: Toward the DSM–IV*. New York: Guilford.

Royce, J. & Powell, A. (1983). *Theory of personality and individual differences: Factors, systems, and processes*. Englewood Cliffs, N.J.: Prentice-Hall.

Rubini, V. & Cornoldi, C. (1985). Verbalizers and visualizers in child thinking and memory. *Journal of Mental Imagery, 9*, 77–90.

Runyan, W. (1983). Idiographic goals and methods in the study of lives. *Journal of Personality, 51*, 413–437.

Rushton, J. (1980). *Altruism, socialization & society*. Englewood Cliffs, N.J.: Prentice-Hall.

Rushton, J. (1981). The Altruistic Personality. In J. Rushton & R. Sorrentino (Eds.), *Altruism and helping behavior*. Hillsdale, N.J.: Erlbaum.

Rushton, J. (1984). The Altruistic Personality. In E. Staub, D. Bar-Tal, J. Karylowski & J. Reykowski (Eds.), *Development and maintenance of prosocial behavior*. New York: Plenum.

Russell, J. (1979). Affective space is bipolar. *Journal of Personality and Social Psychology, 37*, 345–356.

Russell, J. (1980). A circumplex model of affect. *Journal of Personality and Social Psychology, 39*, 1161–1178.

Ryan, R. (1982). Control and information in the intrapersonal sphere: An extension of cognitive evaluation theory. *Journal of Personality and Social Psychology, 43*, 450–461.

Rychlak, J. (1968). *A philosophy of science for personality theory*. Boston: Houghton Mifflin.

Sample, S. (1988). Engineering education and the liberal arts tradition. *IEEE Transactions on Education, 31*, 54–57.

Samples, B. (1976). *The metaphoric mind*. Reading, Mass.: Addison-Wesley.

Santostefano, S. (1978). *A biodevelopmental approach to clinical child psychology*. New York: Wiley.

Santostefano, S. (1986). Cognitive controls, metaphors and contexts: An approach to cognition and emotion. In D. Bearison & H. Zimiles (Eds.), *Thought and emotion: Developmental perspectives*. Hillsdale, N.J.: Erlbaum.

Sayers, J. (1986). *Sexual contradictions: Psychology, psychoanalysis, and feminism*. London: Tavistock.

Schacter, S. (1964). The interaction of cognitive and physiological determinants of emotional state. In L. Berkowitz (Ed.), *Advances in expermental social psychology, Volume 1*, New York: Academic.

Schacter, S. & Singer, J. (1962). Cognitive, social and physiological determinants of emotional state. *Psychological Review, 69*, 379–399.

Schmeck, R. (1983). Learning styles of college students. In R. Dillon & R. Schmeck (Eds.), *Individual differences in cognition, Volume 1*. New York: Academic.

Schon, D. (1987). *Educating the reflective practitioner*. San Francisco: Jossey-Bass.

Schoon, C. (1985). Methods for defining and assessing professional competence. *Professional Practice of Psychology*, 6, 144–155.

Schuyler, G. (1982). Forest management and chemical spraying. In Concerned Parents Group (Eds.), *Brief to Select Committee on Environment*, New Brunswick Legislature, Fredericton, New Brunswick, Canada.

Schwartz, S. & Bilsky, W. (1987). Toward a universal psychological structure of human values. *Journal of Personality and Social Psychology*, 53, 550–562.

Scorer, R. (1977). *The clever moron*. London: Routledge & Kegan Paul.

Scott, W., Osgood, D., Peterson, C. & Scott, R. (1979). *Cognitive Structure*. Washington, D.C.: Winston.

Sewell, W. (1974). The role of perception of professionals in environmental decision-making. In J. Coppack & B. Wilson (Eds.), *Environmental quality*. Edinburgh: Scottish Academic Press.

Shade, B. (1984). Field dependency: Cognitive style or perceptual skill? *Perceptual & Motor Skills*, 58, 991–995.

Shapiro, D. (1965). *Neurotic styles*. New York: Basic Books.

Shaver, P., Schwartz, J., Kirson, D. & O'Connor, C. (1987). Emotion knowledge: Further exploration of a prototype approach. *Journal of Personality and Social Psychology*, 52, 1061–1086.

Shevrin, H. & Dickman, S. (1980). The psychological unconscious: A necessary assumption for all psychological theory? *American Psychologist*, 35, 421–434.

Shipman, S. & Shipman, V. (1985). Cognitive styles: Some conceptual, methodological, and applied issues. In E. Gordon (Ed.), *Review of research in education, Volume 12*. Washington, D.C.: American Educational Research Assn.

Shore, B. & Carey, S. (1984). Verbal ability and spatial task. *Perceptual & Motor Skills*, 59, 255–259.

Shore, B., Hymovitch, J. & Lajoie, S. (1982). Processing differences in relations between ability and field independence. *Psychological Reports*, 50, 391–395.

Simonton, D. (1988). *Scientific genius: A psychology of science*. Cambridge: Cambridge University Press.

Singer, J. & Kolligian, J. (1987). Personality: Developments in the study of private experience. *Annual Review of Psychology*, 38, 555–574.

Skinner, B. (1987). Whatever happened to psychology as the science of behavior? *American Psychologist*, 42, 780–786.

Smail, D. (1984). *Illusion and reality: The meaning of anxiety*. London: Dent.

Small, S., Zeldin, R. & Savin-Williams, R. (1983). In search of personality traits: A multimethod analysis of naturally occurring prosocial and dominance behavior. *Journal of Personality*, 51, 1–16.

Smith, H. (1974). *Personality development*. New York: McGraw–Hill.

Smith, T. (1984). Type A behaviour, anger and neuroticism: The discriminant validity of self-report in a patient sample. *British Journal of Clinical Psychology*, 23, 147–148.

Smith, T. & Anderson, N. (1986). Models of personality and disease: An interactional approach to Type A behavior and cardiovascular risk. *Journal of Personality and Social Psychology, 50,* 1166–1173.

Snow, R. & Farr, M. (1987). Cognitive–conative–affective processes in aptitude, learning and instruction: An introduction. In R. Snow & M. Farr (Eds.), *Aptitude, learning, and instruction, Volume 3: Conative and affective process analyses.* Hillsdale, N.J.: Erlbaum.

Snyder, M. & Gangestad, S. (1986). On the nature of self-monitoring: Matters of assessment, matters of validity. *Journal of Personality and Social Psychology, 51,* 125–139.

Sommers, S. (1984). Reported emotions and conventions of emotionality among college students. *Journal of Personality and Social Psychology, 46,* 207–215.

Sommers, S. & Scioli, A. (1986). Emotional range and value orientation: Toward a cognitive view of emotionality. *Journal of Personality and Social Psychology, 51,* 417–422.

Sorrentino, R. & Higgins, E. (1986). Motivation and cognition: Warming up to synergism. In R. Sorrentino & E. Higgins (Eds.), *Handbook of motivation and cognition.* New York: Guilford.

Spence, J. & Helmreich, R. (1983). Achievement-related motives and behaviors. In J. Spence (Ed.), *Achievement and achievement motives.* San Francisco: Freeman.

Srull, T. & Wyer, R. (1986). The role of chronic and temporary goals in social information processing. In R. Sorrentino & E. Higgins (Eds.), *Handbook of motivation and cognition.* New York: Guilford.

Stark, J., Lowther, M., Hagerty, B. & Orczyk, C. (1986). A conceptual framework for the study of preservice professional programs in colleges and universities. *Journal of Higher Education, 57,* 231–258.

Stelmak, R. (1981). The psychophysiology of extraversion and neuroticism. In H. Eysenck (Ed.), *A model for personality.* New York: Springer.

Stern, S. (1984). Professional training and professional competence: A critique of current thinking. *Professional Psychology: Research and Practice, 2,* 230–243.

Sternberg, R. (1977). *Intelligence, information processing and analogical reasoning.* Hillsdale, N.J.: Erlbaum.

Sternberg, R. (1987). Intelligence and cognitive style. In R. Snow & M. Farr (Eds.), *Aptitude, learning and instruction, Volume 3: Conative and affective process analyses.* Hillsdale, N.J.: Erlbaum.

Stoppard, J. & Miller, A. (1985). Conceptual level matching in therapy: A review. *Current Psychological Research & Reviews, 4,* 46–68.

Storr, A. (1973). *Jung.* London: Fontana/Collins.

Strayer, J. (1987). Affective and cognitive perspectives on empathy. In N. Eisenberg & J. Strayer (Eds.), *Empathy and its development.* Cambridge: Cambridge University Press.

Sullivan, H. (1953). *The interpersonal theory of psychiatry.* New York: Norton.

Tellegen, A. (1985). Structures of mood and personality and their relevance to assessing anxiety, with an emphasis on self-report. In A. Tuma & J. Maser (Eds.), *Anxiety and the anxiety disorders,* Hillsdale, N.J.: Erlbaum.

Thayer, R. (1985). Activation (arousal): The shift from a single to a multidimensional perspective. In J. Strelau, F. Farley & A. Gale (Eds.), *The biological bases of personality and behavior, Volume 1*. Washington: Hemisphere.

Thayer, R. & Miller, M. (1988). Further evidence for the independence of hedonic level and emotional intensity. *Personality and Individual Differences*, 9, 425–426.

Thayer, R., Takahashi, P. & Pauli, J. (1988). Multidimensional arousal states, diurnal rhythms, cognitive and social processes, and extraversion. *Personality and Individual Differences*, 9, 15–24.

Thirgood, J. (1988, October). Present realities and future possibilities for forestry education. *The Forestry Chronicle*, 434–436.

Thomas, A. (1985). Affective response tendency. In E. Gordon (Ed.), *Review of Research in Education, Volume 12*. Washington: American Educational Research Association.

Tomkins, S. (1962). *Affect, imagery, consciousness* (2 volumes). New York: Springer.

Tulving, E. (1985). How many memory systems are there? *American Psychologist*, 40, 385–398.

Turk, D. & Salovey, P. (1985). Cognitive structures, cognitive processes, and cognitive-behavior modification: I. Client issues. *Cognitive Therapy and Research*, 9, 1–17.

Udwadia, F. (1986). Management situations and the engineering mindset. *Technological Forecasting and Social Change*, 29, 387–397.

Vanderburg, W. (1989). Professionals and social responsibility: Some patterns. *Journal of Business Ethics*, 8, 209–215.

Van Der Werff, J. (1985). Heyman's temperamental dimensions in personality research. *Journal of Research in Personality*, 19, 279–287.

Van Melsen, A. (1980). Evaluation. *Agriculture and Environment*, 5, 143–172.

Veroff, J. (1982). Assertive motivations: Achievement versus power. In A. Stewart (Ed.), *Motivation and Society*. San Francisco: Jossey-Bass.

Veroff, J. (1986). Contextualism and human motives. In D. Brown & J. Veroff (Eds.), *Frontiers of motivational psychology*. Berlin: Springer-Verlag.

Veroff, J. & Veroff, J. B. (1980). *Social incentives: A life-span developmental approach*. New York: Academic.

Voss, J., Tyler, S. & Yengo, L. (1983). Individual differences in the solving of social science problems. In R. Dillon & R. Schmeck (Eds.), *Individual differences in cognition, Volume 1*. New York: Academic.

Wagner-Martin, L. (1987). *Sylvia Plath: A biography*. New York: Simon & Schuster.

Walker, L. (1984). Sex differences in the development of moral reasoning: A critical review. *Child Development*, 55, 677–691.

Wallach, M. (1962). Commentary: Active–analytical v. passive–global cognitive functioning. In S. Messick & J. Ross (Eds.), *Measurement in personality and cognition*. New York: Wiley.

Wallach, M. (1970). Creativity. In P. Mussen (Ed.), *Carmichael's manual of child psychology, Volume 1*. New York: Wiley.

Watson, D. & Clark, L. (1984). Negative affectivity: The disposition to experience aversive emotional states. *Psychological Bulletin*, 96, 465–490.

Watson, D. & Tellegen, A. (1985). Toward a consensual structure of mood. *Psychological Bulletin*, 98, 219–235.

Watson, D., Pennebaker, J. & Folger, R. (1987). Beyond negative affectivity: Measuring stress and satisfaction in the workplace. *Journal of Organizational Behavior Management*, 8, 141–157.

Weiss, D., Mendelsohn, G. & Feimer, N. (1982). Reply to the comments of Block and Ozer. *Journal of Personality and Social Psychology*, 42, 1182–1189.

Wenger, M. (1950) Emotion as visceral action: An extension of Lange's theory. In M. Reymert (Ed.), *The second international symposium on feelings and emotions*. New York: McGraw–Hill.

Wenk, E. (1988). Social, economic, and political change: Portents for reform in engineering curricula. *Engineering Education*, November, 99–102.

Westcott, M. (1985). Volition as a nag. In F. Brush & J. Overmier (Eds.), *Affect, conditioning and cognition*. Hillsdale, N.J.: Erlbaum.

Wessman, A. & Ricks, D. (1966). *Mood and personality*. New York: Holt, Rinehart & Winston.

West, S. (1986). Methodological developments in personality research: An introduction. *Journal of Personality*, 54, 1–17.

White, R. (1959). Motivation reconsidered: The concept of competence. *Psychological Review*, 66, 297–333.

Whyte, L. (1967). *The unconscious before Freud*. London: Tavistock.

Wicker, F., Lambert, F., Richardson, F. & Kahler, J. (1984). Categorical goal hierarchies and classification of human motives. *Journal of Personality*, 52, 285–305.

Widiger, T. & Frances, A. (1985). The DSM–III personality disorders. *Archives of General Psychiatry*, 42, 615–623.

Widiger, T., Frances, A., Spitzer, R. & Williams, J. (1988). The DSM–III–R personality disorders: An overview. *American Journal of Psychiatry*, 145, 786–795.

Widiger, T. & Kelso, K. (1983). Psychodiagnosis of Axis II. *Clinical Psychology Review*, 3, 491–510.

Widiger, T., Knudson, R. & Rorer, L. (1980). Convergent and discriminant validity of measures of cognitive styles and abilities. *Journal of Personality and Social Psychology*, 39, 116–129.

Widiger, T., Trull, T., Hurt, S., Clarkin, J. & Frances, A. (1987). A multidimensional scaling of the DSM–III personality disorders. *Archives of General Psychiatry*, 44, 557–563.

Wiggins, J. (1973). *Personality and prediction: Principles of personality assessment*. Reading, Mass.: Addison-Wesley.

Wiggins, J. (1980). Circumplex models of interpersonal behavior. In L. Wheeler (Ed.), *Review of personality and social psychology, Volume 1*. Beverley Hills, California: Sage.

Wiggins, J. (1982). Circumplex models of interpersonal behavior in clinical psychology. In P. Kendell & J. Butcher (Eds.), *Handbook of research methods in clinical psychology*. New York: Wiley.

Wiggins, J. & Broughton, R. (1985). The interpersonal circle: A structural model for the integration of personality research. In R. Hogan & W. Jones (Eds.), *Perspectives in personality*. Greenwich, Conn.: JAI Press.

Wilkinson, C. (1987). The science and politics of pesticides. In G. Marco, R. Hollingworth & W. Durham (Eds.), *Silent spring revisited*. Washington, D.C.: American Chemical Society.

Wine, J. (1982). Gynocentric values and feminist psychology. In A. Miles & G. Finn (Eds.), *Feminism in Canada: From pressure to politics*. Montreal: Black Rose Books.

Winter, D.A. (1985). Personal styles, constructive alternativism and the provision of a therapeutic service. *British Journal of Medical Psychology*, 58, 129–135.

Winter, D. G. (1973). *The power motive*. New York: Free Press.

Winter, D. G. (1987). Enhancement of an enemy's power motivation as a dynamic of conflict escalation. *Journal of Personality and Social Psychology*, 52, 129–135.

Winter, D. G. (1988). The power motive in women—and men. *Journal of Personality and Social Psychology*, 54, 510–519.

Winter, D. G. & Stewart, A. (1978). The power motive. In H. London & J. Exner (Eds.), *Dimensions of personality*. New York: Wiley.

Wispe, L. (1987). History of the concept of empathy. In N. Eisenberg & J. Strayer (Eds.), *Empathy and its development*. Cambridge: Cambridge University Press.

Witkin, H. & Goodenough, D. (1977). Field dependence and interpersonal behavior. *Psychological Bulletin*, 84, 661–689.

Witkin, H. & Goodenough, D. (1981). *Cognitive styles: Essence and origins*. New York: International Universities Press.

Witkin, H., Moore, C., Oltman, P., Goodenough, D., Friedman, F., Owen, D. & Raskin, E. (1977). Role of the field dependent and field independent cognitive styles in academic evolution: A longitudinal study. *Journal of Educational Psychology*, 69, 197–211.

Witkin, H., Goodenough, D. & Oltman, P. (1979). Psychological differentiation: Current status. *Journal of Personality and Social Psychology*, 37, 1127–1145.

Wood, C. (1985). The healthy neurotic. *New Scientist*, February 7, 12–15.

Worster, D. (1983). Water and the flow of power. *The Ecologist*, 13, 168–174.

Wright, G. & Phillips, L. (1984). Decision making: Cognitive style on task-related behaviour. In H. Bonarius, G. van Heck & N. Smid (Eds.), *Personality psychology in Europe*. Lisse: Swets & Zeitlinger.

Yarnold, P., Grimm, L. & Lyons, J. (1987). The Wiggins Interpersonal Behavior Circle and the Type A behavior pattern. *Journal of Research in Personality*, 21, 185–196.

Yeazell, M. (1986). The neglected competency—moral sensibility. *Contemporary Education*, 57, 173–176.

Zajonc, R. (1980). Feeling and thinking: Preferences need no inferences. *American Psychologist*, 35, 151–175.

Zajonc, R. (1984). On the primacy of affect. *American Psychologist*, 39, 117–123.

Zajonc, R., & Markus, H. (1984). Affect and cognition: The hard interface. In C. Izard, J. Kagan & R. Zajonc (Eds.), *Emotions, cognition and behavior*. Cambridge, Mass.: Cambridge University Press.

Zeldin, R., Savin-Williams, R. & Small, S. (1984). Dimensions of prosocial behavior in adolescent males. *Journal of Social Psychology*, 123, 159–168.

Zuckerman, M. (1979). *Sensation seeking: Beyond the optimal level of arousal.* Hillsdale, N.J.: Erlbaum.

Zuckerman, M. (1985). A critical look at three arousal constructs in personality theories. In J. Spence & C. Izard (Eds.), *Motivation, emotion and personality.* Amsterdam: Elsevier.

Zuckerman, M., Kuhlman, D. & Camac, C. (1988). What lies beyond E and N? Factor analyses of scales believed to measure basic dimensions of personality. *Journal of Personality and Social Psychology, 54,* 96–107.

Zukier, H. (1986). The paradigmatic and narrative modes in goal-guided inference. In R. Sorrentino & E. Higgins (Eds.), *Handbook of motivation and cognition.* New York: Guilford.

Zukier, H. & Pepitone, A. (1984). Social roles and strategies in prediction: Some determinants of the use of base rate information. *Journal of Personality and Social Psychology, 47,* 349–360.

Zuroff, D. (1986). Was Gordon Allport a trait theorist? *Journal of Personality and Social Psychology, 51,* 993–1000.

Sources

Parts of Chapter 5 are from the author's "Psychosocial origins of conflict over pest control strategies." *Agriculture, Ecosystems and Environment*, 12, 235–251. Copyright © 1985; reprinted by permission of Elsevier Science Publishers.

Figure 1 is a modified version of Fig. 2-3 and Fig. 2-4 from *Personality: The Scientific Study of Complex Human Behavior* by Alan O. Ross. Copyright © 1987 by Holt, Rinehart & Winston, Inc.; reprinted by permission of the publisher. Figure 2 is modified from *Personality development* by H. Smith. Copyright © 1974 by McGraw–Hill Inc.; reprinted by permission of the publisher. Figure 3 is from *Pattern and growth in personality* by G. Allport. Copyright © 1961, G. Allport. Figures 4 and 12c are adapted from *Personality and individual differences* by H. Eysenck and M. Eysenck; reprinted by permission of M. Eysenck and Plenum Publishing Corp. Figure 5 is from *Individual differences: Traits and factors* by Allan R. Buss and W. Poley. Copyright © 1976, Gardner Press; reprinted by permission of the publisher. Figures 6, 14, and 22 and Table 7 are from the author's "Toward a typology of personality styles." *Canadian Psychology*, 29, 263–283. Copyright © 1988, Canadian Psychological Association; reprinted by permission. Figures 7 and 8 are from the author's "Cognitive styles: An integrated model." *Educational Psychology*, 7, 251–268. Copyright © 1987, Carfax Publishing Co.; reprinted by permission of the publisher. Figure 9 is from *Cognition* by A. Glass, K. Holyoak, and J. Santa. Copyright © 1979 McGraw–Hill, Inc.; reprinted by permission of the publisher. Figure 10 is from "Articulation of the conceptual structure in obsessional neurosis." *British Journal of Social and Clinical Psychology*, 9, 264–274, by F. Norris, H. Jones, and H. Norris.

Copyright © 1970, The British Psychological Society; reprinted by permission of the publisher and H. Norris. Figure 11 is from "Toward a consensual structure of mood." *Psychological Bulletin*, 98, 219–235, by D. Watson and A. Tellegen. Copyright © 1985, American Psychological Association; reprinted by permission of D. Watson and the publisher. Figure 13 is from "The interpersonal circle: A structural model for the integration of personality research" by J. Wiggins and R. Broughton (1985). In R. Hogan & W. Jones (Eds.), *Perspectives in personality*. Copyright © 1985, JAI Press; reprinted by permission of the publisher. Figure 15 is modified from "A personality theory of adulthood and aging" by J. Conley. In R. Hogan & W. Jones (Eds.), *Perspectives in personality, Volume 1*. Copyright © 1985, JAI Press; reprinted by permission of the publisher. Figure 17 is from "Cognitive styles as predictors of artistic styles." *Journal of Personality*, 52, 22–35, by M. Loomis and E. Saltz. (1984). Figure 18 is from *The optimal personality: An empirical and theoretical analysis* by R. Coan. Copyright © 1974, R. Coan; reprinted by permission of the author. Figure 19 is reproduced with permission of authors and publisher from Powell, A., & Royce, J. "Paths to being, life style, and individuality." *Psychological Reports*, 1978, 42, 987–1005. Figure 20 is from "The categorical representation of personality disorder: A cluster analysis of DSM–III–R personality features." *Journal of Abnormal Psychology*, 970, 314–321 by L. Morey. Copyright © 1988, American Psychological Association; reprinted by permission. Figure 21 is from "Evaluation of a circumplex model of DSM–III personality disorders." *Journal of Research in Personality*, 23, 525–538 by D. Romney and J. Bynner. Copyright © 1989, Academic Press.

Index